December 8, 1942

Happy Birthday to
the dearest momie
& the best pal a girl
ever had,

Carol

The American Album of Poetry

The American Album
ℰ of Poetry ℈

FROM **BETWEEN THE BOOKENDS** OF

Ted Malone

BOOKMARK PRESS — CAMDEN, N. J.

First edition, December 1938
Second edition, September 1939
Third edition, January 1940
Fourth edition, July 1940
Fifth edition, December 1940
Sixth edition, January 1941
Seventh edition, August 1941
Eighth edition, January 1942
Ninth edition, August 1942

To Bubbles

And all the boys and girls

who will be the poets of Tomorrow

INTRODUCTION

I am not in the habit of writing introductions. I feel that prefaces, as a rule, are parasitic and unnecessary. But this is the exception which proves the point. Ted Malone's AMERICAN ALBUM OF POETRY is not just one more anthology. It represents a cross-section of the popular mind and the democracy of emotion.

We all have in our libraries, whether those be small or large, two kinds of poetry books. We have books by individual authors. These are selected and cherished because of the personal appeal of the particular book to the particular owner. It has been said that if one reads a man's library, one knows that man. And then we have anthologies which, in a manner of speaking, are reference books. We may read an anthology purely for pleasure; but we may also use it as a sort of encyclopedia or dictionary, to look up some poem or poet.

Here is a third, and new, kind of poetry book. It is an Album.

An Album is an intimate collection in which each item has some personal association with the owner of the book. The Family Album of photographs rightfully excludes classic reproductions in order to make room for the blurred and fading daguerrotypes of great-aunts and uncles. So in this book you will find scarcely any poems which have been reprinted in the usual anthologies, but you will many, or perhaps all which recall familiar scenes, faces, memories and thoughts.

This Album is made up of poems written by poets—but these are the poets who in daily life are housewives, business men, professional people, teachers and students, and their poems are composed wholly for the joy of self-expression.

The Album is not a "vanity publication." The inclusion of the poems has not in any case been contingent upon a subscription or the purchase of a copy of the book. Every poet has been expressly invited by the editor. There are many more that he would wish to have included, but time and space made that impossible. They will come in the next Album.

The treatment of the Album is distinctive. There are twenty-six sections, each with a fresh and engaging title. And throughout the book, connecting poem with poem, is Ted Malone's friendly running comment. These comments supply the same important intimacy which makes your Family Album of photographs interesting to your friends. You say, pointing out a picture, "The old lady in the chair is my Grandmother!"—"The boy by the tree is Frank when he was just thirteen!"—"Remember this old high school picture?" Such comments link your Family Album into a chronicle. And so Ted Malone's remarks tie his collection of unassociated poems into a book with one idea behind it. You may think that some of these remarks have almost nothing to do with the subject matter of the poem—some are most flippant (and in these cases it is hoped that the authors will not be annoyed, as the pointed phrases are not in any sense personal)—some are just typically Ted Malone, whimsical, puckish, and friendly, but all of them serve a determined purpose, and that purpose is to make the book readable as a continued story.

Ted Malone believes that these are the purposes of his book of poetry: that it shall be read, that it shall be fully understood, that it shall serve as an Album, to hold pictures that recall personal incidents—the joys and sorrows of our own lives—and that it shall be a human document in which the reader has a real and rightful part.

Here it is then, an unprofessional Snapshot Album of The Great American Family, casual, quick with life, never retouched or prettified by the hand of the studio photographer—as immediate as a newspaper, as important as a parlor or an attic in the memory.

JOSEPH AUSLANDER.

Director of Poetry
Library of Congress, Washington.

ACKNOWLEDGMENTS

The task of gathering these poems . . . locating the poets . . . obtaining their permission . . . seeking out the original publications presenting a particular poem . . . has fallen on a small staff of people who have worked incessantly these autumn days that there might be no oversights in the giving of credit where credit is due. So let me name them first, the ones who really did the work: Roma Nickles, Jean Kilkenny, and John Keith Hanrahan . . . Then let me bow a sweeping bow of gratitude and toss an armful of orchids to the little lady who has put up with my bad temper all these evenings . . . my tardy arrival home to dinner and my constant demand for special research . . . and copying . . . and recopying in the little den during the wee hours of the morning . . . who has willingly appeared amused when I read the "comments" I thought funny and likewise never cracked a smile when I presumed I was serious . . . my appreciation . . . my gratitude . . . and my love . . . to Verlia . . .

And to these newspapers . . . magazines . . . and publishing houses which are furthering the cause of poets and poetry in America . . . who generously made possible the inclusion of many poems in this book: The American Scholar . . . American Weave . . . Avon . . . The Bard . . . Blue Moon . . . The Boston Evening American . . . The Boston Herald . . . Candor . . . The Chinatown Monthly . . . Chiropractic Home . . . Christian Observer . . . Christian Science Monitor . . . The Coast . . . Creative . . . W. B. Conkey Company . . . Driftwind . . . The Dune Forum . . . The Educational Forum . . . The Forge . . . The Frontier . . . Frontier and Midland . . . The Front Rank . . . The Goldsmith-Woolard Publishing Company . . . Good Housekeeping . . . The Garret . . . The Gypsy . . . The Hartford Courant . . . Hill Trails . . . The Husk . . . Journal Post . . . Kaleidograph . . . Kansas City Star . . . King Features . . . Ladies' Home Journal . . . Life . . . Los Angeles Saturday Night . . . Los Angeles Times . . . The Lutheran . . . The Maryland News . . . Macmillan Company, Ltd., of Canada . . . Montana Woman . . . Muncy's Magazine . . . Muse . . . McCalls

. . . New England Dusk . . . New York Sun . . . New York Times . . . Oakland Tribune . . . Opinion . . . Oregon Journal . . . Pasque Petals . . . Poetry Caravan . . . Poetry World . . . The Portland Oregonian . . . The Post Chaise . . . Reflections . . . Saturday Evening Post . . . Saturday Review of Literature . . . Silhouettes . . . Skyline . . . The Spinners . . . Spirit . . . Sunset Magazine . . . Talaria . . . Tavern Post . . . Unity . . . The Villager . . . Voices . . . Wall Street Journal . . . Walter Winchell's Column . . . Western Poetry . . . Western Revue . . . Westward Magazine . . . Wings . . . and of course . . . of course Pictorial Review Combined with Delineator. . . .

There is another long list of titles I should like to include here: a list of book titles. Some are books already published from which a part of these poems have come, while even more are books still in manuscript form but which some day will grace the libraries of many people. Because of the lack of space, and even more, lack of accurate information, these lists cannot be included.

In conclusion let me acknowledge the interest in Poets and Poetry of Herbert R. Mayes, Editor of Good Housekeeping, under whose leadership "Between the Bookends" became a department in a National Magazine, and Miss Mabel Search, Editor of Pictorial Review, combined with Delineator, who has enthusiastically given more encouragement, space and support to American Poetry than any other national magazine editor. Let me pay a sincere tribute to the program departments of the Columbia and Mutual Networks for their interest in poetry—and particularly point to the Program and Educational departments of the National Broadcasting Company which, having been distinguished by their service to America in the field of great music, are going to be satisfied with nothing short of an equally outstanding performance in the field of Literature.

To the poets who have made the book possible, I invite you, the reader, to make acknowledgment by becoming an enthusiastic patron of the poet or poets whose works interest you. Poetry has many fans; what it needs is friends.

TED MALONE.

SECTIONAL INDEX

WHAT IS A POEM?

Ask him who knows the secret of the seed
  That germinates within the womb of earth;
What force is back of all transcendent need
  To bring a fragile blossom into birth.

Ask him who bears the burden of the sun,
  Who wears a shawl of stars about his shoulder,
Where silver threads of moonlight mist are spun;
  Ask him who is as old as Time—and older.

Ask him whose mouth has known the kiss of danger,
  Who knows no alien heart, nor ever will;
Ask him who makes a friend of every stranger
  And keeps a tryst with Life beyond the hill.

And if, perchance, you are a kindred soul
  He'll point you back to pathways he has trod
And say to you—"A Poem is a goal,
  A mounting step on stairs that lead—to God."

CARMEN JUDSON.

But, Definitely!

Mothers since the world began . . . the mothers of . . . Noah . . . Cleopatra . . . Judas . . . Sir Galahad . . . Shakespeare . . . and now Mrs. Dionne . . .

THE GRANDEST BOAST

Never do I hear a woman say
That she is author of a book or play,
Or hear her proudly boast of something great
Achieved in art, but thoughts of mine go straight
To her who said: "Ignobly born in Thrace,
I have not Grecian culture, caste, nor grace,
But let Greek women scorn me, if they please—
I am the mother of Themistocles!"

DEAN SETTOON MERNAGH.

Leaning against the railing of a New York roof garden . . .

EFFICIENCY EXPERT

Through dreamy eyes she gazed into the night
And murmured this, "Some day I'll buy an isle
Out there. . . ." (The sweeping gesture of her arm
Took in a generous portion of the world.)
"Some place that you and I can call Our Paradise;
Where life will be as simple as
In Eden; where all things will be—"

"But, dear,"
He spoke with genuine concern, "Now who'll
Deliver all our groceries? And what
About a Frigidaire? And as for lights
We could resort to lamps, I guess, but who
Would fill them up with oil and trim the wicks;
And . . . Dear, in short, why I foresee all sorts
Of difficulties!"
"So do I," she muttered.
"Shall we dance?"

LLOYD STONE.

18

In a change of mood he bought her a lodge in the Berkshires . . . and she . . .

CITY GIRL

What can you do with a place like that?
  Look at it!
Twice as hard to keep as a flat—
  Look at it!
Miles from town, hemmed in by trees,
Choked with flowers and birds and bees—
  Look at it!
What can you do with a place like that?
  Look at it!
A cow and a horse, two dogs and a cat—
  Look at it!
A view and a river instead of a street—
He calls it a beautiful snug retreat—
  Look at it!

MARIE MEDORA.

Here we submit . . . is a question that deserves an answer . . .

FOR WHERE IS SHE SO FAIR?

O noble poet, I have loved thee well,
  But foolish man or wise thy songs to sing
In wooing of a frigid damoiselle,
  I must confess, I am still wondering.
Was she a living woman, can it be
  That woman lived who listened to such suit,
And could so callously refuse thy plea?
  Or was she marble, and thus safely mute—
Some goddess, Heaven designed to guard thy youth,
  And foster inspiration's sacred flame?
Had she been woman, beautiful in truth,
  With lasting loveliness (a warmer aim),
Ere twenty of thy ardent songs were spent,
  She had caught fire, and proven thy intent.

BERTHA DEAN FOSS.

19

REVISED EDITIONS OF GREAT POETRY

How do I love you? Let me tell you, ducky,
    I warn you it's the kind that never dies.
The sort of love that makes me think I'm lucky
    To dance with you till daylight—then to rise
At seven just to see you eat your toast
    And drink your coffee from behind the news!
Enough to murmur, "Yes, dear," when you boast,
    And hang enraptured while you air your views.

Enough, my love, to let your wandering eye
    Approve a streamlined hussy now and then,
Enough to never let you see me cry,
    (My crying's not the sort that charms the men.)
Be warned, my man, your sentence is for life;
    One can't escape an ever-loving wife.

BEATRICE MCELWEE.

One can't escape an ever-loving wife . . . not even with twin beds . . .

TWIN BEDS

Now I can twist and turn and scratch my knees
And no one says, "Lie still! You make a breeze
That chills me when you haul the sheets away!
What is the matter with you anyway?
For Heaven's sake get set! It's almost day!"

I twist and turn and then lie upon my back
But sleep just will not come, alas alack!
Though I count sheep, my eyes refuse to close,
I'll have to crawl in bed with you I 'spose—
Twin beds are swell—but I can't sleep—
I'M FROZE!

FLORENCE M. KEELER.

20

So soon ... so soon ... the Album's first romance ... and like so many first affairs ...

FRUSTRATION

I walked with Paul in starlight—
    He asked me if I'd wed him;
Then Peter, touched by moonlight,
    Told of the chase I led him.

But I loved not in starlight,
    Nor yet 'neath pale young moon,
But in the fresh-washed sunlight
    Of an April afternoon.

You bent your head till it and mine
    Were very close together
And then you asked, oh heart of mine,
    How I liked the weather!

ANNE SCOTT.

The first lovers' quarrel ... this romance is certainly running true to form ... our fears ...

RUSTY KEY

You didn't care that that first kiss
    Was not for one who borrows ...
I meant it as a tacit key
    To all of my tomorrows.

I found it just the other day
    Outside my door quite rusted
And knew that things too simply gained
    With boredom soon are crusted.

Well, now that key is hard to get—
    Your lesson, Lad, was thorough ...
My kiss is for a long-term lease
    And not just till tomorrow!

EDITH MILLER REID.

MY FAVORITES

Inordinately fond am I
Of coffee, cheese and hot mince pie,
Of pickles and potato chips,
And any kind of midnight nips.
I add, to make my list complete,
The Wagner operas, the neat
Precision of the Bach motet.
The symphony I don't forget,
Nor candle light nor shades of blue,
Nor curve of silvered moon—nor you.

Some of my favorites are such
That they will never hurt me much,
As for that German from Beyreuth
He's calmed my soul from early youth,
And though some find him quite a bore
I would that I might hear him more.
But you, my love, and mid-night tea
I find are very bad for me,
For after each I lie awake
And often nurse a lingering ache.

ESTHER WOLLAM.

All . . . all is lost . . . and only we and the heroine know . . . the poor blind fool never guesses . . .

LOST

You never knew when I stopped loving you:
    Our voices murmured on in conversation's thread;
You walked beside me on the highway wide,
    Nor ever saw the cloud which overspread
The sun when love for you within me died.

But shadows on the land are shelt'ring friends:
    The cloud gave glad surcease to me from scorching love;
I gained in freedom from the price you cost.
    And life still flows along its patient groove,
With you, you never guessing you have lost.

MABEL STAFFORD.

And when the poor blind fool's eyes are opened . . .

CAUSES

Because I was too carefully correct in everything I said;
Because I was too primly proud in everything I did;
Because I tired of antiquated things, and longed for new;
Because I would find fault in everything you'd do;
Because I knew no endless ecstacy and felt no haunting fear;
I lost you—
Because I was too sure of you, my dear.

MARION THOMAS.

But lo the worm has turned . . . he adds . . .

RECIPROCATION

You believed the words I said—
    That I'd never loved before you;
Cocked your pretty little head,
    Heard my ardent "I adore you."
In your diary, my sweet,
    Boast how well your charms deceived me,
But be sure that you repeat—
    You believed me!

ESTHER BALDWIN YORK.

*One day his mother made him stay in the house . . . and she said she
sure didn't know what he was coming to . . . and she didn't . . .*

PRISON ETCHING

Numbered his back, and shaven his head,
And empty his heart for his dreams are dead,
Muted his lips, and his eyes pain-veiled,
With his soul as well as his body jailed.

An old man stares at the prison sky
With never a hope—save that all men die.

RALPH W. HUNTER.

23

Poetry is no exception ... even in a romance in the Album the lady must be given ... "the last word" ...

DENOUEMENT

Your shoulders were so neatly square
And that faint crinkle in your hair
Made me forget the Winter cold
And all the lovely lies you told.

When Spring revealed her lovely hue
My eyes were closed to all but you.
The days sped by—then, all too soon
We walked beneath a Summer moon.

Oh, all went well until that day
We journeyed to the beach to play.
You lost your charm—forgive me, please,
But, darling, I loathe knobby knees.

ELIZABETH LOU SELLERS.

So ends our sad romance ... And without giving vent to a terrible pun leering at me from the posterior of my cerebellum ... we shall get down to fundamentals ... but, definitely ...

BARELY POSSIBLE

Consider now the nudist's lot—
   As carefree as a flower.
He broileth in the burning sun,
   Is dunked in every shower.

Upon his broad, perspiring back,
   Mosquitoes, joyful, park,
And when he resteth in the grass,
   The ants enjoy a lark.

So when in careless nudity
   He through the thistles goes,
Methinks it barely possible
   He longeth for some clothes!

INEZ GEORGE GRIDLEY.

CHURCH

My church is one
  With a big broad creed;
Where you are left alone—
  Judged by your deed.

Where a Ladies' Aid
  Doesn't exist
And differences are settled
  By blows of a fist.

We worship at a shrine
  In the great open air;
Shooting ducks on Sunday—
  Golf, when it's fair.

The church—it is round
  And built on the level
So it's an impossible task
  To corner the Devil.

BRUCE EARLY.

A current Broadway show . . . young liberal . . . can't get in right with
"left wing" . . . left out by "right wing" . . . gets both wings clipped . . .

A SONG FOR THE UNPOPULAR FOLK

Let us pray by means of song,
For unpopular folk—called wrong,
Who unloved, misunderstood,
Deemed too bad, by those called good—
Deemed too good, by those called bad,
Are alone, in world gone mad —
A la mode.
With these few, let us include
Prayer for us—the multitude.

MABEL GRANT SUND.

Hurry past this verse . . . it's much too true . . . we never should have printed it . . .

CURVE AHEAD

Her prudence was a white fence
Around the danger curve of her desires.
Not strong enough to keep Love
From dashing down the precipice below,
But white enough to catch the traveler's eye.

ROSA ZAGNONI MARINONI.

The singular thing about this single error . . . is its singular plurality . . .

THE SINGLE ERROR

I may be a miser,
A scheming deviser,
    At keeping the grocery bill down;
I may be a wizard,
A slithering lizard
    In getting through traffic downtown;
I exercise magic
Avoiding the tragic
    Disaster of baking too brown;
I'm really quite clever
In wearing forever
    Old shoes or a made-over gown;
But—I let myself go on my hats.

I try to be patient,
I'm never complacent,
    In dressing, I seldom am slow.
I never talk nonsense,
I'm the very quintessence
    Of feminine charm.   And also
I diet in silence
With strictest compliance
    To all his desires; although
When he stares at me boldly,
Contemptuously, coldly,
    With looks of dismay, then I know
That I've let myself go on my hats.

VIVIAN PIKE BOLES.

26

A letter to conclude this little section, all of which seemed to us quite unusual . . . likewise this letter, but, definitely . . .

A LETTER FROM FATHER

My Dear Daughter:

You ask me if your husband should stay in his present position at an "adjusted" salary, but you forgot to tell me what he would do if he didn't. You and he couldn't very well come here just now. Your brother Sheridan's salary has just been "reconsidered," so he moved into his old room at home, and brought his wife.

Your sister, Eloise, telegraphed the next day that Wilfred has just been offered a new contract that was an insult, so your mother is airing out her room. Wilfred never could endure insults. Your sister, Frances, whom you will recall has been a private secretary, wrote last week that if anybody thinks she is going to drop to the level of a common typist, they are mistaken, so we expect her any day.

What with those and the younger children, I imagine that as long as Rupert's salary is merely being "adjusted," he had better stay. An adjustment is nothing like a reduction. It's hard for me to keep up with the new language of big business, but as I understand it, an "adjustment" is the equivalent of a raise. Of course, Rupert wouldn't know that; he has been working only since 1928; he should ask some old-timer to explain what a raise is.

My own business is coming along fine. It was sold on the courthouse steps last Friday, but there were no bidders, so the sheriff let me keep it. That makes the best month I've had since the upturn.

Your affectionate Father.

UNKNOWN.

"Even Man Creates Images . . .

What shall one call the images of poetry . . . the pictures . . . the meta-phors and similes . . . wait . . . here's a word . . . a perfect word . . . we'll call them . . . call them . . . call . . . it's gone . . . I had it on my tongue's tip . . .

POET'S HUNTING SONG

Just now there was a word: a silver fox
  That leapt the mind's high hedge and sped away.
Be after him, my thought! (Strange paradox,
  That he should come at all if not to stay.)
Now, every crying hound of memory,
  Circle the woods, where speech is wont to hide.
And find my sleek and silken word for me—
  The sly young fox that lately left my side.

Hurtle him back, the while I make a thong
  Of strong emotions, grown articulate,
To tie the tiny trickster to a song;
  Where I can sit and muse upon his fate,
Or shut him up within the printed page—
  And watch the curious stroke him in his cage.

                              HELEN FRAZEE-BOWER.

I like this one, but if you figure out what it means . . . please let me know . . .

EVEN AS THE GRASS

Lay not your pencill'd cheek where love may read,
  Your em'rld eyes are dripping tears of scorn,
And where the moon-drowned shadows beg and plead
  Like some unsounded bell the ages mourn.
The sunbeams spear the windows of your home
  And dew lays pearls across your velvet breast,
Reflecting drifted stars on drowsy loam
  While lovers seek your couch, to pause and rest.

If storm and rain put stubbles in your hair,
  And wipe your brow with laces sprayed in mist
March on, for duty drops the web of care,
  Where morning sieves a rainbow on your wrist.
You know the bitter tune the wind may sing
  But love can play a chord on bits of string.

                              RUTH ENCK ENGLE.

30

Flying west . . . a Pacific sunset with beams of gold into the infinite blue . .

THE ARTIST

The copper hills of sunset
And low Sierra trees
Are tinted by the solar god
On iridescent seas.

A canny master craftsman,
His color scheme is hurled
A paltry ninety million miles!
His canvas is the world.

GENE MOORE.

Rolling hillsides in Spring . . . New Hampshire . . . Minnesota . . . North Carolina . . . Washington . . . and China too . . .

RETURN TO EARTH

I

I am the cool, green earth where lovers lie.
No mother could be kinder than am I.

Their slim, young bodies merging for a breath
Will never know that such is part of death.

That life has lured them to this little hour
To brand their souls with pain's bright, passion flower.

They come to me and lie upon my heart,
And I am silent, I have done my part.

II

I am the deep, dark earth where pulsing life
Is eager for the pageantry of strife.

Where worm and seed alike mature and spring
Upon my breast prepared to live and sing.

I let them go. It is their destiny
To suckle once and then return to me.

INA DRAPER DeFOE.

31

Don't let this French title fool you . . . it must have been in Oklahoma . . . Oklahoma has a corner on starlit nights . . .

LES ÉTOILES

Last night
I reached out the window,
Took three twinkling stars
Off their tacks,
Crumpled them
And sprinkled the stardust
Over my closed eyelids.
And what do you think?
I dreamed of you!

MILDRED POTTER.

This ought to pop your vertebrae . . .

CALISTHENICS

Your soul
Is a little stooped.
I should recommend
For its posture
This exercise:
Hands over head,
Now, touch a star. . . .

LOLLY WILLIAMS.

I know some people for whom you would have to change this to a dandelion in an ice cube . . .

TRANSPARENCE

Love peering at me
Thru the indifference of your eyes
Reminds me of an orchid I once saw
Frozen in a block of ice.

ROSA ZAGNONI MARINONI.

GOOD MORNING, SPRING

Earth yawned
Really
A very ill-mannered yawn.
Stretched
Quite
An exaggerated stretch.
Frowned
Into a mirror.
Horrors
Such baggy clouds under my skies!
And so drab
My hair
Must need green rinse . . . tonic.
O confound
These kinks in my trees.
A bit of limbering up for me.
But now
Ah yes.
My pipe, please.
There are tulips to be bubbled!

MARY MORRISON.

And the old time clock . . . slows down . . . tick tock . . .

TEMPO CHANGE

I can remember days when Time
    Led us a merry chase:
Her unbound hair free in the wind
    And blowing in her face.

Now you are gone, Time lags along
    And stops to braid her hair
Beside a quiet pool and sees
    Her sad reflection there.

H. TOTMAN.

33

*If this question bothers you . . . and you're really becoming dissatisfied
. . . go back and read the letter on page 27 . . .*

SONG OF A QUIET LIFE

If I can find a loveliness
  In diamonds in the snow,
If I can hear a symphony
  Wherever tree-tops blow,
And if I'm dressed in cloth of gold
  While standing in the sun,
Should that not be quite wealth enough
  For me, or anyone?

If I can find a palace here
  Within four little rooms,
If warm spice cake and apple pie
  Are rarest of perfumes,
And best of all my husband is
  A prince in dungarees,
Am I a fool to be content
  With simple things like these?

MARION KILROY.

*Dunes . . . dunes . . . melancholy names . . . dunes along Lake Michigan
. . . dunes along the Pacific . . . dunes . . . dunes . . .*

SHADOW ON THE SAND

Here where old sea-trails
  Curve to the land
Dark calls to darkness,
  Moonlight to sand.

Here on the lost dunes,
  Naked and white,
Grief is a ghost-wind
  Wailing at night.

DEDIE HUFFMAN WILSON.

34

"Ashes to ashes . . .

CLINKERS

She claimed her love for him
Had burned to ashes.
But when she went to clean out
The little stove of her heart
In order to start a new fire,
She could not shake the grate—
For the clinkers.

ROSA ZAGNONI MARINONI.

A poet is likely to be a meticulous individual . . . punctilious about punctuation . . . and why not . . . when a simple sign can signify as much as . . .

PUNCTUATION LANGUAGE

An exclamation point
   Is a soldier on review
With head held upright
   Bright polish on each shoe!

A question mark's a lady
   With her back bent double
From carrying through life
   Inexplainable trouble?

Colons are the chubby twins
   With cunning feet and hands
Going everywhere together
   In home or foreign lands:

And dashes have a hurried look
   Such breathless-reckless ways
Rushing giddily about
   Without any stays—

A period is so steady,
   The dependable kind
Who always stops
   When he's said his mind.

OLGA EDITH GUNKLE.

35

Of the thousands who lunch on the beach or scatter their papers . . .
burn themselves raw . . . then actually plunge into this picture . . .
so few . . . so few . . . ever see it . . .

SURF — JONES BEACH

White to the lips, the waves
    Suck at the silver beach;
Their breaking tips beyond,
    As far as sight can reach.

Puff balls of foam escape,
    Racing from draining sea;
Blown in the sandy wind
    Back to eternity.

MARCIA NICHOLS HOLDEN.

When one is calm and cool and sitting by a long polished table . . . and
writing with an emerald pen on paper white as snow . . . these things
are true . . . and love is this . . . a virtuous emotion . . .

LOVE

Love has been dragged too often through the mire.
    I would brush it clean and free it from the bars
That would detain it, I would set it up
    High on a cool green hill beneath the stars
Where the wind can blow the clinging dust away,
    And the cool night wash it with its crystal dew.
It matters not what others make of love.
    Mine shall be pure and beautiful for you.

My love is like the shimmer of the stars.
    It has absorbed the radiance of the moon;
Has taken on the glory of the sun
    That climbs the far blue glittering heights of noon.
I am jealous of the name of love. I long
    To lift it high, to hold it like a flame
That no unworthy thing may venture near
    To tarnish the white splendor of its name.

GRACE NOLL CROWELL.

STRANGE HARBORS

Let me set sail for strange harbors, the crescent mouth
Of a languid land, laughing along the south,
Where men, dark bees, swarm, honey-tongued and bold,
Breasting the bar of breakers to uphold
Sweet fruit, soon tasted, gems too gladly sold . . .
Wind, fill afresh the slack sails of my yearning . . .
No footprint on this shore and no returning.

For stranger harbors let me now set forth,
From breathless islands to the lock-lipped north,
Where men, lone trees, stand sheathed in fibers cold,
Indifferent to my figurehead of gold,
Blind to the worth my cargo could unfold:
Candles for starring stark oblivion;
Mirrors, redoubling vestiges of sun.

Hurled by hurricanes from pole to pole
Becalmed in beauty, without peace of soul,
East to West I plow the sapphire loam
And reap no harvest from the fleeing foam . . .
Let me set sail for the strangest harbor—home . . .
Landfall at daybreak, looming spires and slips
Where spent tides still the restless pulse of ships.

There, past slow-turning beacons, glad hands bring
The hawser to the rusted mooring-ring.
(How many years ago did I depart,
With cloud on the horizon of my heart?)
Before me wanderings I cannot chart,
For here a wider sea for questing lies,
And strange new harbors, in remembered eyes.

EDITH CHANDLER HAUBOLD.

37

FARE FOR A GIPSY HEART

The heart of me is like a railroad bum
Who wears a yellow vest and has a pack
Of useless things in red bandana wrapped
To carry on a limb for beggar's luck.

His shoes are overbig; his ancient hat,
Thru many rains, is shapeless as a sponge;
The shirt front where his buttons came undone
Is looped with nails he found along the track.

He planned a solid home for living, once—
But he of clumsy hands was so unapt
That walls and rafter timbers all collapsed
Into a path of ties where life is much
Of dodging dogs and finding doors to rap
Where cups of tea are prelude to a lunch.

LOUIS RAGG.

And Webster dared to build a house to hold such things as this . . . and
there it stands . . . with all it holds . . . the world . . . the dictionary . . .

WORDS

Our words are flame and ashes, fleet as breath,
Plumes for adventure, pageantry of death.

Our words are color—yellow, blue, and red,
Drumbeat for marching, prayer for bed.

Words are our armor, they are our intent,
The coin we used along the way we went.

GRACE MANSFIELD.

Yes, but what does one do in case of twin beds . . .

3 A. M.

Night has an entity, a shape
    Of darkness, skeletoned with fear,
And few there be who can escape
    Some chill acquaintanceship with her.

Night has a manner of speech, a voice
    Which she can properly disguise:
A mouse's business . . . the small noise
    Of crumbling embers, or the sighs

In empty corners, or the creaks
    Of doors ajar at no one's hand.
In such masked syllables night speaks,
    And all her listeners understand.

Yet, when I lie with you, my love,
    Curved to your side, and warm, and well;
So proud, so gracious night doth move
    I'd swear she were an archangel;

Who otherwhile were grim to hear
    In bodiless presence through the gloom,
And heavy on the frightened ear
    Her subtle footfall in the room.

SARA HENDERSON HAY.

Go get in the closet and hold your ears . . .

WINDY NIGHT

The lightning witch is mad again!
Amid the night and rain,
She streaks her skinny fingers down,
She strikes the tallest spires in town
And screams with wild disdain.

CHRIS REAL.

39

All right, you can come out now, but it's really a shower . . .

RAIN

A man sinned today
And God, seeing, wept
Crystals, jewelling
The way.

Some dashed
Against my pane;
Some tapped the tin roof
Tumbling into
The drain.

A window
I would be
Or even the pipe
God's handkerchief
. . . Me.

MARGARET MCCORMICK.

Do see the rain blowing first one way then another . . . as far as eye can see . . . rain . . . rain . . .

RAIN IS LIKE A WOMAN

Rain, in silver, wanders
    Up and down the hills,
Strolls across the meadows
    As her whimsy wills.

Rain is like a woman
    Walking with her lover,
Back and forth upon the road,
    This side and then over.

Moving on the garden,
    Touching every flower,
Yet not thinking of it
    Hour after hour.

Wind must be her lover,
    Tall and white and slim;
Silver rain and white wind,
    She will follow him.

MARY WILLIS SHELBURNE.

Storm is over at last ... dripping trees ... wet streets ... little puddles everywhere ...

PUDDLES

Little puddles have a way
  Of fixing up at night . . .
In apricot and apple-green,
  In rose and petalled-white.

In lemon-yellow they've been seen,
  In bronze and golden-glow.
And sometimes they are carnival
  And hems of scarlet show.

Round about the set of sun
  You will see them flower . . .
Glist'ning in the country lanes
  For a sunset hour.

Little puddles have a way
  Of turning black and deep . . .
Save the favored few that find
  A star or two to keep.

Nights are long and nights are drear
  Go clock hands fast or slow . . .
What do little puddles do
  That have no stars to show?

                                        RUTH ECKMAN.

When you think of the secrets old Mother Nature has ... remember nobody knows ... where anything comes from ... or anything goes ...

SECRETS

When drowsy Time discards her spangled dress,
Angelic touches carefully caress
  Its secret folds
And place it, womanlike, within a vault
Where tenderness can smooth the earthly fault
  Each wrinkle holds. . . .
                                        LILLIAN EVERTS.

41

The paper says it will rain tomorrow . . . that means shopping will have to be postponed . . . the youngsters will have to stop running in and out . . . rain . . . rain . . .

I SAW GOD WASH THE WORLD

I saw God wash the world last night
  With his sweet showers on high,
And then, when morning came, I saw
  Him hang it out to dry.

He washed each tiny blade of grass
  And every trembling tree;
He flung his showers against the hill,
  And swept the billowing sea.

The white rose is a cleaner white,
  The red rose is more red,
Since God washed every fragrant face
  And put them all to bed.

There's not a bird, there's not a bee
  That wings along the way
But is a cleaner bird and bee
  Than it was yesterday.

I saw God wash the world last night.
  Ah, would He had washed me
As clean of all my dust and dirt
  As that old white birch tree.

WILLIAM L. STIDGER.

Here is a poem about overcoats, and overshoes, and coal bills . . . and hot water bottles . . . and snow and sleds . . .

YEARS END

Calm nature, old and withered, seeks the rest
That follows summer's hot and burdened days.
Now winter's shivering night slowly pulls down
Her blue-black mantle round her silvering head.

EVELYN SWANSTROM.

THE CLOAK

The cloak Life made for her was gray in hue
  And shaped to hide her lissomness of line,
But from the scrap-bags of the folk she knew
  She cut and fashioned many a gay design
And made a border full of fruit and flowers,
  Orange and green and gold, with here and there
A butterfly that danced away the hours,
  Or red-bird darting through the sun-filled **air.**
A scrap of song a lover sang one day,
  The kiss a mother gave her latest born,
The happy laughter of a child at play
  Were fashioned all her gray cloak to adorn.
And neighbors, passing in and out her door,
Envied the glorious garment that she wore.

ANNA LOUISE BARNEY.

BLOWING BUBBLES

A breath of air—
A delicate ball,
A frail illusion mirroring all.
Slowly drifting—
Quivering still,
Pastels of spring on a crystal hill.

BEATRICE PAULA BYRNES.

"I Never Like to Gossip, But . . .

As long as we're old friends ... and she's not here ... and since you won't ever tell her I said this ... but ...

GUEST

Each time I go to her house
  I wear my very best.
I touch the bell sedately
  And am a proper guest.
I nibble at my wafer,
  I sip just half my tea.
And while I view the garden
  She cuts some blooms for me.
I utter proper praises
  About her well-kept lawn ...
But oh, it takes me hours
  To smile when I have gone.

But when I come to your house ...
  Heigh-ho! The clothes I choose.
My dress is faded gingham,
  I've pollen on my shoes.
The knocker's never lifted,
  The bell's not touched at all.
I push the door wide open
  And call you from the hall.
There is no cup to balance,
  There is no cake to munch.
We hunt a sunny meadow
  Without a thought of lunch.
I trot along beside you
  With zeal no miles could faze.
And heart so full of singing
  It lasts for days and days.

Ruth Eckman.

No, she never married . . . people said there was a reason . . . something about her daddy . . . there was other talk . . . she herself just said she didn't want a man . . . but . . .

NEXT DOOR NEIGHBOR

She was very little,
   Only so high;
Her eyes were the color
   Of an April sky.

Once she was a wild one,
   So she said,
Shaking gaily
   Her snow-white head.

She'd have been married
   But her daddy wouldn't let her.
She was just as glad—a man
   For worse or better

Would be a bother,
   And she had her cat,
And her grand piano,
   And a lavender hat.

No, she didn't like
   babies a bit—
She'd rather have tabby
   When the lamp was lit.

So she said.
   But one afternoon
I caught her singing
   A funny little tune

And rocking my baby,
   With her bright, blue eyes
Looking like tear-wet
   April skies!

FRANCES M. FROST.

INTIMATE APPAREL

She braids her hair in rivulets of sun
    And binds her wrists
And brow with buds of pomegranate,
    Her throat with amethysts
Of glittering laughter—
    The most alert
Would not surmise that next her flesh
    She wears a haircloth shirt.

IRENE WILDE.

*Words under the breath . . . gossip of the mind . . . at a girl in a club
. . . in a Spanish dance . . .*

POOR LITTLE COQUETTE!

Your mouth is as crimson, as crimson as sin!
    Your breath is the breath of a flower;
Dull gold and amber the tints of your skin
    Under spangles, and bangles
That jangle . . . and yet . . .
What falls and gleams on your bodice of jet?

Chantilly laces and ruffles that swirl,
    Swathing your half-ripened charms;
Satin shod feet that untiringly twirl . . .
    Revealing, concealing,
Appealing . . . and yet . . .
What is ashine on your bodice of jet?

Stamp your small slippers and toss your high head,
    Snap your slim fingers and smile,
Deep in your bosom a love-dream lies dead
    As swaying and playing . . .
Your bold castanet
Must deny that you cry . . .
Poor little coquette!

FRANCISCA VALLEJO MCGETTIGAN.

48

*Rich, what do you mean rich ... I could tell you a few things about her
life ... poor old soul ... rich ... humph ...*

THE GOOD PROVIDER'S WIFE

"With all my worldly goods I thee endow,"
　He stood with her one purpling dusk and said,
And from that glamoured hour until now
　She has not wanted raiment, roof and bread.
But Fate could not have destined her to face
　More devastating poverty than this:
Deep hunger for his unbestowed embrace,
　The chill of his perfunctory, cool kiss.

Sometimes, though long unbidden, come to her
　Dreams of an ardent Prince of Ne'er-do-Wells,
With outheld arms, whose whisper once could stir
　Her thoughts to cadences like chiming bells.
But some strong fiber in her warp and woof
　By loyal, brave foremothers woven fast,
Holds her beneath the staid, Remote One's roof,
　Intent to warm and win his heart at last.

She sits outside its gateway, proudly dumb,
A wistful beggar, waiting for a crumb.

JULIA CLAY BARRON WEBB.

Now take those twins ... both lovely girls ...

TEMPERAMENT

Martha dusts an empty room,
　Mary gathers heather,
Martha leans upon a broom,
　And Mary on a feather.

Martha gives a man content,
　Her routines never vary.
But, due to some bedevilment,
　Men string along with Mary.

ELEANOR STANLEY LOCKWOOD.

49

A strange combination, I'd say . . . it doesn't seem right to talk about her . . . she meant well, I guess . . . and yet . . .

SHE TALKED SO MUCH

She talked so much that often what she said
Made others miserable, and oftentimes afraid;
She went to church, put something in the plate,
And always saw when some one came in late;
She criticized the few in sporty clothes,
And sniffing said, "They're short enough, land knows!"
She made the finest cake, salt rising-bread
From recipes kept solely in her head,
But when her boy came for a bite to eat,
She'd crossly call, "Again? Go wipe your feet!"
Yet when that stranger's lad was sick and died,
She was the very last to leave his side;
She doubted love and happiness to be;
Said when one wed, "Well, you just wait and see."
And when a certain tragic afternoon,
That pretty Benton baby came too soon,
Her version of it shocked the neighborhood:
Yet every day she prayed that she be good.

DAISY CRUMP WHITEHEAD.

You know how it is . . . when you just overhear a part of a conversation . . . it isn't clear . . . although it was to them . . .

OLD NUNS' TALK

I do not fear for Margaret.
All their thoughts of her
Are autumn reveries of brown leaves dropping
And powdered apples clustering on the boughs.
Forgotten spring as if it never blossomed
Hints of deep winter and the death of snow;
I do not fear for Margaret.
It was October when she first knew earth,
And after darkness it was late July;
She shall be old forever. And I know
It will be spring forever in her mind.

SISTER MARGARET.

50

When local scandal fails us . . . we can always fall back . . .

CELESTIAL SCANDAL

Whoever hangs the stars at night
   And takes them in by day
Must need a million filing clerks
   To get them put away.

Sometimes a clerk must lose his job
   And know the reason why,
If a star has not been properly
   Fastened to the sky;

For what a scandal there would be
   If one of them should dare
To place Orion's belt and sword
   In Cassiopeia's chair.

                          ELVA R. RAY.

Doesn't she look natural . . . yes, it is too much rouge . . . but she always wore too much . . . her funeral will be the biggest social event of the season . . . if all her highbrow friends attend . . .

THE SNOB

She knew a Lord. "I met him once, my dear,
   In London"—and her eyes shone at the thought;
"And Baron So-and-So, a dashing peer."
   A young Lieutenant whose grandfather fought
At Flodden Field had led her out to dance.
   She had a button that adorned a king,
A ribbon from a Chevalier of France;
   Gossip to last you through an evening.

Her name high fashion's charities has graced,
   Yet sick and beggared passed her unaware;
No poor relation ever could have faced
   Her jeweled Lorgnon, with its brittle stare.
Now she is dead she greets Christ with a nod,—
(He was a carpenter)—But She Knows God.

                    VIRGINIA MCCORMICK.

She had two sons . . . oh yes, the famous one . . . and then his older brother . . . he didn't come to much . . . he stayed with her . . .

SONS

She did not love one son the more
   For that he climbed the steps to fame,
And placed a green, perennial wreath
   Above her name.
She loved as much the other one
   Who could not rise above the rest,
And who had need of her and love,
   And she was blest
In two fine sons she always said,
   And hung their pictures side by side—
A nation's favored, and the one
   In whom her love was satisfied.

ISABELLE BRYANS LONGFELLOW.

Have you heard of what finally happened . . . she came down from her pedestal . . . oh yes . . . everybody is laughing . . .

CAREFULLY

Carefully, on the safe and solid rock,
   She knew how wise she builded, and how well;
How cunningly she fashioned bolt and lock
   To seal the portal to the citadel;
How smooth and gleaming were the battlements
   That nowhere offered foothold to the foe;
How high the guarded window, and how dense
   The thorny boughs that hedged it round below.

And so she knew, and savored to her core,
   How stark, how more than bitter is defeat
To one whose own swift hand unbars the door,
   Who sees her towers toppling in the street,
And who herself delivers up the key
   To the amused, victorious enemy.

ETHEL JACOBSON.

Of course if you could read my mind . . . you might be surprised to know what I'm thinking about you . . . even now . . .

TOUCHÉ

Your little cat is soft and warm,
  Your babe is dearer still;
I envy you your tiny house
  With roses and a hill.
I'd like to have that willow ware,
  Those what-nots tucked in nooks;
And stay at lovely home all day
  And read from novel books.
I wouldn't want to be you, though,
  Not now—nor evermore
And have a husband who comes home at night
  And slams the door!

RUTH STEWART SCHENLEY.

Even the servants love to gossip . . . the fat mammy cook tells her "chillun" of her mistress . . .

LATE TER GLORY

She am late gittin' up,
  She am late gittin' meals,
She am late to retiah,
  An' she'll know how it feels
Ter be late gittin' inter Glory.

She am late ter de church,
  She am late ter de meetin'.
She'll be late ter de gate
  When her soul hab gone fleetin',
She'll be late gittin' inter Glory.

She wuz late ter de weddin'
  An' she kep' her man waitin'.
She'll be late ter her fun'el,
  But she'll cheat Ol' man Satan
Bein' late gittin' inter Glory.

EMMELINE LOWE.

BALLAD OF THE LADY IN HELL

The Devil was bored with the whole affair.
He yawned while he lolled in his judgment chair,
Impatient with even the ones who swerved
From God and themselves that his ends be served.
Three fiends slammed the door of the draughty hall
And all Hell gazed on a woman—small—
Defiant—though tortured—with mouth still sweet
With mortal caresses at Satan's feet.
The Devil is fair, though he plays to win.
"Just what," he inquired, "was the lady's sin?"
The first fiend bent low, "She was one man's wife—
She loved two men dearly through half her life."
The second fiend spoke, "Though she sewed straight seams
And swept her floor clean—still she dreamed her dreams."
"She bore one man's children," the third fiend said,
"She pledged him her soul—but her soul is dead!"
"Just what," said the Devil, "do you imply?"
"We state," the three shouted, "she lived a lie!
She gave one her body—she shirked no task—
Her song was a shield and her smile a mask!
Her dreams were a gossamer road that ran
From year on to year to another man."
The Devil smiled thinly, "From what you tell
I judge that the lady has had her Hell."
The gate against sinners was half ajar.
The lady slipped by the celestial bar.
An angel approached with a flaming sword—
"What boon dost thou ask of the kindly Lord?"
The lady was weary and very sad.
"I came though unbidden, for once I had
The gift of all gifts and I could not pay
In full—I seek only to kneel and pray.
I pray to forget him who came too late!
I want to go back through the star chained gate—
To dream the old dreams that I cherished when
I knew but one voice in the world of men.
To see one man's face and to be soul free
For Him would be Heaven enough for me."

* * *

While down on the earth two—unheeding—slept
The angel and God and the lady wept.

ANNETTE PATTON CORNELL.

54

Before I forget . . . you know your neighbor's new cook . . . of course she's pretty . . . she's been around . . .

SAILOR'S WILL

Red slippers from a princess's feet
Bought for a song in a Persian street;

A string of beads and a kiss, or a peck,
In each dull stone upon her neck;

A stolen book from a grey convent
With its broken chain and Latin print;

All of these she gathered in,
But the last was a Spanish mandolin.

(In the northeast storm the other night
The crew of the Molly S. drowned outright.)

Now she's put by slippers, beads and book
And has got a job as a lady's cook.

But that mandolin on the wall will play
Songs of her men to her dying day.

ANDREW HEWITT.

But let's talk about the new president of the club . . . Her husband is a liberal . . . she shouts it every meeting . . .

SHALLOW WATERS

She thinks I'm narrow-minded,
    Because my thoughts don't flow
Along the same small channel
    Where hers are bound to go.

ELVA R. RAY.

55

I always suspect people like that . . . so proper and precise . . . behind
their doors and windows . . . their maids could tell us quite a lot . . .

MILADY KNITS

Milady, at the open window, sits
With countenance serene and look demure,
Her downcast eyes contributing allure.
The blush upon her cheek that glows and flits,
Adds glamour that demoralizes wits;
And waning sun with touch so light and sure,
Makes of her hair a golden halo pure.
But modestly, Milady simply knits,
Intent upon the swiftly rhythmic flash
Of gleaming needles that is never stopped—
While world and I adore her beauty fair.
But now I rise and quickly close the sash,
For I have noted that a stitch is dropped,
And World—you must not hear Milady swear!

OPAL BLAISDELL LENOX.

Not the grocer's wife . . . have you seen her baby . . . poor thing . . .

CHASM

She and I
Can never be friends!
Our babies are the same age,
But not
The same weight.

MARY LANIGAN HEALY.

56

Having spared no one in the community . . . we should hardly hesitate to dig up a little scandal among trees . . .

CLANDESTINE LOVE

Two poplars rose for years,
Slim and proud, on each side
Of an old stone wall.
Their arms lifted to the sky.
They looked conventionally
Impersonal,
Last summer—
The drouth killed them.
Today they were uprooted.

Under the dividing wall
Their roots embraced.

ROSA ZAGNONI MARINONI.

It's been so nice visiting with you . . . if you find out what really happened when the banker's wife left him . . . call me up won't you . . . it must be worse than people say.

WARNING

Who drinks of Rumor's unguent brew
  Will never quench her thirst,
For she will crave succeeding cups,
  More spiced than the first.

ELIZABETH SAWYER.

"All the World's a Stage—
and All the Men and Women Merely Players . . .

At the opening of a play the plot may seem so futile . . . a hero and a heroine . . . so hopelessly apart . . .

DARK BLESSING

Physicians said the chance was very dim
That she might ever see the face of him
Who had grown dear by painting leaden skies
In brilliant colors, lending her his eyes.
Her fingers on his face were cool. The tips
He kissed as they brushed lightly past his lips,
Her fingers could not feel the cruel streak
That zagged its fire-marked way across his cheek;
And he who thought a broken spirit dies,
Had found himself in her unseeing eyes.

JESSIE FARNHAM.

Costume play . . . with Indians . . . scouts . . . plainsmen . . .

GRANNY'S RECEIPT

I found it deep in Granny's trunk,
  Beneath her Sunday petticoats,
A yellowed paper, old and worn,
  Shuffled and lost among her notes.

In girlish writing, round and straight,
  It marches brave, across the page,
"My husband Jim's best-liked receipt,
  Dressing made with prairie sage."

I followed her receipt one day,
  Although I had no glowing fire,
Built by a prairie schooner's door,
  Blown by a prairie wind's desire.

Yet somehow in its flavored depths,
  I saw a little maiden stand,
And say, "I made your dressing, Jim,"
  And touch him with a sun-browned hand.

I saw brown prairies meet the skies,
  And love and laughter in their eyes!

HAZEL GOLDING.

60

Pantomime . . . the greatest art of all . . . the most and least satisfy-ing . . .

MAIDEN LADY

She built herself a little house
    Upon a quiet street
And lives a lonely, sterile life,
    Sufficient and complete.

No guests have ever entered there
    But strangers passing by
Report the oddest kind of sounds,—
    A word, a kiss, a sigh.

And oftentimes on stormy nights,
    Above the thunder's roar
They hear a ghostly pit-a-pat
    Go toddling 'cross the floor.

KATHERINE KELLY WOODLEY.

Mountebank . . . Charleston . . . Fort Sumter . . . Cypress and Magnolia gardens . . . the slave market . . . King Street . . . Meeting Street . . . against this back drop . . .

THE GULLAH CRY

Centuries old is the Gullah's cry,—
Calling his wares in Charleston,—
"Hur's de *bes-t*—ter bu-y!
Buy,—bu-y-e,-e'ry-son-er-de-gun,
De velly bes-t 'n Char-lees-ton!
Dey sell-e by de pint ur de ton,—
De *velly* best in Char-lees-ton!
Veg-e-bubbles! *G-u-d-e* veg-e-bubbles,—
Cure ye uv *all* yer trubbles!
Strawber-ee, an-e fresh, an-e fine,—
An-e right off e-vine!
Strawber-ee! Nathin' sa fine
'Pun e-vitch t' dine!
Strawber-ee,-n-e fresh an-e fine,
An-e right off e vine!

Nothing's so old under the setting sun,
As the *Gullah's Cry* in Charleston.

ELEANOR FOX PONDER.

61

THE TEA TRADER

Jackson at his counter packing tea—
Storing little bags away
For the rush hours Saturday.
On the tea-bins' painted faces
Are quaint names and quainter places,
And a Geisha waves her fan
And allures him to Japan!
'Mid the syrups, soaps and sodas
Jackson muses on pagodas,
And the tea's pervasive smell
Works an opiatic spell
On the old clerk's stuffy brain. . . .
He goes sailing to Formosa
And to Java and Hong Kong;
He goes trafficking in Pekoe
And Bohea and Oolong!
Then a voice, "Six lemons, please,
And a pound of English cheese!"
Jackson's ship has come to shore
In McConnell's grocery store!

DANIEL HENDERSON.

BARGAIN

"Thirty pieces . . . I will sell.
   I will sell them, God.
Fools! to think that they can hold
   Stem of Jesse's rod."
Torch-lit swords reflect the kiss.
   Pierce the night with sorrow:
God escapes to self as God
   With the blood-bought morrow:
Drenched, the silver-driven hope
Mocks the bargain with a rope.

MABEL NATALIE ERICKSEN.

SOPHISTICATE

Old friends are but a graveyard where the dead
  Lie unentombed and have a final fling;
    A potter's field, with gay bones bellowing
Forgotten things far better left unsaid.
Yesterday is a hearty corpse, well fed;
  An old lover; a long outmoded thing;
    And yet persistently re-echoing
An existence which has since been shed.

Today I go serenely on my way
  Until a face looms from the past; I greet
Not just this friend, but all of yesterday—
  A kiss, a tear, a triumph or defeat.
Oh God! It seems more strange with passing Springs
That I should have outgrown so many things.

ETHEL BARNETT DE VITO.

QUIEN SABE?

A Mexican couple
Oblivious of the staring crowd,
Climbing the old Court House steps;
The bride in a billowing white veil
And the proverbial orange blossoms.

Across the street stands the County Jail,
From which the groom has been released
Under a solemn oath
He would no longer be a bad *hombre*.

And in the basement of the Court House,
Conveniently located,
Presides a stern judge,
Who dispenses divorces
For wife beating.

MINA SHAFER.

ANN'S WAY

Ann has a way that's different, some way.
  She makes a game of every little thing . . .
Her suds is just a white-cap on the bay;
  Her copper kettle has a song to sing;

If biscuits burn, it's incense trailing there
  With fragrant scent, and weaving filmy dreams
About her head; she laughs at every care,
  And always is quite happy, so it seems.

When sonny hurts his hand or stubs his toes
  She says: "Now here's the hospital, I'm nurse."
And then she laughs and wrinkles up her nose,
  And sonny soon gets better, 'stead o' worse!

But when she thinks no one will see her, well . . .
  She seems to look away, way off somewhere,
And falls into a kind of dreamy spell,
  And moves her lips like one in silent prayer.

ESTELLE E. WILSON.

THE KNITTING

"What will it be when I am done?" she said,
"A self-compounded morphine of the soul;
A sedative administered by self
For want of any other to prescribe.
The stitches small? Yes, you may find them so,
And even; as the restless work of hands
Which find no meaning in the task they do
Sometimes may be. Having no larger goal,
They seek to do a small thing perfectly;
Hoping some miracle may make it seem
Important to themselves.
Were I to watch this window, here, and sit,
I should go mad more quickly; so I knit."

MARGARET BARBER.

The ingenue . . . no painted lily . . . no dream of beauty . . . just a simple girl to prove the oldest adage of romance . . . love . . . true love . . . is ofttimes blind . . .

THE ANSWER

"Dear God," she used to pray, "when I am grown,
　Make me as beautiful as sister, please,
With curly hair that's dark and fine and long,
　And not a freckle for a boy to tease."
The years could scarcely change the braids of red
　To chestnut curls or hide the freckles, quite,
And mirrors did not answer with a dream
　Of loveliness until one magic night
When someone said, "You are so beautiful.
　Within his eyes she saw her dream come true,
And did not guess that she had found, at last,
　The kindest mirror ever woman knew.

ISABELLE BRYANS LONGFELLOW.

Character part . . . how shall he be interpreted . . . he who knew all height and depth . . . how was he at the end . . .

NAPOLEON AT SAINT HELENA

Quicksilver courage had escaped his hand;
The kelp was blanching on the ocean's lawn;
His face was wrinkled flotsam, white and drawn;
The little Corsican longed to join his band.
Napoleon cringed upon the lonely sand;
He gibbered, cursed at night's eternal dawn.
His leering warden took him for a pawn:
An ivory king brushed from the chessmen's land.

Was he remorseful in his final hour,
Accused by misty mothers of the slain,
Convicted by fog-jurors of the west?
The claw of twilight crunched his dream of power
While gnats and flies of doubt besieged his brain;
The drum grew silent in his craven breast.

M. G. WILLIAMS.

IN NICOTINA

Oh! she was a gay little cigarette
  And he was a fat cigar,
And side by side on a tabouret
  They stood in a ginger jar.

Though nary a word could I understand,
  For they chatted in Actobac,
Yet wonderful things I am sure they planned
  Like lovers all do—alack!

Today she's a sad little cigarette,
  For gone is her brave cigar,
And all alone on the tabouret
  She stands in the ginger jar.

Now Love is a marvelous thing, 'tis true,
  And many a fault will cloak,
But often it ends as the dream of these two,
  In nothing at all but smoke!

RENA SHEFFIELD.

*Realism . . . the modern play . . . no footlights or spotlights . . . no color-
ful curtains . . . just empty stage . . . front . . . center . . .*

UNSEEING EYES

A blue-bird sings his heart out at her window—
  She doesn't hear him as she scours the pane,
Great drifting clouds are gathering in the heavens—
  She only thinks, perhaps it's going to rain.

She scrubs the porch with concentrated vigor,
  White and smooth it gleams, beneath her work-worn hands;
Some children pass her gate with quiet swiftness,
  Their laughter hushed . . . she never understands.

A butterfly rests on a vine beside her,
  Lifting and lowering dusty golden wings—
But she is all unconscious of its beauty . . .
  Her life's obsession . . . is material things.

GERTRUDE S. STINSON.

TWO MARYS

I wonder if Mary, heavy with Child,
Counted her stitches and softly smiled
At the feel of wool that would keep Him warm,
As she knitted a sleeve for a baby's arm;
Knitted and counted, woman-wise,
And looking up to meet the skies,
Saw camels trudge across the sand
Loaded with jeweled contraband.

I know a Mary who's knitting for
An unborn child where the steady roar
Of a China Clipper against the sun
Brings the scene to the present one.
And never a king with gifts of myrrh
Will kneel at the shabby feet of her;
And never a star will lend its flame
To halo a son without a name.

And yet I feel, because of Him;
That other Mary in the dim
Cathedral of a manger bore,
The world will have compassion for
This little one whose Christmas cry
Will mingle with the roar of high,
White planes that winter clouds emboss . . .
Two Marys shadowed by a cross.

VIVIAN YEISER LARAMORE.

PARADOX

It seemed a paradox, that she whose placid days
Were anchored by four walls, and garden paths ...
Prim rows of hollyhocks, delphinium and phlox,
And the tranquil tenor of domestic verities,
Should mother a storm-tossed lad, who "must away",
Following the salt-tides and the flying spray,
Compassed by stars ... the rolling deck, his home.

"Is it not strange", in wonderment men asked,
"That son of hers should sail before the mast?"

Her answer held the flash of gull-swept skies,
For all the magic of the seven seas
Shone from her eyes!

MAGDELEN EDEN BOYLE.

Tableau ... purple and grey mountains on beyond ... beams of rainbow color ... a trail winding onward and then ... in the soft light ... a man walking slowly toward a maiden awaiting him ...

TRAILS TO THE GREY EMPERORS

He is one in whom the gypsy gods delight,
Journeying with the wind for compass, at night
   Kindling his fire by some stream
Where waters rustling darkly over stone,
And willows chanting in silver monotone
   Set music to his dream.

At dawn again upon his far nomadic way,
Up blue flights of hills sky-mounting where the grey
   Emperors brood above eternal snows,
And down through canyons widening to green,
Far-sweeping waters where the wind cuts keen
   And spray-light glints and glows.

But there will come a day in some thronged place,
When he will glimpse a shy miraculous face ...
   The sombre cloak of loneliness will fall
Upon him and his trail-worn steps will turn
Down some old street where quiet tapers burn
   Beyond an ivied wall.

IRIS LORA THORPE.

68

All the world's a stage ...
      and after the play ...
               the curtain ...

'TWIXT MAN AND MAN

I

My dear Mrs. Kenneth:

This goes to you tonight with a box of arbutus blossoms —the flowers you told me you loved best. As your flowers, I thought of you as I searched the woods for them. You will not refuse them a welcome. Let them tell you, if they can— if anything can—of my reverence for you. Their fragrance is but faintly typical of the sweetness your life has breathed upon mine. In the presence of these pure blossoms—in your presence, I tremble as I allude to the last dance on the lawn.

Perhaps you will forgive me the exquisite joy of that half- hour in the moonlight, when I tell you that since yesterday, when I learned the truth, my hair is almost white. You were so young; you had come all the way from Washington— I did not catch your name, and then when you were chosen maid of honor, I felt sure. I am a worldly fellow, Mrs. Kenneth, but I think, as I sit writing here alone tonight, that in that other world where souls are unveiled, you will not blush to have inspired the worship of even a worldly fellow's heart —the worship my heart will always give you.

Faithfully yours,

JOHN THURSTON.

March 8, 1902
Calumet Club, New York

II

My dear Mr. Thurston:

Your box of arbutus came last Sunday morning. Dolly, my wife, died the night before. When I had read your letter, I laid the blossoms in her hands. I, too, am a worldly man. I had grown used, I fear, to the precious things of life. I can not put a finger on my regrets—I never knowingly hurt her; but as your letter lies before me now, it comes to me with bitter pain that I did not always worship on my knees.

In that world where souls are unveiled, Dolly sees clearly now, and it may be that she knows you loved her best. God forgive me; she was worth the homage of both our lives. Her death leaves me quite alone. When you are in Washington you can find me at the University Club.

Yours truly,

RICHARD KENNETH.

March 12, 1902
University Club, Washington

"First Person, Singular . . .

NOT WHOLLY CHAINED

Beloved, if you love me, leave me free.
   I shall be twenty times your own, if I
   May keep my old communion with the sky,
The pool that holds it, and one ancient tree,
Green meadows, and all lovely things there be;
   If I may dance when autumn moons are white
   With old, familiar spirits of the night,
Not wholly chained to domesticity.

For sometimes I have neither sex nor age,
But just the urge of one strong heritage:
   To view an outspread world from heights above;
And seeing all the kingdoms of the earth,
Beloved, I shall measure best the worth
   Of this small one we founded upon love.

FLORENCE B. JACOBS.

*This is a true story . . . it took place . . . corner Church and Chapel
Streets . . . New Haven, Connecticut . . .*

I SHOULDN'T HAVE BEEN STANDING THERE

I know, I shouldn't have been standing there in everybody's
   way.
I shouldn't have been standing there at that busy time of day.
When he came around the corner he must have been goin'
   lickety-split
'Cause I thought a mountain toppled when our two full bodies
   hit.
He sure must have been in a hurry by the way he fussed and
   swore.
And he didn't even notice, when I promised I wouldn't stand
   there any more.
But I guess only 'cause he was ruffled that's why he was so
   downright unkind
For I just know he'd have acted differently if someone had
   told him I was blind.

MARKEY SULLIVAN.

74

SKYLINE TRAILS

Smooth grey macadam, or sunshiny rail,
Black-funneled ship, or a gleaming white sail—
Ribbon of highway, or moon-path of sea—
None of these ways will be tempting of me.

Mine is a wanderlust, harder to cure—
Old as mankind, and as certain its lure—
Spring-time or Autumn, the charm never fails:
I go, to the beckon of skyline trails!

Sturdy of boots, but a shoulder-light pack,
Up, then, and over the Mountain's broad back!
Deep-needled pathway, and pungence of pine,
Furry, light foot-prints, companioning mine.

Timberline-hemlock, or vine-maple glade,
Tall firs, that whisper ... and I, unafraid,
Thrill to the scents and the sounds of the wild!—
Kin to the forest—the hill-country's child.

Up, and away with the dawning, I walk,
Singing to chatter of forest-folk talk ...
Noon-day, and silence—that infinite hush!" ...
Night, and the sweet hermit-call of the thrush.

Night, and a finger of smoke from my fire,
Pointing as true as the Mountain's white spire ...
Sleep, and its benison, never once fails!—
I go, to the summons of skyline trails.

BLANCHE DEGOOD LOFTON.

AFTERMATH

People thought that you were dead,
"The dear departed one," they said.
How strange a thing, they never knew
That I had died instead of you.

LOLLY WILLIAMS

*Where is the source . . . of the boundless faith . . . supreme confidence . . .
knowledge irrefutable . . .*

THE SOUL SPEAKS

I shall discover; I shall know—
The reasons for me . . . and, where I go . . .

Through mists of fears I rise and fall—
Obedient to bidding beyond it all. . . .

I, who have died a thousand times
Upon false crosses, live! And climb!
With boundless reach . . . with groping prayer . . .
Strangely, move toward some birth, somewhere . . .

I leave the graves of blood and pain . . .
I go from death, to love again. . . .

No end to me! This Soul must bear
This gift from God . . . to His Somewhere. . . .

SARA ADLER ROSALSKY.

The I . . . that even I must never fully understand . . .

ACQUISITION

Grandmother counted linens,
    Laundered white as snow,
Counted all the silver
    And placed it in a row.
Let a piece be missing,
    She would know.

I never counted silver—
    Pantries were to me
Prison cells for chattel
    And drudgery.

Grandmother now is sleeping,
    All her treasure scattered;
I possess the teaspoons
    Old and frail and battered;
Why do I count them
    Who never thought it mattered?

CLARA HYDE.

The I . . . the ego, I . . . the self-sufficient pagan I . . .

TO APRIL

I am pagan, so are you.
We are pagan through and through.
Some unshriven gypsy strain
Latent through the years has lain
Dormant, smouldering, alive;
Curse that priest could never shrive.

We have lived in other climes,
Lived and died full many times;
Dwelt with Isis, body-free,
Pagans still—eternally.
Suns and seasons serve their turn,
Pagan fires forever burn.

Spirit held by spirit hands
Danced in thought, so spirit bands;
Waltzed into the here and now—
Ask me not, I know not how.
This I glean from vale and hill:
You and I are pagan still.

We have danced to rites of Set,
Dimly I remember yet:
Wild the music, mad the dance,
Great the gods of circumstance
Ruling water, earth and sky—
You are pagan, so am I.

DAVID INNES.

The thirst that is unquenchable . . .

POVERTY

My cup is full; yet oft I think
    It holds scarce anything at all!—
Not because life lacks abundance,
    But because my cup is small!

RUTH INSCHO.

77

How many things were you . . . before you became what you are . . .

SONNET

I might have been a hawk's scream, harsh and slow,
    The plaint that's in the whip-poor-will's still cry,
Six turning flakes of this down-drifting snow
    Or neat track of a fox gone stealthy by
The hill field's rim. I might have been the rain,
    March rain and cold or April rain and sweet,
Or scent of hay in June or faster stain
    Across the light of speed to make it fleet.
Why on this earth? As well I might have been
    Far darkness in the starry vast of space,
But I am quick and man, all these have seen.
    I am them all and love for this my place.
Berkshire is mine while atoms, planets, dance
    And tremble round the cynic laws of chance.

JAMES PLAYSTED WOOD.

You can do this with a book too . . .

BLUE WILLOW

My fate might not have been the dreamer's,
    No time for prose and all for froth,
If the ware had not been old blue willow
    From which I supped my daily broth!

A child, I lived the quaint tradition,
    I was the Chinese maid, Kong Shee,
Flitting the bridge with Chang, the lover,
    From the convent house by the willow tree.

I drained my mug at every serving
    To rid it of its milky sea
And bring to light a gull still sailing
    Above the swaying willow tree!

A whimsy thought but one for toying,
    For who has power to estimate
The end of a young poetic fancy
    When nurtured from a willow plate?

MILDRED D. SHACKLETT.

78

"Out of the cradle endlessly rocking . . .

THOUGHTS OF A MODERN MAIDEN

Throb of my heart, throb of my heart,
How did you get here, where did you start?

Ages ago in some lowly thing,
Pulsating since with unceasing spring?

Through countless lifetimes, from mother to young,
Heart throb, heart throb, a rhythm has sung.

Once in a queen, twice in a slave,
Wife of a prince, wife of a knave.

Mother to daughter, down through the years,
Some heirs to gladness, some heirs to tears.

Defended by vassal, seized by a lord,
Sentenced to death but saved by a word.

Women of virtue, women of scum,
Women of desert, women of slum,

Down to my grandmere, sweet and demure,
Down to my mother, patient and pure.

Why was I forged as a link in this chain?
What of the past shall I break or maintain?

Heart throb, heart throb, wonder past knowing,
Where did you come from, where are you going?

EDITH M. ROBERTS.

The yesterdays . . . unlived . . .

SAD HARVEST

For years, it seems, I've only plowed
    Furrows, back and forth, around fields
Of hard-turned earth, when time allowed;
    I did not sow—now, no abundant yields.

CLARA S. HOFF.

79

I wonder who the first singular person was to say this . . .

TRAILER

When people say a witty thing,
   I never have a comeback.
I'm silent as a calendar
   Impaled upon a thumbtack.

But when the chance to speak is gone
   And finished are the quips,
The answers that I think of then
   Undoubtedly are pips.

Ah, me! The smart and funny cracks
   On ice within my brain,
Awaiting opportunities
   That will not come again!

               CONSTANCE R. DOWD.

Don't let the title lead you astray . . . this is but one of them and a lesser one at that . . .

MY SECRET SIN

If I were a modest violet
   I'd have a secret sin,
I'd want to be a hollyhock
   Tall and gay and thin;
I'd want to reach up toward the sky
   And throw my flowers about,
I'd hate to hug the soft damp earth
   And just grow wide and stout.

I'd want to whisper to the winds
   And feel the clouds sail by,
I'd want to flirt with humming birds
   Way up there in the sky;
I'd hate to feel the crawling things
   Around my little feet,
I never could be satisfied
   With being stout . . . and sweet.

             MARGUERITE V. YOUNG.

There is a chemical formula given to college freshmen . . . detailing with great accuracy the amount and variety of each chemical of which the body is composed . . . but it does not cover all . . .

DISCOVERY

I looked at me one day, one day,
    And made a strange discovery;
I am not me at all, at all,
    But all this that pretends it's me.

I am a laugh that some one liked,
    I am a walk that I acquired;
I am a scent of long-gone hours,
    Of lullaby and dreams half-fired.

I am a scrap of poetry,
    I am a prayer I learned to lisp;
I am that hidden unnamed fear,
    I am the first shy-given kiss.

Although I am not me at all
    I had to laugh at fate's bland tease,
That I who thought that I was me—
    To think that I am all of these.

CAROL PHILLIPS.

A poem on a piece of paper . . . from an envelope . . . from a girl . . . all . . . all golden brown . . .

I AM BROWN

I am Brown—as brown as Autumn trees
Shimmering gently thru the breeze.
I am Brown—because God made me so.
He must have loved me tho'
For it took time to make the dye
Then wait for me to dry.
I am not one who idly grieves,
Thanks God, for me and Autumn leaves.

ORALEE BROWN HARRIS.

81

WE KNOW

My heart and I know many things:
We know why singing birds have wings;

Why moths, enthralled by mad desire
Would rather die than shun the fire;

Why spirits bruised can make brave show,
While happiness must softly go;

Why music's mystic trinity
Holds peace, heartache and ecstacy;

Why Woman, since the world began
Feeds drop by drop, her heart to Man;

How daisies dance and grasses wave
Impartially above each grave;

Why bees must hive, fruit fill the pod;
How each soul fashions his own God.

My heart and I know many a thing,
Why tides must rise and poets sing.

MARTHA TAYLOR BROWN.

So spake the mother of Themistocles . . .

WEALTH

I never had an orchid in all my life;
Dimes loom large, economies are rife;
For me no mink will ever come to harm,
The lowly little rabbit keeps me warm;
One tiny diamond is the sum of my gems;
I've never seen Vienna, the Louvre or the Thames;
Yet many a pampered beauty could pay me jealous tears—
For I have had a son for sixteen years.

MARION SCHMIDT.

DEVOTION

When all your days are bright and fair,
I do not mind, too much, just where
Your sunny hours are gayly spent.
Content to know that you exist;
Brief moments, even, I resist
That longing, all your life to share:
Content then, if not happy, too,
I live—I breathe away from you.
But when your life by storm is rent
No longer can I rest content;
Heart throbs suspended or perturbed,
Hard-won placidity disturbed;
My spirit yearns to hold you fast
Against each hurt till all is past.

BERTA G. McGUIRK.

*The I . . . the calm courageous human I . . . the lyrical, laughable, lovable
I . . . At long last the last long I . . .*

RENDEZVOUS

I, too, have a rendezvous with Death,
    But, woman-like, I'll keep him waiting,
Grumbling beneath his icy breath,
    Impotently execrating
Mothers who will not leave their young
    To go adventuring in the night
'Til the last lullabye is sung,
    The last, soft cover tucked in tight,
And all the out-grown books and blocks,
    The cover-alls and little dresses,
The well-worn shoes and tiny socks
    Stored in the attic's dim recesses.
But patience, Death, when I have done,
    I shall come smiling down the stair,
And whisper, "Come, impatient one,
    I'm ready now for anywhere!"

WINIFRED STODDARD LeBAR.

83

LOST — A BOY

I lost him,—I, who should have been his friend and guide.
Through early years I led his eager feet;
But when he came to me with questions grave and deep,
With eyes that brooked not sham or sophistry,
I lost him—I was his church.

I lost him,—who was mine to love and rear.
A nurse girl salved his early woes and shamed his fears.
Time fled; an eager lad rushed home from school,
With some small triumph, ill concealed,
Or with a problem that called for sympathetic handling,
Or perchance it was a boy's appetite, seemingly insatiable,
And was greeted by a cold and empty house.
I lost him—I was his mother.

I lost him,—who should have been my pride and recompense
    for labor.
His eager questions and shy efforts at companionship,
His hidden hero worship small sons have for "Dad,"
Were met with sharp impatience, "Some other time, I'm
    busy."
One day I called to him for a son's companionship,
And lo, he was a stranger.
I lost him,—I was his father.

KATE BRINGHURST JOOR.

DOUBTING THOMAS

My friend the skeptic sees no truth in man,
While I believe all things I rightly can.
My friend is honest—others' honesty
Is lost to him, and all sincerity.

Who's fooled the more—my skeptic friend or I?
The one who doubts the truth, or trusts a lie?
I may be duped, deceived. I shan't repine.
My friend would give his soul for faith like mine.

LILLIAN F. HODGES.

MARGARETTA'S BOOK 1816

The ink grows pale upon the page
   A century and more
Has rolled away since last she closed
   This book of ancient lore.

They said her hair was like the sun,
   Her body slim and white.
She looked on death with quiet eyes
   And passed into the night.

Smiling she went away with him,
   Gentle and unafraid;
Why does she stir my thoughts today,
   This ghostly little maid?

Upon a grey and lichened stone
   Are scarcely to be read
The simple words that mark the place
   Where lay her golden head.

I wonder why, this April dusk,
   When air is cool with dew,
A message seems to come to me
   From one I never knew.

KATHERINE VAN DER VEER.

I WONDER

I wonder, with a shuttle warped
   As mine is, if a life can still
Be woven well. Perhaps it can
   If I command a greater skill
In weaving than one whose shuttle's true.
   And it may take more thought to design
A pattern, strong, complete, for me
   To weave, whose shuttle's out of line.

ELVA R. RAY.

"Wit or Without . . . Brevity Is the Soul . . .

If you don't get the point ... you should be sat on ...

MEMORY

Memory is a fragile thing;
A bee's honey, and its sting.

VIOLET WIGGINS NEWTON.

Name of the lady on request ...

MODERN LULLABY

Hush-a-bye, baby, life's just a blight,
Man is a monkey, Barnum was right;
Ma's gone a-voting, Pa's buying clothes—
But the name of the lady, nobody knows.

ELEANOR STANLEY LOCKWOOD.

The flowers that bloom in the spring tra la ...

FRIENDS

Some are true;
Others are not.
They'll either love you,
Or what you've got.

BEA MYERS.

Blooming idiots ...

A MEAN TRICK

April showers
Bring May flowers
That perhaps might well be true,
But *one* shower
On the flower
Of my hat—and it is through!

DOROTHY QUICK.

88

Defective detective yarn . . .

WARNING TO WHODUNIT FANS

You like your murders gory when they're safely in a story,
    But here's a little warning I will offer free of charge:
It used to be the butler, but the readers like 'em subtler
    So they're running out of suspects and the criminal's still
        at large.
Do you think you can recover when some author does discover
    That the reader is one character he has never thought to
        brand?
For he'll pin the crime on you, and you won't know what to do
    When you awake and find yourself with a murder on your
        hand!

INEZ GEORGE GRIDLEY.

Monument works . . . please copy

When the last person
Here is dead,
Who'll put a tombstone
At his head?

LEONORE EVERSOLE FISHER.

Blame this on the apple too . . .

SOMETIMES THIS HAPPENS

She liked tall things—
High heels,
Sunflowers
And slender sky-bound trees.
She succumbed to the force of gravity
And married
A gentleman
Of circular rotundity.

LOUISE HAYNES.

The Infinite sense of humor . . .

"HUMORESQUE"

He must have smiled a little, I suppose,
  When He saw plus and minus disagree,
And elbows never could contact one's nose—
  He must have laughed aloud when He made me!

CONSTANCE ANN HALL.

The ultimate utter . . .

ANATOMICAL OBSERVATION

A chicken's skin hides
Its interesting insides.

LENORE EVERSOLE FISHER.

But when he's old and bald . . .

PREDICTION

The baby's hair is just a timid fuzz,
  And innocent of prophecy, although
It has its own persistent human way
  Of going just the way it wants to go.

ELLEN ACTON.

You may count on your fingers . . . to figure this out . . .

INFINITY

To the ever-rising sun
  There is no time, no age—
Tomorrow yesterday are one;
  That which was and is to be
Doth with *now* as one become.
From whence we glean *infinity*.

EDWIN N. ACKERMAN.

"Silence is golden . . .

MUTES

Vivacious, nutant poppies,
On each slender stalk,
Mute but not expressionless,
Smile and talk.

And aunt in fresh starched apron,
Troweling the sand,
Deaf and mute these sixty years,
Still can understand.

EDITH L. JOHNSON.

Maybe . . . for a poet . . .

IT IS ENOUGH

A lovely thought—if that is all you know of me.
It is enough—oh, quite enough to satisfy;

I cannot think of one thing more I'd rather be,
Than one fine thought to last through all Eternity.

ESTHER FRESHMAN.

This will burn you up . . .

BIT BY BITTER

His hair was so splendidly flaming
I'd not be denier;
His mind was brilliant past taming
And set it on fire.

But now he is bald and much older,
'And only a smoke
Of moustache reveals that there smoulder
Hot words that he spoke.

RALPH CHEYNEY.

91

Thank goodness it isn't red ink . . .

FUTILITY

I'm burning the well-known midnight oil,
    And using endless bottles of ink,
In trying to write with flaming pen—
    But all my stuff is *pastel pink!*

CHARLOTTE BLAISING.

Starlight . . . starbright . . .

NIGHT IS SO LONG

A strip of void fastened to my window frame,
    And one assertive star;
Chastising me, purging me in its white flame,
    Where all tomorrows are.

MARY CALUORI.

Mutual admiration party . . .

BABY PICTURE

So You were I. . . .
Somehow
I can't think thru
To that forgotten time
When I was You.
Could your clear eyes
Read
What is in my own,
Would You
Feel disappointment
At the Me
To which
You've grown?

AMY ATWATER.

92

QUERY

Wishful thinking . . .

Because I am
So short and fat
Quite like
A butter ball,
I
Wonder
Why
My
Shadow
Is
So
Thin
And
Straight
And
Tall!

HELEN YOUNG.

I knew a girl once . . . in Paris, Missouri . . .

IMPRESSIONS OF PARIS

Apache dance!
I can't forget:
A small dark girl,
A cigarette.

A puff of smoke,
A glittering gun;
And fat Americans
On the run.

NORMA PAUL RUEDI.

93

I have tried my best to think of some appropriate little remark for this little poem . . . but invariably the remark turns out to be longer than the poem it is supposed to introduce and that is unpardonable . . . so if you will just ignore all this . . . I'll strike off something casual like . . . Mountain music . . .

OLD WOMEN TREES

The pine needles click . . .
Click . . . knitting stray wisps of wind
Into scarves of song.

DOROTHY MARIE DAVIS.

Memorize this one . . .

RAINBOW-ROOM

Almost any rainbow
Finds a place to start,
In a rain-stained heaven,
Or a tear-stained heart. . . .

LILLIAN EVERTS.

Alibi . . .

GOOSE AND THE GANDER

It wasn't lovelight
For me in your eyes,
That I knew;
But it was alright,
I was telling lies
To you too!

FRANCES FARFONE.

"It's an ill wind . . .

OZARK FUTILITY

Peach trees in bloom again
Pink petals blow . . .
Down across the pig-pen
Beauty wasted—so!

RUTH H. TYLER.

Sorry This Section Ran Short . . .
Brevity Is That Way Sometimes . . .

"I Went to the Animal Fair . . .

Along the Boston Post Road . . . out in front of a stand piled high with apples . . . pumpkins . . . squash . . . potatoes . . . onions . . . peppers . . . cider . . .

SIGN BY THE ROAD: *KITTENS FOR SALE*

Can you imagine anyone selling his kittens?—
Young kittens with eyes like plops of opaline dew?—
Kittens with twitchery ears and little pink candy-heart
      noses?
And bellies of snowy fluff and paws like feathered roses?

If I hadn't two cents to my name I wouldn't sell kittens;
Not if they rolled underfoot and clawed runs in my hosiery,
Or meowed incessantly for cream and expensive cat-ration,
Or were littered in batches of twelve *twice* every lunation.

For never were light-flash or shadows so nimble as kittens—
(Dart-legged, eld-worshipped, deemed sacred, and mummied
      in spice!)—
Nor so deft, nor so daft swifts, junebugs or squirrels—so
      winning
Knaves, elfmen or pixies—adepts at frank amiable sinning.

I can imagine one selling his shirt or his ancestors' kettles,
Or his pottage, or his cottage, or—in China—his daughters,
Or his collection of stamps, or his car, or his old driving
      mittens;
But *never,* not *ever* black, white, tabby or calico kittens!

Bettie Sale.

Have you ever read a finer tribute to dogs . . .

BRIEF WORSHIP

So short a time they have
    Before life ends,
These dear companions,
    These beloved friends—

So brief a while to frisk
    In utter glee
Or droop in dire disgrace
    Upon severity.

And man is somehow greater that,
    For his one nod,
They'd scale the frowning heavens and
    They'd bark at God!

Virginia Scott Miner.

*Some people who buy kittens . . . grow careless of their treatment . . .
they let them go hungry . . . they let them get lost . . .*

LOST KITTEN AT THE DOOR

Purr softly . . .
For surely someone will decide to let you in.
Cold loneliness is not for such a gentle thing
As you. And then besides, a worried Mother Cat
Is counting out her little brood and praying that
A kindly soul somewhere will stroke your tiny paw
And let a bit of friendly fire her truant kitten thaw!

Purr softly . . .
For folks will know you're weary of your little fling,
And soon their altruistic hearts will start to sing
Because of you. A problem kitty though you be,
You soon will doze in undeserved security;
And Mother Cat, her final pussy prayer a-said,
Will put the others of her little brood to bed!

EMILY TEMPLETON.

*Some people who buy kittens . . . treat them quite as richest royalty . . .
I know a kingly Persian . . . and his name . . . Honey Boy . . .*

HONEY BOY

Like mountain honey, richly red
From tip of tail to regal head,
A thing of beauty, and a joy
Forever, is my Honey Boy.

Akin to lilies of the field
Who neither toil nor spin, yet yield
Their fragrant beauty to the earth;
And, yielding, justify their birth.

He lives his life of silken ease,
And strives none but himself to please;
Yet walks in beauty all his days,
And thus his debt to life repays.

BILLIE MARIE CRABB.

99

CHIMNEY SWALLOW

The chimney throat is old and wide;
A questing swallow's downward glide
Precipitates him in my room—
To him strange world with threat of doom.

The frightened swallow with magic wings
Beats futilely the pane and clings
At last, despairing, to the curtain's lace.
And I, the dreaded monster of the place,
Approach with outstretched hand. He quakes;
Whatever prayers a swallow makes
Are timely now. With fast-closed eyes
He waits. Now in my hand he lies,
Inert, defenseless—nor can guess
That I am sharing his distress.

I hasten to the door and fling
It wide—the thorny small feet cling
Tight to my finger! Can it be
He scorns the gift of liberty?

One moment till bewildered brain
Discerns that he is free again;
One breathless moment till he flies
Into the glory of the skies!

Souls, too, have wings for flying far
If they could sense how free they are.

B. Y. WILLIAMS.

*By the light of the moon . . . "the big baboon" . . . saw a creature crawl
from a cracked cocoon . . .*

DISCOVERY

A caterpillar squirmed
   Up to a lettuce leaf
And panted at the top
   In woolly-worm relief.

On pancake world of green
   And dizzy depths of brown
It gaped: "Now I've seen everything!"
   And slowly slithered down.

DOROTHY SIGMUND.

100

*For the erudite scholar we submit this as technically one of one hundred
twenty thousand varieties of the Lepidoptera . . .*

A MOTH FOUND ON THE FLOOR

Were I an entomologist,
I'd call you by your proper name
That's likely long and difficult, but now
You're just a dead grey moth—the grist
Of circumstance.

I touch your tame
And quiet wings, and then allow
Their spangled dust that lies like dew,
Or pollen on a flower, to glint
Upon my fingers—spread your wings;
Although they're drab and dull of hue,
Upon them lies a patterned print
Of intricate black stencilings
That shows a master craftsman's ink.

And here are hidden wings inside
Of velvet black, and on each lies
Surprisingly, two bars of radiant pink. . . .
Who taught you wisdom, Moth, to hide
Your loveliness from casual eyes?

EDNA M. BECKER.

To the fair . . . to the fair . . . the best in the county were there . . .

THE ROAN COLT

His awkward legs have not learned how
To ease the rhythm of a plow;
The harness on his back is not
Like anything he has been taught.

He shakes his head; his back is wet;
He pulls to pay an unknown debt;
His years of laboring begin
To earn his dole from stack and bin.

I know there is no help for it
As long as time controls the course,
But I must always grieve a bit
To see a colt become a horse.

KEITH THOMAS.

101

MY NEW CLAM

A funny creature is my clam:
He doesn't seem to give a damn
About how anxiously I am
   Watching to see him move.

Without the use of feet or toes
Hands or fingers, eyes or nose,
Straight across the sand he goes
   And leaves a groove.

I cannot tell which way he'll face,
When travelling from place to place:
He may bewail his slothsome pace
   In much exasperation,

And still, if he could talk aloud
He *might* be very, very proud
That Nature had *so well* endowed
   A clam with transportation.

'Tis plain he's Master of his Soul;
He asks no aid to find his goal,
Nor even hollow out a hole
   Wherein to dwell:

He has no worry, nor a care,
His food is in the water there,
And when the gold fish come and stare,
   He shuts his shell.
               STEPHANIE L. BINCKLI.

If they are grasshoppers . . . in Kansas . . . it's a plague . . . if they are dreams . . . in the heart . . . it's a vision . . .

MIGRANT WINGS

They are moving down the star-lanes,
Down the star-lanes, curving under;
They are plowing through the darkness
   Of the sky.
And the beat of whirring pinions
Makes a faintly sounding thunder
That my heart awakes to answer
   As they fly!
               RALPH J. DONAHUE.

*Lest you be tempted by the sea food . . . be assured . . . this lonely clam
is simply on exhibition . . .*

MISAPPELLATION

I've named my Clam, Irene, although
I'm sure it is a male, and so,
Before his spirit gets too low,
   I want a female for him.
His right Divine to be a sire,
(There is no aspiration higher),
Shall justify his deep desire
   For baby clams who would adore him.

For each male creature is at loss
If he has not someone to boss
And blame things on, when he is cross:
   (The gold fish quite ignore him),
So he should have a Mate, to maul,
A wife on whom to blame his "fall",
And little clamlets who would bawl
   And for clemency implore him.

If you've a female clam to sell,
And she would amiably dwell
Within his heart, but her own shell,
   And if she's "for" him,
He now extends this invitation
To come and share his habitation,
And there is just one stipulation—
   She must not bore him.

Which merely proves I'm not an intellectual—
Surely I should have known clams are asexual.

STEPHANIE L. BINCKLI.

MIZZ NOAH

Mr. Noah he build him an ark,
  A hundred feet both long an' wide,
An' den he open up de doah
  An' bid de animals come inside;
An' in dey walk, come two by two,
  De fat ones and de thin,
But Mizz Noah jus' sigh, and say:
  "Wipe yo' feets as yo' come in!"

Mr. Noah he set him down
  Well inside, away from rain,
An' den he make a long, long prayer,
  An' den he pray again;
But Mizz Noah she sweep up hair
  An' get de animals fed,
While Noah say he'd a long, hard day
  An' he gwine right to bed.

Mr. Noah he made his task
  To count de day and night,
Ontil he count up forty time,
  Den set de dove to flight;
An' he say: "I expeck from this
  To be in histories . . . "
But Mizz Noah say "Don' bother me,
  Dese animals got fleas."

So Mizz Noah comb and comb and comb
  An' give 'em bath and bath,
While Mr. Noah he make a speech
  When de dove points out de path;
He tells de animals farewell
  Like one ob Royal Blood,
But Mizz Noah wring out her mop
  An' start clean up de mud!

ELIZABETH EVELYN MOORE.

From one Missourian . . . to whom it may concern . . . this is exactly what the name describes . . . an ordinary mule . . .

THE MULE

I saw him standing in a barren field,
Head a-droop, as in a dream.
His shoulder blades and vertebrae
Had almost pierced the dried and rusty skin.
This Mule had plowed a hundred thousand rows,
And pulled a million pounds
In twenty years of unrequited drudgery
And aching toil.
No rhyme nor reason in his life.
And now the end.
His carcass soon would feel the beak
Of yonder vulture circling overhead.
He shuddered and a ripple,
Like wind-crinkles on a stagnant pool,
Ran through his almost hairless hide.
Perhaps a fly had bit
Into that raw place
Where the hame had rubbed;
Perhaps (Who knows?) he felt
Strange stirrings in his blood,
Vague atavistic memories of a day
Far back in his ancestral stream,
When Jesus on a lowly ass
Was hailed triumphantly as King.
Could he have been thus solaced
As he dropped upon his buckled knees
And yielded up the ghost?

J. T. COTTON NOE.

LINES ON A CANARY
SINGING TO AN ELECTRIC BEATER

There is no call for him to rise and sing
  No plump gold female comes to be his wife.
Alone forever in a gilded ring
  Of curving bars, he flutes his lonely life.
No paean this to feathered fatherhood
  When bursting eggs declare his progeny.
The whirring beater drones thru golden foam
  A monotone discordant symphony—
And thru it peals his bursting yellow notes
  Expending all the love in his lone breast;
To this strange heartless electricity
  He hymns the notes that never found a nest—
Like some starved soul who finds in his machine
  More beauty than the fields, farflung and green.

AMY LEE SPENCER.

A PRAYER FOR LITTLE BEASTS

O guard, dear Pan, so great and wise,
All little beasts with frightened eyes
Who sniff and scrabble in the night
Then skurry off alive with fright.
Hide them in burrow, nest or den
Far from the gins and traps of men.
They ask so little, only these;
Grain from the farmer, mouldy cheese,
A wormy apple in the grass
And nuts for winter store, alas,
How they are hunted out of hand
All up and down their noisy land!
O guard, dear Pan, so great and wise,
All little beasts with frightened eyes.

BEULAH MAY.

UP-STREAM

Little brown bear,
  Went up-stream to die.
Where the alders bend,
  The water-lilies lie,
  They heard little brown bear whimper and cry.

They had seen the man;
  There was time to run.
The rabbits and the foxes,
  They had seen the gun.
  Little brown bear lay asleep in the sun.

Slowly by the field
  Where the blackberries grew,
Softly by the hole
  Where he lay new,
  Close by his mother the late spring through:

Little brown bear
  Cried and snuffled.
Past the berries
  He lurched and shuffled
  Along the stream where the shade lay ruffled.

Where the willows dip
  And the birds go by,
Where the rabbits run
  And the foxes lie
  Little brown bear lay down to die.

KATHERINE KELLEY TAYLOR.

"Sugar and Spice . . .
              and
"Snakes and Snails . . .

Try this one on your own neighborhood . . . it takes me back to a neighborhood circus one spring day . . . net profit . . . ninety-one cents . . .

ON OUR STREET

We almost know the season of the year
    By what the boys are doing on our street.
In fall it's always football; then we hear
    Shouts and thudding of their heavy feet.

In winter it is sleds and maybe skis,
    Cries of delight when someone takes a "spill".
In spring it's flying kites, and then one sees
    Our boys on stilts showing each his skill.

In summer there is sure to be a stand
    Where muddy-looking lemonade is sold
For only a cent a glass, we understand,
    From nearly naked salesmen ten years old.

LOUISE GOODSON.

This poem hangs on the wall of a maternity ward . . . in the middle west . . .

BIRTH

Little we know what stranger enters here,
What traveler from a weird and distant shore,
What passionate pilgrim groping through a door
Of fog, in mute bewilderment and fear.
Little our eyes can trace, from year to year,
The soul's approaching turmoil; or explore
The fury, the hope, the anguish that may pour
Flood-like along the wanderer's veiled career.

Strangely, we do not question; do not see
How in this little wizened hairless thing
Is born anew the burden of all life,
Its pain, its wonder and its mystery.
In this wee shape, the choiring ages sing,
And generations bleed, and groan with strife.

STANTON A. COBLENTZ.

MIRACLE MODERNE

My baby, a being of little size,
Little accomplishment, little, lies
In his crib, and I, above him stare
At the miracle, all unaware in sleep.
Mother of God, there's been given me
Wealth in such showering litany
This shivering soul had succumbed to dust
If, while body grew great in its pregnancy
My soul also had not grown in trust.

ELAINE M. MOORHEAD.

*The battle of bedtime ... the mind of the child ... the unspoken thoughts
that provoke his resistance ...*

GOING TO BED

Time for bed and the stairs are dark,
And the room is so large and still.
You must be brave—there's nothing there,
Nothing under the bed.
Nothing at all in the closet door,
And nothing behind the blind.
If only the pussy could come up, too,
Warm and furry and soft—
If only the pussy could come!
Nothing at all is very scary,
Nothing at all in the dark.
If it were light, there would be the walls,
Castles and roses and flying birds—
And the small little chair,
And the little red table,
And the drawers with bright brass knobs.
Something has swallowed them all—all up,
And it's something no one can see.
Nothing has swallowed them up in the dark—
And you can't see nothing-at-all!

MARIAN McMUNN.

111

This poem was the birthday present of the author to his son . . . in lieu of cake or candles . . .

SKY-BOY

In the time before forever;
In the land of Never-Never;
Lived a boy.
Lived a boy who played forever
   With the stars;
Played forever chasing moonbeams;
Played forever catching star-gleams;
Chasing comets; playing cross-tag
   With the little shooting-stars.

But the game he played most often—
The game he loved the best—
Was to balance on a moon-beam
   On his toes.
Then, tripping, tripping, tripping,
Up the moon-beam he'd go skipping,
'Til he'd strike the poor old Moon-Man
   In the nose.

Other times, he'd slip up slyly,
'Round behind the old Moon's back
And he'd whisper in his ear;
   "Watch the skies!
Watch for comets! Watch for star-gleams!
Watch for frisky little sun-beams!
Watch! And tell me if you see one
   Going by!"

There he'd wait with stars a-beaming,
Sun a-gleaming, comets streaming;
Wait, until the Moon should whisper;
   "One is near!"
Oh, then how the comets darted!
How the little sun-beams started!
When he jumped out on them, crying;
   "I'm a bear!"

112

When the time before forever
Turned to now and ever-ever
And the Land of Never-Never
    Turned to Now and Everywhere,
Little Sky-Boy started falling
And the stars began a-calling;
Falling, calling; calling, falling;
    Down to here.

But he landed very gently
In the Here from out the There,
He just scooted down a rainbow
    Made of dew.
Loving eyes looked up and sought him.
Loving arms reached up and caught him,
And the Sky-Boy now is My-Boy!
    Yes! He's You!

EDWARD P. GILCHRIST.

*The road of life is lined with many milestones . . . and one may laugh and
one may weep . . . as the selfsame stone is passed . . .*

BABY

Baby smiled today,
    Her first wee smile,
And all the room was brightened
    For awhile!

Baby spoke today,
    Her first soft word,
And everyone within the cottage
    Heard!

Baby walked today
    So shaky stepped,
And mother, watching closely, quietly,
    Wept!

FERN L. MOLLOY.

113

BEYOND UNDERSTANDING

A little boy just half-past three,
  On a sunny day in May,
Asked his mother childishly,
  "Where is God today?"

The mother, quite confused
  As to what to do or say,
Tried so hard to explain to him
  In a very simple way.

"He's in the flowers and grass," she said.
  "He's part of the birds and trees,
He makes the sun to shine so bright.
  He's the keeper of the bees.

"He makes the raindrops patter down,
  He makes the waters flow;
He's part of everything, and all
  The things we love below."

The little child, so innocent,
  Listened to every word she said,
And when she had finished,
  Scratched his little head.

Looking up so sweetly,
  His wonder never ceases,
"Ma, I love God awful much,
  But, He's in so many pieces."

MARION WALLEY.

In every land and every language . . . mothers sing their lullabies . . .

LULLABY

Hush, my little sleepyhead, the stars are in the trees,
  The wind in carpet slippers shuffles by;
Crickets rubbing rosin on their little fiddle knees,
  Moon is blowing bubbles down the sky.

Lightning bugs are sprinkling little cups of golden dew,
  The swallow's head is underneath his wing;
The goblin in the cotton tree is bringing dreams to you—
  Can't you hear me coaxing him to sing!

Fill your little arms with sleep and close your tired eyes
  And sail across the Sandman's golden sea;
But when the moon has gone away and when the last star
    dies—
  My little sleepyhead, come back to me!

BERT COOKSLEY.

Had you ever thought of this . . .

THE LITTLE BOY NEXT DOOR

Suppose the little boy next door
Should grow to fame like lads of yore,
And all his friends, like you, and me,
Were put in a biography.

It really gives one food for thought,
Have we reacted as we aught
Towards a celebrity?

If he should chase our pussy cat,
Or soil our wash, or this, or that,
Could it be said we failed to see
His charming personality?

So let us be more circumspect,
And give to him all due respect,
In view of our publicity.

HELEN MALLORY SCHRADER.

115

ADVENTURE ON THE WINGS OF MORNING

A boy upon a Shetland pony,
(Sing, bonny bluebird, sing!)
Is riding down a lane of maples
To high adventuring.

Within the meadow may be danger,
But this lad doesn't care—
When summer winds are calling to him,
A lad rides anywhere.

Within the forest may be pirates
(Who knows?) in secret caves;
But no brave lad of seven's ever
Afraid of daring knaves.

This rider has a heart that's valiant;
(Hush, bluebird, your refrain!)
The courage that a nation's needing
Is jogging down my lane!

RACHEL ALBRIGHT.

*On the New York Central . . . rolling through the Bronx . . . a thousand
little frocks on the clotheslines Monday morning . . . and always more in
spring than in fall . . .*

TREASURE

April still is far away
And Autumn's gold is gone,
But I've a lovelier garden
To feast my eyes upon—

Spring will come with tulips
And flowering lilac trees,
But I've a wash-day garden
More colorful than these.

Men have died for lesser things,
For far less Adam sinned—
A small girl's bright-hued dresses
Blowing in the wind.

BERYL V. THOMPSON.

116

This brings back memories of a field of oats in Oklahoma . . . the sun was so hot . . . we shocked by the moon . . . some sow them . . . some shock them . . . the same harvest moon . . .

SENT FOR WATER

He was only a little lad
  Shocking oats with the men,
And jugs of water that they had
  Were quickly drained.
He had to take them to the springs again
  And he complained.

He took the jugs and found
  The springs, by the willowtree,
Gurgling and cold from underground.
  Then filled to the brim
He hurried the jugs to the field where he could see
  Men waiting him.

He was only a little lad
  Shocking oats with the men,
And he kept thinking if he had
  The time it took
He'd splash cool water in a cloud and then
  Just sit and look.

Then, watching his father drink
  From the sweating jug he brought,
He saw him smile once more—and wink:
  "In threatening weather
We men (and there was comfort in the thought!)
  Must work together!"

GLENN WARD DRESBACH.

A prodigy and his problem dad . . .

THE CHAMPION

My daddy is the strongest man in this whole world, I'll bet!
 When he plays golf, he drives the ball so far it's out of sight.
And he can swim and ride a horse and everything and yet,
 When we play games at home, why, I just beat him every
 night.

Sometimes we have a boxing match, with Mother looking on,
 And my, he's strong! But so am I, so it's a reg'lar fight.
And Mother always claps for me and smiles when I have won;
 She doesn't seem to think it strange I beat him every night.

Sometimes I think because I win, it makes my daddy sad.
 Tonight if he should say to me directly after dinner,
"Let's run a race together to the gate and back, my lad,"
 Would it be cheating, do you s'pose, if I made him the
 winner?

LIDA WILSON TURNER.

A new baby in a cradle . . . and her critic's first "review" . . .

A LITTLE WRINKLED SOUL OF LOVELINESS

She was a little wrinkled soul of loveliness,
If souls of earth inhabit bodies of their size:
(Souls which were never crumpled by the ugliness
Of life, may not recapture beauty when she flies).

This soul drew lucid rays, convergent in her face,
Disclosing concentrated goodness of her sires,
Reflecting out beyond position, pride and place,
The coals of character at white heat in the fires.

Disarming judgment in evaluating man,
Critic of beauty, she was beauty's aged elf:
Beauty like a new polished gem, is lovely when
In youth or age it but reflects the inner self.

WILLIAM BYRON CHARLES.

This may be merely "a free translation" of the previous poem . . . with adequate attendant color . . .

PICKANINNY

Black-eyed pickaninny
    Someone's little tot,
On a pile of cotton
    Where the sun is hot.

Someone's lump of sugar,
    With a curly top.
Tiny feet a kicking
    Little candy drop.

With a sack to shade you,
    While the darkies sing.
Black-eyed pickaninny
    Mammy's little King.

ELLEN EARL.

A story the storybooks never tell . . .

OF SUCH . . .

I visited the squirming second grade
Where forty pencils crept a painful pace,
And sadly watched the downward anxious face
    Of one near-sighted twisted boy who made
My throat close sharply on my heart's tirade
Against his fellows' heedless lively grace;
I sighed to see him shift his heavy brace
    When the dull bell the waiting silence frayed.
But as he darted off to get his cap
    He flashed at me a look of happiness,
Rejoicing like a bird from unsprung trap,
    Feeling the others' joy no whit the less,
And whispered, with a stealthy, gleeful clap,
    "She lets us play Red Rover at recess!"

ALICE DOUGAN GASS.

119

DAUGHTER AT ARITHMETIC

Difficult as it is, she sits
Dividing numbers into bits,
Sucks the eraser, hums off key,
Figures with brief intensity.
Outside the day is lush with spring,
Sunshines and the crickets sing,
The dog barks and a train goes by
Brushing smoke along the sky.
Silence in the house is fat
And somnolent; the mother cat
Walks slowly past, her tail a plume,
To kittens in another room.
The chairs are sober, curtains fall
Neatly by windows, on the wall
The pattern of the paper goes
In quaint shapes, here a ship, a rose . . .
She starts, and guilty, looks around
But dreaming has not made a sound.
She writes again, then drums upon
The table, but her heart has gone
From working—she can't make it stick—
Most girls detest arithmetic.

DOROTHY MCFARLANE.

Aesop's fables to the contrary . . .

STORY TIME

Tell them the moon is lemon ice,
  That kittens once had wings.
They will love any freakish tale
  Of cabbages or kings.

Your oceans may be orangeade,
  Your ships sapphire or coral.
Their only stipulation is:
  Don't try to add a moral.

NAOMI REYNOLDS HESS.

120

Now we know how embarrassed Uncle Sam must feel . . . when some of his "patriots" make a speech . . .

A FATHER'S DILEMMA

He did not know that I was in the woodshed, my young son.
He did not know that I could hear him talking to his chum.
I'd scolded him that morning, told him what I hated most
Was listening to little boys who'd stand around and boast.
"Be what you are," I told him; "for the time will come, some
    day,
When you will have to answer for the things you do and say.
You want me to be proud of you, don't you, when you're a
    man?
Well, then, don't boast that you can do a thing, until you can."

"I won't," he promised solemnly, and now, behind the shed,
He argued with the lad next door, and this is what he said:

"Aw, watcha talkin' 'bout? A lion bigger'n the two
That we saw fightin', Sunday, in their cages at the Zoo?
You mean he chased your daddy, down yonder in the wood,
An' your dad couldn't lick him? Huh! I betcha *my* dad
    could!
Your Dad must be a 'nawful coward! Aw, shucks, I bet he is!
My Dad could lick a half-a-dozen lions! Why, gee whiz!
I betcha he could lick 'em with one hand behind his back!
My Dad sure packs a wallop! . . . Race you to the house an'
    back."

Well, I sat there in the woodshed with my chin upon my
    hand . . .
And I did a lot of thinking. . . . He deserved a reprimand. . . .
'Twas nothing less than boasting . . . yet, why quarrel with
    the lad?
You shouldn't disillusion little folks . . . about their Dad!

E. PEARL DANCEY.

121

Little boys seek adventure in caves ... mothers find it in pockets ...

ESSENCE

Why do little boys' pockets
  With all of their contraband
Always hold in the bottom-most fold
  A fingernail of sand?

Sand with the other treasures—
  An essence with tangles of toys—
Seems a bit of substantial grit
  That's part of all little boys.

Boys with wings of young wisdom
  Find moths in their self-spun berth,
And seek the root of stalk and fruit
  Full length on the hard, warm earth.

Or press inquisitive noses
  To clovery timothy land ...
Pigeonholes of little boys' souls
  Are dusty with golden sand.

DOROTHY BURNHAM EATON.

And still they say ... it's the woman who pays ...

SMALL BOY'S RESIGNATION

For weeks he tried to interest her
  With stones of red and blue;
She snubbed his efforts, every one,
  As only girls can do.

He turned handsprings and hung from trees,
  Till clothes were in a wreck;
As last resort, so great his love,
  He washed his ears and neck!

RALPH J. DONAHUE.

122

This one will catch you . . . hook . . . line . . . and sinker . . .

THIS I REMEMBER

A cloudless sky,
  A sun-warmed brook,
Crooked old pole,
  Bent pin for a hook.

Barefoot boy with
  A piece of twine,
Knotted and spliced,
  For a fishing line.

Lunch in a bag
  Smoky frying pan,
Wriggling worms
  In a rusty can.

Big bear-hug, a
  Kiss or two;
This I remember,
  Fisherman . . . do you!

ELISABETH CHANNING ALLEN.

In all fairness to the dads . . . they do have problems . . .

MODERN YOUTH

I used to have to be so good,
  And do as Papa said,
Or else he'd spank me soundly as
  He sent me up to bed!

But everything is different now,
  Since Mama "studies" me,
And goes to class to learn about
  This child "psychology."

She says I must not be "suppressed,"
  Which drives poor Papa wild,
But, gosh, it's fun since Mama found
  That I'm a "Problem Child!"

RUTH VIVIAN KIDWELL.

123

PATSY NELL

She is a child of divorce.
I have not known her very long.
She always comes as quietly and gently
As flakes of falling snow, or rose petals,
Or Autumn leaves, and I am unaware
That she is near, until looking up or down
As it may be, I find her standing there.
She is so little—so wistful—and just six.
And she is beautiful, with a beauty
That plays upon the harp strings
Of the heart.
Her hair is the color of rich old mahogany,
Sheened as burnished copper, in the sun;
It softly frames her brow and face
With curling tendrils, that resemble
A lovely pattern of fine old lace.
Her eyes are twin pools of beauty,
The beauty of a limpid shaded stream.
Her mouth—one just knows
Could only have been fashioned
From a new-born baby rose.
The gracious curves of her little neck,
And arms and limbs,
Like pure white marble gleam.
She is the very essence of
An old master's sculptured dream.
She is exquisite as some rare flower
Found only in a secluded dell,
Yet—she is a child of divorce,
This gentle, lovely Patsy Nell.

LOUISE POBAR.

124

*My grandmother having lived to an old age . . . saw with difficulty . . .
she wore bifocals . . . she told me once . . . she held her chin high and
through the bottom of the lenses saw things close . . . as she lowered her
head and looked through the upper portion she could see things distant
. . . then I asked how far she could see when she bent her head and
looked high over the top of the glasses . . . she smiled and told me when
she bent her head . . . all she could see was God . . .*

SHE WALKS IN BEAUTY

My little daughter who is patient, being blind,
Most dearly loves to walk, her hand in mine,
Across the fields and through the woods of Spring,
Where every flower blows and every wood-thrush sings
It seems, for her alone. And this I know is sure—
That each small blossom is more known to her
Than ever it will be to me, poor clod,
For I have only eyes, and she has—faith in God.

JOHN B. COOK.

Just in case you are still haunted by those "knobs" back on page 24 . . . here are the virtues of one's knees . . .

A NINE-YEAR-OLD BOY'S DEFINITION OF KNEES

Knees are pretty important.

They're the things
that push holes through your pants
when you play marbles.

They're the things
that get the hard bumps and skinned
when you fall.

They're the things
that help your legs bend
when you walk.

They're the things
that shake
when you're scared.

They're the things
that you sometimes open doors with
when you're carrying bundles.

They're the things
that your daddy puts you across
when you're bad.

They're the things
that you hug
when you're cold.

They're the things
that you sit on
when you say your prayers.

And they're the things
that you lean against
when you tell your mother stuff.

Most people never stop to think
that knees are pretty
important.

SARA D. LEWIS.

126

YOUTH'S AMBITION

At five he wants to be a fireman
And has a veritable passion to wear red;
He dreams of hatchets, hose and ladder,
And saving little Cousin Lucia's life;
At seven a picturesque cowboy strikes his fancy,
And Tom Mix becomes his cherished idol:
He visualizes the colorful Western prairies
And the excitement of the rodeo;
When his years advance to ten he feels the urge
To be a G-Man, and secret codes cause
His little bròw to wrinkle with intensity;
He now captures bandits on a large scale.
At twelve he wants to discover new worlds
And sail the heavens in a gigantic plane;
Now **Lindbergh** is the hero of the day,
And welcoming crowds acclaim his glory in parade.
At fifteen he yearns to build a temple to the sky,
That dwarfs the Empire State Building fifty feet
And is the most majestic in all the world;
Now he preaches a stirring sermon to the masses.
At seventeen he dreams of winning the Pulitzer Prize
For a literary achievement that is without peer,
That brings in royalties by the millions
And makes him eligible to the Hall of Fame.
And the years roll on in enthusiastic sequence;
He envisions himself as another Alex Carrel,
A Henry Ford and, eventually, President of the United States.
But at twenty-four he's married to dark-eyed Loraine
And renting an ivy-covered bungalow on the outskirts
Of a grubby little town that has no special place upon the map.
And he's wondering if he might summon up courage enough
To ask the boss for another raise ... !
After all, he *is* the chief-shipping-clerk and
Quite indispensable.

                                        ANNA GRACE BOYLES.

"LISTEN, SON:"

I am saying this to you as you lie asleep with one little paw crumpled under your cheek and the curls stickily wet on your plump forehead. I have stolen into your room alone. Just a few minutes ago, as I sat reading my paper in the library, a hot, stifling wave of remorse swept over me. I could not resist it. Guiltily I came to your bedside.

"These are the things I was thinking, son: I had been cross to you. I scolded you as you were dressing for school because you gave your face merely a dab with a towel. I took you to task for not cleaning your shoes. I called out angrily when I found you had thrown some of your things on the floor. At breakfast I found fault, too. You spilled things. You gulped down your food. You put your elbows on the table. You spread butter too thick on your bread. And as you started off to play and I made for my train, you turned and waved a little hand and called, "Good-bye, Daddy," and I frowned, and said in reply, "Hold your shoulders back."

"Then it began all over again in the later afternoon. As I came up the hill road I spied you down on your knees playing marbles. There were holes in your stockings. I humiliated you before your boy friends by making you march ahead of me back to the house. Stockings were expensive and if you had to buy them you would be more careful. Imagine that, son, from a father. It was such stupid, silly logic.

"Do you remember later when I was reading in the library, how you came in, softly, timidly, with a sort of hurt, hunted look in your eyes? When I glanced up over my paper, impatient at the interruption, you hesitated at the door. "What is it you want?" I snapped. You said nothing, but ran across, in one tempestuous plunge; and threw your arms around my neck and kissed me, again and again, and your small arms tightened with an affection that God had set blooming in your heart and which even neglect could not wither. And then you were gone, pattering up the stairs.

"Well, son, it was shortly afterwards that my paper slipped from my hands, and a terrible sickening fear came

128

over me. Suddenly I saw myself as I really was, in all my horrible selfishness, and I felt sick at heart. What has habit been doing to me? The habit of complaining, of finding fault, or reprimanding, all of these were my rewards to you for being a boy. It was not that I did not love you; it was that I expected so much of youth. I was measuring you by the yardstick of my own years.

"And there is so much that is good, and fine, and true in your character. You did not deserve my treatment of you, son. The little heart of you is as big as the dawn itself over the wide hills. All this was shown by your spontaneous impulse to rush in and kiss me good-night. Nothing else matters tonight, son.

"This is a feeble atonement. I know you would not understand these things if I told them to you during your waking hours, yet I must say what I am saying. I must burn sacrificial fires, alone, here in your bedroom, and make free confession. And I have prayed God to strengthen me in my new resolve. Tomorrow I will be a real daddy. I will chum with you, and suffer when you suffer and laugh when you laugh. I will bite my tongue when impatient words come. I will keep saying as if it were a ritual: 'He is still a boy—a little boy.'

"I am afraid I have visualized you as a man. Yet as I see you now, son, crumpled and weary in your cot, I see that you are still a baby. Yesterday you were in your mother's arms, your head on her shoulder,—I have asked too much, too much.

"Dear Boy, Dear little son, a penitent kneels at your infant shrine, here in the moonlight. I kiss the little fingers and the damp forehead and the yellow curl. Tears come, and heartache and remorse, and also a greater, deeper love, when you ran through the library door and wanted to kiss me. Good-night, Sonny—from this hour on we're pals, you and dad."

* * *

I do not know of a better shrine before which a father or mother may kneel or stand than that of a sleeping child. I do not know of a holier place, a temple where one may come nearer to seeing and feeling God.

UNKNOWN.

IF YOU HAVE A LITTLE BOY

If you have a little boy
All your very own,
Then you have enough and more
To make a happy home.

And if but once each day
You should see him smile,
That would be enough and more,
To make your life worth while.

Or, say you have a little boy
To read to every night,
That would be enough and more
To make your evenings bright.

And if each night at bed time
You can kiss this little lad,
That will be enough and more
To make you very glad.

And if you see him in the evening
When he kneels to pray,
That will be enough and more
To make a perfect day.

OMA CARLYLE ANDERSON.

"Sugar and spice and everything nice . . .

In the breast of a bulb
Is the promise of spring;
In the little blue egg
Is a bird that will sing;
In the soul of a seed
Is the hope of the sod;
In the heart of a child
Is the Kingdom of God.

W. L. STIDGER.

YOUNG LAUGHTER

Eeny, meeny, miney, mo . . .
Pocket full of posy . . .
Wrote a letter to my love . . .
O ominous counting-out rhymes, O delirious
Ring-around-a-rosy, and tremulous hide-and-go-seek.
Ready or not, you shall be caught . . .
(Ready or not, by the full-grown years!)
O strenuous tag, and dangerous London Bridge—
And the fumbling and laughter of blindman's buff,
The lyrical suspense of drop-the-handkerchief,
The popularity contest of the-farmer-in-the-dell.

Now dear is this carefree heritage,
These happy-go-lucky rigmarole ditties
Which children have lightheartedly chanted
To their dancing and running, spring
After spring, up the centuries' turning!
What rollicking, nonsensical jingles,
What catches and rounds to their frolicking!

This is the green grass of tradition,
The vernal revival of song in young veins,
The yearly renewal of lilt in young limbs,
The attuning of new hearts to the ancient race rhythms,
The annual amalgam of the endless generations.
This is the young laughter of the language,
The perpetual April of poetry.

ROBIN LAMPSON.

MISTAKE

My daddy said my sleeve was out
Of the elbow; I can't believe
He knows just what it's all about—
For my elbow's out of my sleeve!

LENORE EVERSOLE FISHER.

131

"Listen My Children . . .

Read this once . . . hurriedly . . . it's true . . . it's true . . . but it isn't any fun . . . and shouldn't have been written . . .

I'D RATHER BE YOU, LITTLE WIDE-EYED BOY

Yes, little boy, I am old as you say,
I've sailed the ocean and ridden a train,
And flown over the mountains in a plane.
I've studied books and been off to schools,
And I've shaken the hand of a king who rules.

But, I'd rather be you, little wide-eyed boy,
Watching the squirrels in the tree so high,
Wondering what makes the bluebirds fly.
Than any old man with a wise bold look,
And a head full of notions out of a book.

FLORENCE DAVIDSON STROTHER.

What must the young mother bird in the nest . . . do with her heart . . . when she literally pushes her babies away . . . away . . . away . . . she pushes her babies away . . .

TO MY BABY

When first I held you in my arms,
   That day as dawn awoke the skies
I looked beyond the vault above
   And prayed to Him that your dear eyes
Would ne'er on aught but beauty look
   As through the years you made your way.
I said—Dear God I give thee thanks,
   For thou hast brought me joy today
In trusting to my care this child.
   Please make me strong, yet gentle too,
Then when the time comes I can say—
   I gave the best in me to you.

A babe you were just yesterday;
And now you've gone so far away.

MARGERY STEVENS WARNER.

134

And the old mother duck . . . when she shoves them out to sea . . . such
a deep . . . deep sea . . . if this time they couldn't swim . . .

FOR MY SON

These years have been so very short—
The years when you have clung
To me for comfort and support—
And you are still so young,

So full of hope, and so untried,
I wish that I might save
You from the grief to come, and guide
You still. But you are brave,

And eager. Dear young heart, forgive
The many times when I seem slow
To learn it is your life to live.
It is so hard to let you go.

ELIZABETH GREY STEWART.

Listen my children . . . don't tell your little sister . . . but

SANTY ISN'T SANTY CLAUS

Maybe you think Santy Claus
Is just a jolly elf,
With lots of toys and reindeer.
I thought so once, myself,

But when I saw him in the street,
And found him in the store,
And went around the corner,
And there he was some more,

I felt real sad about it,
But I could tell right then,
Santy isn't Santy Claus,
He's just a lot of men.

ELIZABETH PORTER KESSLER.

135

AUTHOR TO HIS CHILD

When you were born
We called you,
"Little Poem."
Your mother liked
Gay verses—
But God wanted her
For part of His Great Poem. ...

You were a funny little verse—
She would have liked you.

Then—
You were a Short-short.
An incident or two—
And yet, a story;
Complete, in your way.

Now you are grown.
Privately,
I call you a Novelette.
A story. . . .
But not fully characterized.
Plotted. . . .
But no counter-plots.

A few more years—
And you will be a Novel.
A Complete Book-length Novel!
. . . . I hope I've helped.
I hope we've created
A good Novel.

One your mother will read with pleasure.

FRANCES AIRTH.

*This is the sermon all parents preach and never practice . . . never . . .
no never . . . never . . . well hardly ever . . .*

FOR AN OPEN MIND

I must grant you, my son, the right to think,
    I must not fill your mind with outworn fears;
You must remain an open soul to drink
    The changing ideas of the changing years.
Great seems my wisdom to you now you're young,
    I must take care lest I too think it so;
Too long, I fear, to ancient forms I've clung,
    You must not heed my credo; you must grow.

The things I work for, how I vote or pray;
    May foolish seem to you, or even wrong.
Well, you are free to seek a better way!
    Your mind is healthy when your doubt is strong.
Too long has age been synonym for truth;
    My son, seek your own answers; you are youth!

VERA WHITE.

*They've known it for a thousand years . . . but never changed the pat-
tern . . . yet . . . not yet . . . but some day soon . . .*

Tongue in his cheek, Youth climbs the path
    That leads atop the hill Success,
Too well aware that he will find,
    When he has reached the crest,

A crazy, topsy-turvy world,
    With people fighting bout on bout
For everything they do not want
    But dare not do without.

HELEN DOREMUS.

137

Copy this for your daughter's eighteenth birthday . . . she will cherish it her whole life through . . .

MOTHER TO DAUGHTER

It is not just because you might be fair
    As that magnolia blossom opening wide
Its curved white petals to the sunny air—
    That, watching you, I glow with artists' pride;
It is because—as from the blossom's rim
    Fresh waves of sweetness ripple into space—
Your eyes, your lips, your very gestures brim
    With springs of joy so rich they might embrace
All arid wastes, all frozen poles of grief,
    And make them flower. . . . It is because such joy
Lingers like incense for the world's belief;
    Because like gold, untarnished by alloy,
It shines in doubt's grey palm—therefore I lift
My head as one who shaped a priceless gift.

MARGUERITE STEFFAN.

Copy this for your sons . . . it is a mother's heritage to youth . . .

SONG FOR THREE SONS

Here lie the kingdoms of the world, my sons,
For all to claim and none at last to keep.
This interlude dividing sleep from sleep,
This crystal glass through which the bright sand runs
Brings each his dawn and each the dark that stuns
The subtle brain and stills the proud heart's leap.
And those who know their own and make a heap
Of that alone become the gifted ones.

Here lies all treasure but a man must choose,
Lest too much in his grasp should forfeit all;
Or make his hoard of greed a shining bar
To destiny. Some things you must refuse
But pledge yourselves to these beyond recall:
One rose, one dream, one woman and one star.

ANNETTE PATTON CORNELL.

138

MY SON-IN-LAW

Somewhere, a little boy plays now,
  My daughter's husband. As things go
By averages, I'm thinking how
  They'll meet in twenty years; from what I know
Myself, of life and love. Grow strong,
  My little unknown son, be not too free
With life—she is all gold and song,
  This little girl, so dear to me.
Watching her with her dolls today,
  A mother in the bud—it does not seem
Too foolish of me, son, that when I say
  My prayer for her, I send some little boy a dream.

RUTH SCHENLEY.

All brides are child brides in a mother's eyes . . .

BRIDE'S MOTHER

They see you as a woman, as a bride,
  Sweet in a modeled gown of creamy lace;
Your blue eyes turned to him in trust and pride,
  Your golden curls a halo for your face.
Yet I, your mother, see you not as this
  Alone: I see you as a baby in my arms,
Helpless and small, mine to adore and kiss;
  I see you as a child of three whose charms
And childish laughter are for me alone;
  I see your first, brief step beside my knee;
I see you in the years when you have grown
  Into the lovely woman that they see.
A thousand priceless memories I keep
  Within my heart. Forgive me that I weep.

CHRISTIE LUND.

139

In New York . . . at the cathedral . . . bridesmaids . . . flower girls . . .
best man . . . ushers . . . a brilliant wedding party that filled the
pews . . .
In Kansas . . . at a country church . . . just "her and him and the
preacher after the Sunday sermon" . . .
New York . . . Kansas . . . always . . . mother's hearts saying good-
bye . . .

THE MOTHER-IN-LAW

She was my dream's fulfillment and my joy,
  This lovely woman whom you call your wife.
You sported at your play, an idle boy,
  When first I felt the stirring of her life—
Within my startled being I was thrilled
  With such intensity of love, it filled
The Universe! But words are vain—
No man can comprehend that wild, sweet pain.

You smiled in childhood's slumber while I felt
  The agonies of labour; and the nights
I, weeping, o'er the little sufferer knelt,
  You, wandering on through dreamland's fair delight
Flung out your lengthening limbs and slept and grew,
While I, awake, saved this dear wife for you.

She was my heart's loved idol and my pride—
  I taught her all those graces which you praise;
I dreamed of coming years, when at my side
  She should lend luster to my fading days,
Should cling to me (as she to you clings now)
The young fruit hanging to the withered bough.
But lo! The blossom was so fair a sight
You plucked it from me, for your own delight.

Well, you are worthy of her—oh, thank God—
  And yet I do not think you realize
How burning were the sands o'er which I trod
  To bear and rear this woman you so prize.
It was no easy thing to see her go—
Even into the arms of the one she worshipped so.

140

How strong, how vast, how awful seems the power
  Of this new love which fills a maiden's heart,
For one who never bore a single hour
  Of pain for her; which tears her life apart
From all its moorings, and controls her more
Than all the ties, the years have held before;
Which crowns a stranger with a kingly grace,
And gives the one who bore her—second place.

She loves me still. And yet were Death to say,
  "Choose now between them." You would be her choice,
God meant it so to be—it is His way—
  But can you wonder if, while I rejoice,
In her content, this thought hurts like a knife;
"No longer necessary to her life?"

My pleasure in her joy is bittersweet.
  Your very goodness sometimes hurts my heart,
Because for her, Life's Drama seems complete
  Without the mother's oft-repeated part.
Be patient with me. She was mine so long
Who now is yours. One must indeed be strong
To meet the loss without the least regret.
And so, forgive me, if my eyes are wet.

ELLA WHEELER WILCOX.

What will he do at recess time . . . when the boys all play Red Rover . . .

MY LITTLE BOY

My little boy is only four
  And restless when the children shout,
I see his eyes, at once, alight
  With longing, as they run about;
I can stride swiftly to and fro
  Or sit at leisure, as I choose;
Oh, God, to think I used to frown
  Upon a worn-out pair of shoes!

ELVA SMITH.

CRY OF A LONELY HEART

I want a boy, a small boy,
A not-so-very-tall boy,
   A boy of ten, eleven, or perhaps, thirteen.
I want a boy to talk with,
To take a long walk with,
   Then home again, to chatter over what we've seen.

A gay little, square boy,
A sure-of-playing-fair boy.
   A boy that I can chum with, and mother, and pet.
A boy who will love me
And never weary of me . . .
   D' you know a boy like this, that I might get?

A motherless, tired boy,
An ambition-fired boy.
   A boy that I can pamper, in every small whim.
A hungry little, sad boy . . .
A dirty little, bad boy . . .
   I want a boy . . . who needs me as I need him.

E. PEARL DANCEY.

She kept a lamp in the window . . . she waited up until he came . . . and sometimes it annoyed him . . . he didn't know her secret joy in his late hours . . . he didn't know . . .

WOMAN WITH A SON

That was the front door I heard gently closing.
The book is shut. I have been dozing.
Quiet. Slip into bed. The dawn is rosy.
Would anyone have thought I should be nosey?
Pull up the blanket. Frost's white airy fingers
Are in my hair, yet understanding lingers
In my heart. Ho hum, some memories are very nice,
And I have not forgotten. Let that suffice.

GRACE MEREDITH.

Memorize this . . . for stormy days when dreams wear thin . . .

HOLD FAST YOUR DREAMS

Hold fast your dreams!
Within your heart
Keep one still, secret spot
Where dreams may go,
And, sheltered so,
May thrive and grow
Where doubt and fear are not.
O keep a place apart,
Within your heart,
For little dreams to go!

Think still of lovely things that are not true.
Let wish and magic work at will in you.
Be sometimes blind to sorrow. Make believe!
Forget the calm that lies
In disillusioned eyes.
Though we all know that we must die,
Yet you and I
May walk like gods and be
Even now at home in immortality.

We see so many ugly things—
Deceits and wrongs and quarrelings;
We know, alas! we know
How quickly fade
The color in the west,
The bloom upon the flower,
The bloom upon the breast
And youth's blind hour.
Yet keep within your heart
A place apart
Where little dreams may go,
May thrive and grow.
Hold fast—hold fast your dreams!

LOUISE DRISCOLL.

Sons can be used for so many odd jobs . . .

ROOM — TO LET

I've had a vacancy for years
    Within an empty heart;
A furnished room with furbelows
    With love was set apart.
For the little girl, who never came
    To burst my heart with joy;
But what a glorious substitute
    When God sent me a boy.

Now I know that you, my son
    And deft propinquity
Will make a goodly choice for me
    And fill this vacancy.

                    RAE ANGELO OCKERMAN.

Three strong links   . the endless chain . . . generations of life . . .

MOTHER-TO-BE

What is that look in your lovely eyes?
    What is it, darling, you see?
Have you and the fairies some glad surprise,
    Dear Little Mother-to-be?

What is that smile on your trembling lips,
    So full of a sweet mystery?
Why do you thrill to your finger tips,
    Dear Little Mother-to-be?

What are the words of the song you sing
    In that soft tender key?
Is it a lullaby on the wing,
    Dear Little Mother-to-be?

Why is your heart-beat so strong and true,
    Keeping close to the heart of me?
I know—because I am the mother of *you*,
    Dear Little Mother-to-be!

                    SOPHIE E. REDFORD.

144

*And so the ageless attempt to bargain with time . . . to slow up the hours
. . . to cling to the seconds . . .*

TO A YOUNG MOTHER

Little mother, hold her tightly;
You would never guess how lightly
Slip the years,
And your tears
Too soon shall flow.

Little mother—tired? Maybe.
But you still can clasp your baby
Closely near;
Oh, my dear,
Be glad it's so!

Little mother, Time goes reeling,
Womanhood too soon comes stealing;
It will make
Your heart ache—
I know! I know!

HELEN DARBY BERNING.

*Listen my children . . . with all these pretty speeches . . . on life as we
would have you live it . . . we are right back to the beginning . . . what
do we wise people know of here or the hereafter . . . wisdom isn't important . . . it's love . . .*

HEAVEN

What can the wise men know of heaven?
    What can the ancient know at all?
But we, tonight, while the world is sleeping,
    We two, breathless, have scaled its wall.

Heaven is not a stately city,
    Set on a hill, with streets of gold.
Heaven is only you to want me,
    Heaven is not yet being old.

MARY CAROLYN DAVIES.

"Ode to . . .

An anonymous soul that hangs from the window of the corner tenement
. . . third floor rear . . . she stares at the strange wild world below . . .

ANNE BOLEYN O'SHAUGENNESY

Anne Boleyn O'Shaugennesy
Bent over her laundry-tub.
Her red, rheumatic hands gave one
Decisive, final rub.

But O! the fierce blue blood of kings
Pounded hard within,
And there looked out from tired eyes
The soul of Anne Boleyn.

RUTH CRARY CLOUGH.

A little grave lying north and west of General Grant's tomb . . . Riverside
Drive . . . New York City . . . the stone bearing the inscription . . .
"Erected to the memory of an Amiable Child, St. Claire Pollock, Died July
15, 1797, in the fifth year of his age." . . .

TO "AN AMIABLE CHILD"

In the shadow of a tomb
Where in homage men have filed,
Under sod is one at rest
Called "An Amiable Child."
Voices hushed, in solemn mien,
Mortals guard a nation's shrine,
But the boy is sentineled
In the whispering trees' confine.
In his grill-enclosured grave
Lies sweet innocence at rest,
In the marbled sepulchre
Is reposed a medalled breast.
And though manhood brought the man
To a death-defying fame,
Yet how good it is to know
That the lad is free from blame.
Stern, the General's glory rode,
Borne upon a nation's grace,
But the gentle child won fame
By a smile upon his face.

MABEL N. LAWSON.

148

BALLADE OF A DREAM ADDICT

I have no will to weep if love should leave,
   No wish to wear the scar of memory's brand
Upon my heart. For mind will interweave
   The past with dreams, and fabricate a band
Of shimmering fancies following my command;
   Empowered to heal the wound with subtler art
Than hot desire inspired within some gland.
   The drug of dreams will ever ease the heart.

I have no will to tug at fortune's sleeve,
   No wish to break the soil of arid land—
Or grope in office gloom—and so receive
   The right to jingle silver coins in hand.
An hour of solitude!--and thoughts expand
   To gather treasure unknown to public mart;
A purchase poverty cannot countermand:
   The drug of dreams will ever ease the heart.

I have no will to struggle—climb—achieve—
   No wish to build in steel, or tunnel sand,
For hands are prone to blunder. Dreams conceive
   The perfect races—alter maps—demand
The world shall wear a face benign and bland.
   I fumble facts, but never lose the chart
Which leads me toward this self-created strand.
   The drug of dreams will ever ease the heart.

Envoi

Oh, God! In illusion born of mist I stand;
   Engulfed—embalmed in wishes—set apart
By knowledge, poison-filled, and contraband:
   The drug of dreams will ever ease the heart.

VIRGINIA SCOTT.

A sales clerk in the bargain basement ... where frantic customers blessed and abused and bought everything but her dreams ...

SPENDTHRIFT NANCY

So what do you own at the end, Nancy,
   The end of everything?
"Oh, some of them gave me a grateful word,
   And some gave a word to sting."

But what have you then to keep, Nancy,
   Of all it was wise to save?
"Nothing but this for memory,
   They asked of me and I gave."

Then what is the use of it all, Nancy,
   Here at the end of day?
"It was only gifts that I let them take ...
   I never gave dreams away!"

MARGARET WIDDEMER.

The porter in a big hotel ... he enters and leaves by the basement door ... he always has ... he always will ...

SAM

Sam hurls waste paper into canvas bags
   And runs the vacuum over Brussels rugs.
Sam coats a cuspidor to shine with rags,
   Rubs bright and tarnished brasswork while he shrugs
His rounded shoulders in a rustic grace.
   He is a noisy child of fifty-two;
His eyes grab for you from a pudgy face:
   The stage where thought has not a chore to do.

Sucked into toil's waste bag, this awkward actor
   Is grimacing that he may win applause
From owlish men who should not call him cracked or
   Tap their temples. When Sam has time to pause,
He wonders, blots a wistful tear, and blocks
Hiccups that shake his rippling dinner-box.

M. G. WILLIAMS.

A skull of a court jester turned up unexpectedly by an archeologist excavating an old tomb . . .

TONGUELESS LINES

Look at it now
What once was I!
You'd scarcely think
This empty, naked thing
Once held the potency
To make words sing,
Kings clap.
Yet so it did.
The lauded lump
That chinked the vacant space
Behind these gutted orbs,
This fleshless face,
Once juggled words
More cunningly than you
Into neat rhyme!
This crumbled ear,
A brief and eager time,
Alertly leaned to praise
That made the ego strut; to din
That wreathed the head . . . ha!
(Pardon my lipless grin) . . .
The head . . .
Look at it now!

PAT MERNAGH.

The anemic child on the floor above . . . she goes to church on Wednesday nights . . . comes home . . . dances herself to sleep . . .

TWO HERITAGES

Someone left a willful wish to me,
    A wish to dance beneath the night
While tomtoms drum a heathen chant
    And stars look dim by firelight.

And someone left a body, frail
    As misty clouds of Springtime rain.
I have them both. I do not sigh.
    That willful wish is worth the pain.

MARY BUIRGY.

The lady who runs the boarding house . . . "strictly modern" . . . "convenient to trolley" . . . "popular rates a week in advance" . .

BACHELORS' LANDLADY

The Lord employed a quaint disguise
To clothe a worth He deifies,
When, after haunting us for weeks
With that fat wench whose flat foot squeaks
The tortured boards out on the floor
Beneath the keyhole to our door;
Whose heartless, calloused, upturned hand
Repeats its ornery demand
For rent; whose curt, concise replies
To all our fragile, whitened lies
About the burn, the noise, the scratch,
Are always victor in the match—
This round misprison of His way
He sent to our lean flat today
—God only knows the reason why—
Porting a luscious lemon pie!!!

HYDE CLAYTON.

*Low tide at La Jolla . . . and nostalgic memories . . . of the music . . .
and the moonlight . . . of southern California . . .*

TIDES

Once more you journey outward, weary tide,
    Your questing waters moving toward the sea.
What is it that you seek eternally,
    And, failing, seek again unsatisfied?
In the night hours I heard your voice that cried
    Along the sedgy marshes wistfully,
And thought how beautiful your dream must be
    That baffled through the years, has never died.

Oh, sea, my own unquiet, restless heart
    Echoes your anguish. My tumultuous blood
That surges high when life is glad and fair
    Knows that the transient glory must depart,
Knows that the exaltation born of flood
    Must vanish with the ebb tide's old despair.

INEZ BARCLAY KIRBY.

A sculptured piece of alabaster . . . inanimate and cold . . . to a myth that warmed a lover's heart . . . thirty centuries ago . . .

TO VENUS IN A SCHOOLHOUSE

Rising once more out of the sea
Was Venus in that noise-crammed hall
Where bells pinched immortality.
From her entombing marble she
Ascended, made warm and palpable
And breathing, the lovely skeleton of beauty.
Between the crowd she moved and coolly
Smiling glittered along the wall
Like sudden sunshine when it's cloudy.

This happened once I swear and still
She walks the subterranean
Cool dark of the unconscious.

KATHARINE SHATTUCK.

The politician who meant his campaign promises . . . and foolishly thought that his party did too . . . and learned . . . and wept . . .

TO ANY YET FAITHFUL

You who believed, believe no more in me.
I was no prophet in the wilderness
Crying, "Make ready, for a King will pass!"
No prophet was I, but an old banshee
Keening for splendors lost. I was Dead Sea
Fruit. I was flags nailed to a broken mast.
Herald of no dawn was I, but the last
Flower of a false spring frozen on the tree.

Yet do not say it was an empty cup
That you in your delusion lifted up.
Say only that you happened once to see
Beauty, though small and strange it was, in me
Who have no beauty now. That you once took
A jeweled fish where weeds now choke the brook.

CORAL MORGAN.

153

A man who had one love and two wives . . . and both were faithful to him . . .

WINGED BEAUTY

Mad Audubon, whom failure could not blight,
Saw the Ohio, clear in emerald light,
With topaz ripples where the mallard king
Dived fishing; saw the sudden halcyon fling
A Chinese fan abroad, of azure, bright
As morning-glories; saw the zigzag flight
As of a bouncing yellow ball and swing
On tufted weed-top of that jocund thing,
The jet-winged goldfinch; shared the panic fright
Of chewinks at a buccaneering spright,
The frisking squirrel; heard the mezzo ring
Of blackbirds' carols; felt the fiddle-string
Vibration of the meadow lark's mad flight.
This was the Vision Splendid: everything
Was harmony; again as Adam might
He entered Eden, heard Creation sing
Eternal music, saw in a blaze of light
Triumph at last—to hoard this fluttering
And motile Beauty, ever on the wing!

VIRGINIA PAULINE SPRIGGS.

*A man in a hall of mirrors . . . and some convex . . . and some concave
. . . and some a combination . . . and one straight one . . . but that one
dark . . . and that named "the future" . . .*

SO BIG

"Heil Fuehrer," resounded from glen to glen,
(How big he seemed to his country-men!)

He preened himself as he heard their cry,
(He seemed so big, in his own mind's eye!)

Heartaches littered the path he trod,
(I wonder how big he seems to God.)

ALBERTA M. PARIS.

154

BLUE BOWL

The bowl has very graceful lines
And keenly fascinates the eye
    With wondrous hue,
A work of art in crystal glaze
    Of charming periwinkle blue.

The bowl was bought in China's realm
From store that is war-riddled now,
    Bespattered red
With blood from fierce destruction's curse,
    And sad to say—that clerk is dead.

It seems the bowl has human pride
To hold its treasured memories,
    For when sublime
With lilies, fragrance truly is
    An incense for a vanished time.

EMMET PENDLETON.

All that would have been . . . that could have been . . . but for some sad strange reason . . . isn't . . .

TO ONE BORN DEAD

Not for you alone, though my defenseless
Woman heart grows faint with tenderness
Before the memory of that helpless mold
Of flesh, its story ever now untold,
But for all dreams, ideals, and hopes that lie
Unseen, unknown within life's womb, to die
The death most pitiable of all, the death
That precedes life and never knows one breath—
For all man's noble deeds and dreams stillborn
Condemned by alien force—for these I mourn.

BERNICE CAREY FITCH.

155

*A sentinel . . . standing by the sea . . . cousin of a clanking bell buoy for-
ever ringing out across the bay . . . to guide the ferry boats to Staten
Island . . .*

FOG HORN AT NIGHT

Fashion the feel of it,
Eerie appeal of it
  Into a song
Hurting the heart of me, till it's part of me
  All the night long.

Haunting the wail of it,
What is the tale of it:
  Why does it creep
Out of the fog and gloom, into my quiet room
  Making me weep?

Voice of unspoken things,
Shadowy broken things
  Fallen in flight—
Out from the hidden sea, dreary mist-ridden sea,
Fog horn at night.

HELEN MITCHEL.

*The funny old fellow with tangled beard . . . he sits all day and feeds
sea gulls . . . and wonders . . . and wishes . . . and dreams . . .*

THE DOCK DREAMER

Down at the docks on his lonesome beat,
With broken shoes on his shuffling feet;
Watching the tugs as they come and go,
With a grizzled grin and his eyes aglow;
For he's dreaming of soft sapphire seas,
Far tropic isles and ocean breeze—
And longing again for a lost lagoon,
Or a fiddle's rasp in an old saloon;
But his watch is over, his days are done,
As he sits alone in the noon-tide sun,
Seeing 'em still where his fancy strays
Those gallant ships of his sailing days.

HARVEY MCKENZIE.

A little boy who once upon a time loved to visit neighbors . . . and
devotes his life to calling on his friends . . . doorbells . . . doorbells . . .

POSTMAN

A stereotype? The suit, the sack,
  The step gives such impression?
To handle letters, to retrace steps
  Is in truth a full confession
Of dull procedures, dull routines?
  Therefore, by repetition born,
A dull life? Such logical conclusion
  Is imperfectly drawn.
With every letter goes a passport
  To a roundtrip of romance.
The doorsteps, the shops all shifting ports
  On an odyssey of chance.
Lands glimpsed yesterday are already gone
  From crowded and swift question
Of those today that vanish tomorrow.
For tiny chit-chats and self-suggestion
Transform scenes more than all the paints and tricks the
    artist knows
And open up more worlds than the geography shows.

E. MANFREDA.

A tall old man who commuted thirty years . . . every day for thirty years
. . . the eight forty-seven . . . and now no more . . .

TWENTIETH CENTURY LIMITED

  The train is coming down the track
    With a wish, a whirr, and a shudder—
  It grinds to a stop—
  It's like a ship, with the gleaming rails
    For a rudder.

  Over the hills and through the tunnels—
    It's a puff of smoke by now—
  And although my body is standing still,
    My soul's on the train somehow!

RUTH NORRIS KENT.

THROUGH RIVERS OF BLOOD

Earthlings will yet do noble things,
Fear not,—these bloody underlings . . .
These uncouth, dinosaurish men,
Will reach the place destined for them . . .
They will put the soul's harmony,
Above their fiendish revelry . . .

Pass mountains of hostilities . . .
Purge ugly depths of rivalries . . .
Crumble, One Day, the madman's sword,
One Day, I say, but O my friend,
What mountings on hearts . . . what rivers of blood . . .
And limbs to cross . . . to gain that end!

When, after they have suffered much . . .
Their hands will reach out hands to touch . . .
Despite their grotesque strategy,
They will achieve Fraternity!

SARA ADLER ROSALSKY.

TO AN OLD PLATTER

Old China keeps its secrets.
    Here on this platter—blue and white—I trace
The tiny multitudinous cracks,
    Like wrinkles on a kind old face.

How tiny on its spreading space appears
    The modern butcher's miserly affair!
It is the relic of a fuller day,
    Still carrying that antique well-fed air.

KAY PHILLIPS.

Robinhood . . . to Cupid . . . or Hiawatha . . . to all the archers every-
where . . . who string their arrows . . . bend their bows . . .

THE ARCHER

I saw the bowman bend his straining arc,
  Place on the string a shaft of varied hue,
And call an urchin playing in the park
  To try, to please him, if his aim be true.
The child, exerting all his puny strength,
  Laughing, drew the "pretty" to his cheek,
Released the twanging string; then ran to seek
  The arrow where it fell—at no great length.

Life is a bended bow,—our soul the shaft,
Well-notched, set to the string with master craft,
  And placed a moment in our infant hand:
Simply, delighted with the gaudy lure,
We draw; the arrow, wavering, weak, unsure,
  Sings its short song. . . . How little space is spanned!

CRAWFORD WILLIAMS.

"But the clock stopped . . . never to go again . . .

CLOCKS

Like fashioned rock,
The patterned clock
  Pushes aside the hours each day.
Its tapered hands
Are music bands
  That play an endless roundelay.

In sorrowing,
Or when I sing,
  A clock keeps ticking in my heart;
Through night and day
It ticks away,
  To keep my life and death apart.

TESSA SWEAZY WEBB.

O graceful shaft of steel
    Piercing the city sky,
Holding the panorama
    Of urban life to your eye,
Can you know the glory
    You bring to such as I?

Can you know the friendship
    You bring when I hear you speak,
When I hear the eager voices
    Call from your lofty peak,
As the drifting clouds pat softly
    The shining gloss of your cheek?

You paint me vivid pictures
    Of life both near and far.
When I meet your charming callers
    From here to Zanzibar,
I feel as though I'd travelled
    Like prince or king or tsar.

I see this mighty city
    From night to the warm sun's rise,
In every kind of weather—
    Each mood to me a prize.
You give my life real purpose.
    I'm blind. And you are my eyes.

KATHARINE RENWICK.

*The hide of a haunted beast somewhere . . . the hide tanned and cut and
sewed . . . and fitted . . . once haunted . . . now haunting . . .*

HIS GLOVES

These are his gloves.
Plain, brown, common,
In them, the print of his hands.
His hands—sweet and warm in our wooing,
His hands—kind and gentle when pain racked my body,
His hands—wise and courageous to guide our children,
His hands—gently folded in long, last sleep.
And these are his gloves,
Plain, brown, common,
In them, the print of his hands.

ESTHER HAKANSON.

*A neighbor's yard . . . where every spring . . . a carpet green . . . the
pride and envy of the street . . . becomes suddenly democratic . . .*

THE DANDELION

She's just a little wayward minx
    Conceived in nature's mold
Who spreads her devastating wiles
    With locks of splintered gold.

But soon she finds she is betrayed—
    Gray tresses shade her face,
Derisive breezes snatch her bald
    And leave her in disgrace.

MARTHA E. CUNNINGHAM.

*A poverty-stricken minstrel . . . found in the Bowery with this in his
pocket . . . a scrap of paper and five short words . . . "Dear friends and
gentle hearts" . . .*

TO STEPHEN COLLINS FOSTER

"Dear friends and gentle hearts," he wrote;
Some later date to pen the note
For one more haunting melody,
But by some strange catastrophe
His soul was snatched beyond recall;
Sleep well! oh gentlest of them all!

ELEANORE RANDALL LAMKIN.

161

A shopkeeper's window on Madison Avenue . . . to an ivory goddess that smiled one day . . . to a little box I didn't open . . .

CARVED SANDAL-WOOD

O jewel-casket, sandal-wood,
I would not have you, if I could,
Disturb milady's hour of ease
To voice your scented mysteries. . . .

Tell where you grew, what isle upon,
Perhaps far Fiji, far Ceylon;
What sun first waked your sandal-tree;
What breezes gave you fragrancy;
Or tell what artist's chisel sought
To token all your years have brought
By this skilled carving, whispering
Of jungle tree or jungle spring;
Of vine that gave you love's caress
Like an impassioned Druidess;
Of tropic bird's song from your bough,
An aria ringing even now.
Your beauty tells that craftsman's heart
Will pulsate ever in his art.
Guard well her jewels, paltry things
Compared to iridescent wings,
To blossoms you have known and lost,
To white-capped waves your sea has tossed.

O jewel-casket, sandal-wood,
I would not have you, if I could,
Disturb milady's hour of ease
To voice your scented mysteries.

MATTIE HALLAM LACY.

FAMILY DOCTOR

Out of a world of black ignorance and jagged fear
Standing sturdy like a beacon of guiding light,
Dispelling the horror of a pain-filled night,
You come to us, with your brusque, good cheer.
How quick your hands to probe, your eyes to peer;
What God-given strength lies in your quiet might,
What sinewy muscles you use to win your fight.
It's over . . . and instantly your face is clear
As you smile over a task well done.
Quietly you re-pack your medical kit
And stop a moment long enough to say,
"How bright the room is with the morning sun."
And then you go again, doing your needed bit
To help the world face yet another day.

DOROTHY BLADIN HILL.

The same shopkeeper's window . . . and ivory goddess . . . and sandal wood casket . . . but this time . . . a Chinese gong . . .

TO A CHINESE GONG

Great shining disc of burnished brass, you hold
The soul of China in your gleaming heart!
Perhaps a sorcerer with magic art,
Long years ago before the world was old,
Imprisoned in you one who, grown too bold,
Defied the gods and, haughty, stood apart
With unbowed head, when through the crowded mart
The deities were borne, in chairs of gold.
I strike you with the gong-stick, and you roar
Defiance at the humbling that old spinner,
Fate, has devised for you; but never-more
Shall the celestial sun—Oh brazen sinner!—
Shine down on you. Your punishment is sore;
To summon "foreign devils" to their dinner.

WINONA MONTGOMERY GILLILAND.

THE DREAM THAT CRACKED A WHIP

Dream,
You are too much
For this frail strength.
How can I make you
Less a dream?

Once I thought that dreams
Were fragile as the velvet dust
Upon the wings of moths.
But you are strong;
You lash unmercifully!

Perhaps I am too small
For this great dream;
And,
Failing to bring it into
Conscious being—
Will ever bear its scar.

This dream, unrealized,
Unsung,
Will take its vengeance
Crying for expression.

Dream,
How can I make you
Less a dream?
Be reality,
Or vanish into
Nebulous nothingness.

You are too much
For this frail strength.

FRANCES AIRTH.

164

A troublesome lad who broke the game laws ... and maidens' hearts ...
and all the box office records at London's old Globe Theater ...

SONNET TO SHAKESPEARE

I shall not read you yet. (Some say I should.)
　　I cannot ask for more than I possess;
I know a girl whose slender body could
　　Not hold an atom more of loveliness;
I know a boy whose cool, proud head is fair,
　　Whose lips are strong, eyes—cold; I know starshine;
Bleak days; black nights. For you I do not care
　　Lest I become like him with too much wine.
Ten years from now I shall much wiser be;
　　Of panting eagerness less shall I know;
Then I shall be the blind man made to see
　　To find the wealth you offer me. This so—
I'll save you 'til this now within me dies;
I'll read you when I am mature and wise.

Sara Alice Howard.

Mm–m–m–m–m–m–m–m–m

This is to give you fair warning . . . these poems in this section are senti-
mental . . . if you are under fifteen or over fifty . . . they will be mushy
. . . but if you're in love . . . mm—m—m—m—m—m—m—m—m . . .

DO NOT LOVE ME NOW

The air is ecstasy; to breathe is joy;
  The sky is all one dream of flower blue;
This loveliness must needs have some alloy,
  Or else my swelling heart will break. Ah, do
Not love me now; save love for bitter days
  Of wind and rain, when hearts need comforting
Against the cold. There are so many ways
  That one may capture happiness in Spring
That April love is waste; it should be stored
  Away in some far corner of one's heart
'Til winter grays the world; then the bright hoard
  Can be brought forth. But love should have no part
In Spring and all its beauty; love should be
Dark winter's own—its one bright ecstasy.

VIOLA CORNETT.

The cynic . . .

PERHAPS THIS TIME . . .

My moons are made of green cheese;
  My dreams are all still-born,
And every rose I've stooped to pick
  Has had its piercing thorn.

I've grown so used to this, dear,
  And yet you came my way
And fairy things have happened
  Through this one sunny day.

I've dared to start a new dream.
  I will not count the cost.
I know I shall be happy—but
  I'll keep my fingers crossed.

IRIS LEE HAILE.

SANCTUM

I built a tiny garden
    In a corner of my heart.
I kept it just for lovely things
    And bade all else depart.

And ever was there music,
    And flowers blossomed fair;
Yet never was it perfect
    Until *you* entered there.

BEULAH B. MALKIN.

Haven't we met somewhere before . . .

ON YOUR TWENTY-FIFTH BIRTHDAY

I think I knew, beloved,
The day that you were born.
Although I was not, yet
I think there came to me
Across the infinite reach
Of star-studded heavens
The sound of your first baby cry.
And, in my before-life existence,
I think I heard you, felt my need of you,
Vowed to search you out
When you and I had reached
Our full maturity. . .

This is the time, the place, beloved.
You have waited a quarter of a century,
I a few months less.
We have no need of further waiting,
You and I, no need of further search.
We have each other—soon for life.
For life! For days and nights
Of sweet, warm closeness.
For months and years of hand-in-hand
Companionship. For an eternity
Of living side by side,
Content together. . . .

ADRIAN F. NADER.

REMEMBERING THE DARK

I'd like to be the lightning,
   A golden shaft from God
That strikes into lilies
   And the soft brown sod.

I'd like to be the silver
   That zigzags up and down
Across the blue heavens
   And through the great town.

Yes, I'd like to be electric,
   A quick come and go,
For just being human
   Seems so very slow.

Oh to mix in a motor
   And drive a great machine;
Yes, to be a force eternal
   That never can be seen.

Yet here I stand so puny
   Among the race of men,
While there a great dynamo
   Chants 'lectricity again.

But when I think of loving
   I can't admire sparks;
My mind runs in rhythms,
   Remembering the dark;

And when my heart caresses
   I like to linger so,
My lips seem too human,
   Love won't let me go.

So when it comes to loving
   I'm not a shaft of light;
I'd rather be a woman
   In the soft black night.

ROSALIE GOODYEAR.

170

I hope this won't start an argument ... we were getting along so beautifully ...

DO LOVERS' TONGUES

Do lovers' tongues sound more silver-sweet
By day or night, because a round rich
Phrasing records the fairy-fact complete?

Does any mistress write a better
Letter to her Lover
Because Heloise could cover
Every phase of love in one
Most lovely letter?

Does the woman you love
Bring a passion more resistless
For the songs of Whitman,
For the throngs of loving thoughts
Of which he was the loving master?

Because of them
Can you vow your love
The faster?

GRACE BAER HOLLOWELL.

Sometimes it takes fourteen lines to say "I Love You" ... but what lines ... or what a line ... or what ...

TO AN ADORED ONE

There is no word expressing fragile charm,
But breaks to dust at my hand's clumsy weight.
Thought is a fugitive—I desecrate
The bluest blue of veining in your arm
With offer of the blue a gentian knows.

A sensuous ache throbs on through my prayer,
And I would hold you closely, did I dare,
With no care how the world would have us go.
I will not let those wings of our old dreams
Weigh down with tears that they no longer beat.
My adoration runs through little themes
And falls a breathless poem at your feet.

JULIA A. FRENCH.

171

*If you still doubt this is the sentimental section . . . get a tall glass of ice
water . . . and read this . . .*

INTERVAL OF FLAME

I should have met your tentative caress
    With frosty eyes, or cool deceptive lips.
I should have feigned a somewhat startled air
    And held you off with warning fingertips.
No doubt the old traditions have their place
    Wherein the man pursues, the girl withdraws,
Or simulates a passive attitude—
    And yet, my dearest one, in that brief pause
Before your lips met mine, I quite forgot
    The careful, stilted role I should have played!
I couldn't see your eyes, but at your touch
    Some wild sweet madness stirred my heart and made
Me lift my lips to yours. I took your kiss,
    More tremulous and shaken than you knew
And yet not caring if you dimly sensed
    With how much eagerness I came to you.
Your hands were gentle, and your tenderness
    Was something I had never known before.
I felt as though you took me by the hand
    And led me through a strange enchanted door
Swung open by the magic of your kiss,
    Beyond which there was neither time nor space
Nor anything I knew—except for this—
    An interval of flame in your embrace.

SYLVIA GARDINER LUFBURROW.

Getting sentimental again . . . m—m—m—m—m

EXPECTATION

    Starlight, moonglow,
    Hoofbeats in the snow.

    Lamplight, fireglow,
    Footsteps at the door.

    Lovelight, heartglow,
    In your arms once more.

GLADYS BRIERLY ASHOUR.

Hold your breath while you read this one . . .

SOFT FEATHERS SPURNED

I don't like my pillow—now.
The smug look on its fat and foolish face
Reveals belief that it can take your place.

With pride it cries, "Look at me!
I offer peace—tranquillity."
Oh God! Who wants tranquillity?

I want you—hot lips, warm breath
    To make my pulses leap.
While my poor pedantic pillow thinks
    That I will be content with *sleep.*

RUTH CARROLL.

Close your eyes and read this one . . .

SURRENDER

You are the stars, Beloved, my moon and sun,
    My land and water, darkness, light and air,
    All life was drab until you made it fair . . .
Made life and love with beauty subtly one,
Unconscious of the glory just begun
    With knowing you. Now I no longer care
    For any thing in which you do not share.
Alas for me! This thing that you have done
Renders me deaf and dumb and wholly blind
To everything in which you have no part . .
    In my devotion only I exist.
Yours is my body, soul and quailing mind.
I have no eyes, nor lips nor ears nor heart—
    No will, no inclination to resist.

KATHERINE K. WOODLEY.

We thought we'd ignore
The sudden sweet madness
That came between us.
How casually we spoke!
How carefully we controlled our eyes!
How loudly we shouted,
"I don't believe in love!"

What fools we were. It
Would have been easier
To hide a mountain.
Or stop the thunder,
Or put the prairie in your pocket,
Than to deny the
Existence of sunshine.

BEATRICE FLEMING.

REPLY TO ADVICE TO YOUTH

And what of old age without memories,
    The only wealth life leaves us at the end?
Who would exchange remembered ecstasies,
    A bough of comets, for the cold gray blend
Of comfort and immunity's dry laurel?

Better the acrid embers than no fire;
    Better the blood-thirsty steel of a quarrel
Severing the thundered veins, than no desire.

Only the coward heart refuses love;
    Afraid to suffer, bars its cautious door;
Crouched by its bare hearth fondles the tame dove
    Of peace—unheeding—till love knocks no more:

Then shall silence fall like stone on the mind,
And time stand still, and the last frail hope go blind.

MARION DOYLE.

KNOWLEDGE

Men form all their best designs
To play a public part;
Women keep their purposes
Neighbor to the heart.

Thus when power and enterprise
Crash in public day,
Women in the secret night
Know the things to say.

FRANCIS C. COOK.

Address unknown

A WOMAN SPEAKS ACROSS THE YEARS

Wherever you may be in all the world
This winter night of softly falling snow,
So like the night we went divided ways,
I send this word to you and think you know.

Whatever life and years have done to you,
Whatever life and years have done to me,
Though other greater loves have come to us,
We can never be sundered utterly.

There was too much of beauty that we knew
Together and there was enough of pain;
Two lives that have been bound by these, my dear,
Are never wholly separate lives again.

There was too much we gave each other once,
Beyond our love itself, that stayed to bless
The years that were to be. Some bond endures
When two have shared so much of loveliness.

ADELAIDE LOVE.

175

PHANTOM

Last night when the moon was free
I sent a breeze as messenger
To brush a kiss across your lips.
Did you turn your head, alert
Because it ruffled up your hair
So like my fingers, light as air?
Did you close your eyes to dream
And hear the rustle of the leaves?
It was my echo, whispering
My heart, my soul, belong to you!
And always, when the moon hangs low
Should you but pause and wish for me
You will feel my presence near,
Lingering in every shadow
Beneath the pale moonglow of night.

GUANETTA GORDON.

But when the waiting is over ... it's ... "Where in the world have you been" ...

WAITING

Waiting for you begins
Like softly muted violins.
The tempo quickens . . .
    Rises in intensity
Until it crashes . . . in a symphony
    Of waiting . . . waiting . . . waiting . . .

Then, suddenly, you're home
From far across the foam.
    The music swiftly blends
Into a lullaby of love
    And . . . waiting for you ends.

WINIFRED BURKETT.

176

ARMORED

Your kiss lies hearteningly upon
　　My lips as some high accolade;
Sending my timid spirit forth
　　Quite unafraid.

And from three ageless, golden words
　　A shield is wrought so that no dart,
However keen or venom-tipped,
　　Can reach my heart.

LUCILE HARGROVE REYNOLDS.

A friend kept a scrapbook of poems once . . . I thought it was just a scrapbook . . . and then one day . . . a hint was dropped that there was an incident or story between each line . . . suddenly the old scrapbook held all the romance of a diary . . .

BOOKENDS

Between the bookends
Of my heart
I keep the stories of our love . . .

The one that tells of that first night
When we knew each sweet surrender . . .
Sang our song of love
And found such comfort
In the silent wisdom of the stars . . .

The one that tells of your farewell . . .
(I realize now how wise you were
Not to tie me down
But to leave our love unspoiled)

And so
I treasure dearly the stories
Between the bookends
Of my heart . . .

R. SCOTT BOWEN.

EXCEPTION

"Look cautiously and far ahead
    Before you give your heart away,
And be not hasty," O I said,—
    And always I have paused to weigh
The consequences when I read
    The signs of love, till yesterday.

But yesterday I swear I had
    No time to think how it would be
To love a serious dark-haired lad
    Before he took the heart of me,
And left me weak and wildly glad
    And wretched, simultaneously!

ELAINE V. EMANS.

*It's wonderful as long as she doesn't write it all in her diary . . . then it
sometimes is delicate . . .*

REVEALMENT

Why can I seem to write of naught but you?
I find each day replete with new delights,
And there are moments shining down from heights
To touch and thrill a hungry heart anew.
But when I take my eager pen to trace
The intricate pattern of each lovely day,
I find that there is little I can say
That does not find the image of your face
Impressed so deeply on my heart and mind,
That I can but endeavor to express
The fleeting little lights of happiness
Or sadness I find there, and I am blind
To all the beauties of a radiant world
When your bright flag of beauty is unfurled.

BERT HENDERSON.

Take this with a "pillar of salt" . . .

BIOGRAPHY

I've always heard
  The good die young.
When I am dead
  May every tongue
Deplore my vice,
  For I would be
Methuselah, since
  You came to me.

ANNA LOVELACE GORSUCH.

This is for all who love or have loved . . .

LOVE SONG

Out of all splendor that there is
Remember this . . .
That, for a moment, before day has dwindled
To dark, the sun is hugely kindled
And lights our world with a great, blazing fire,
A furious glory and torment of light
Before night.
So, now, no matter what happens if desire
Be quenched untimely, yet our moment was
When life and love were pure and clear as glass,
Touched by a faint reflection of God's being
For all men's seeing.
You were a witness also, who walked through it,
You knew it.
Whatever we know again, whatever
Sorrow and pain and grief may do to us, what fever
May burn, it was ours more beautifully, the splendor—
Therefore, be tender.
And never deny it, nor shake your head, for you have known
    it.
No one can own it.

DOROTHY MCFARLANE.

179

AVOWAL

Love is a shield to hold against the dark,
 A fire to warm me, shelter from the night;
A lamp forever burning, and the spark,
 The eternal spark that keeps the flame alight.
Love is the merchandise not bought or sold,
 The gift, self-giving, counting not the price;
The deep-embedded vein of hidden gold
 Refined in crucibles of sacrifice.
If I may have your love to keep beside me,
 To hold inviolate, a precious thing,
If I may have its steady light to guide me,
 It will not matter what the years may bring,
Nor what the years may take beyond recall.
If I may have your love I shall have all.

MINNIE MARKHAM KERR.

Even candles can light prairie fires . . . in the right hands . . .

LOVE

You wanted love—not love that I could give you,
 But something that was fire and lightning flame;
And I had only lamplight for my windows,
 And candleshine to greet you when you came.

A prairie fire held warmth that you were seeking,
 That ruthless sweep, high challenge to the bold,
How could you know—when meteors flung red guidance,
 That quiet hearths are best to keep the cold?

You wanted love . . . somewhere perhaps you found it,
 And journey now with scorched heart cold and numb . . .
My candles burn a little every evening . . .
 It may be they will last until you come.

HELEN WELSHIMER.

A poem in prose . . . all for you . . .

TO A FRIEND

"I love you not only for what you are, but for what I am when I am with you.

"I love you not only for what you have made of yourself, but for what you are making of me.

"I love you for the part of me that you bring out.

"I love you for putting your hand into my heaped-up heart and passing over all the foolish and frivolous and weak things that you can't help dimly seeing there, and for drawing out into the light all the beautiful radiant belongings that no one else had looked quite far enough to find.

"I love you for ignoring the possibilities of the fool and weakling in me, and for laying firm hold on the possibilities of the good in me.

"I love you for closing your ears to the discords in me, and for adding to the music in me by worshipful listening.

"I love you because you are helping me to make of the timber of my life not a tavern, but a temple, and of the words of my every day not a reproach, but a song.

"I love you because you have done more than any creed could have done to make me happy.

"You have done it without a touch, without a word, without a sign.

"You have done it first, by being yourself."

After all, perhaps this is what being a friend means.

UNKNOWN.

"Two's Company . . . Three's . . .

It isn't so bad . . . a crowd of people running through your mind . . . but just two or three tramping through your heart . . .

You offer me all that women want;
　　Climbing vines on a cottage small,
Ruffled curtains and a cheery hearth,
　　And tiny footprints in the hall.

He offers me nothing—nothing at all—
　　But a life that is mad and wild at best,
And a searching, hungry, lonely heart
　　With never a quiet moment to rest.

I'll probably marry you, because
　　Women do the things they must;
And I'll eat the cake you feed me, dear,
　　But my soul will long to share his crust.

WILMA ROBERTSON.

It isn't so bad to have a "line" . . . nor to use it to string them all along . . . but if those strings get together . . . it's a rope . . .

LINES TO A PHILANDERER

Your voice no longer holds the power to thrill:
　　Once, lure of all the world was in each tone,
Each love-fraught word. I never had my fill
　　Because I thought they were for me alone.
I learned, at least, five others had a copy.

Just like a lovely dress, once dearly-prized:
　　I thought it, too, was made for me alone;
Now cast aside, although not quite despised,
　　Limp hangs its faded beauty, gone its tone.
I learned, at least, five others had a copy.

BERTA G. McGUIRK.

This poem will seem beautiful to you until you find yourself in the posi-
tion of one of its characters . . . then it will become . . . absurd . . . un-
reasonable . . . and much less effective than fingernails . . .

TO THE OTHER WOMAN

One of us must lose this thing
    For which we've lived and breathed and fought,
And losing, go upon a lonely way,
    Failing to forget how once we sought
For bread and drink within a land laid bare,
Looking for sustenance when none was there.

And if this lost and lonely
    One be you, remember you have met
With ecstacy and harbored something sweet.
    And though your heart breaks and your eyes are wet,
Be grateful for the little you have had, and then
With lifted soul, go out and love again.

And if I be the one to lose
    And must watch bravely while he goes away,
Then hold his love with tender, careful hands
    And keep it always new and bright, I pray.
A thing so dear demands a gentle touch.
And oh, be very proud that God has given you so much!

BETTY MADSEN.

i...f

PLEDGE OF FAITH

    I would not lift my eyes again
        To any male on earth,
    Nor ask his admiration, gifts,
        Companionship, or mirth.
    I would be true to only you,
        Forever thus to be,
    If I could be quite sure, my love,
        You'd be as true to me.

NELDA WOOD MARTIN.

185

Memory is a tricky thing ... time does not enter it ... everything that memory holds is changeless in its grasp ... but we who crowd its portals grow older every hour ...

SONNET FOR THE SUBSTANCE

O, doubtless you'll remember till you die
   The way her bronze curls burned against the white
Pure oval of her flower face; and I
   Have not one gift that's beautiful to fight
These memories so close through dark you see,
   Pale moonlight staining her sweet body gold,
For having known her not so well as me,
   She stays forever young and I grow old.

But that is well and I would wish no harm.
   Her cold high sanctuary's safe from me:
For I may hear you swear at the alarm,
   And turn to find me warmly close, while she—
I think, again, her memories retreat
   When you come shouting late, "When do we eat?"

FRANCES ELEONORE SCHLUNEGER.

There are so many Cynaras ... to whom their loves are faithful ... in their way ...

RIVALS

Oh, well, I know you think you love but me
   And hold your vow of faithfulness is true;
But I am woman-wise, and I can see
   What rival I may fear in mist and who
Of Spring's loose daughters with their mouths of musk
   Are dangerous. Last night I saw you far
Up on the lonely hillside wooing dusk
   And holding dubious traffic with a star. . . .

There is that witch-tree in the wood—oh, yes,
   I heard her whispering all the afternoon . . .
And I have seen the furtive wind's caress,
   And your face hid in long hair of the moon . . .
Oh, well, I know you think you love but me—
But oh, my dear, if you should know the sea!

MARJORY SMITH.

186

FIRST LOVES

Lure of the Orient,
   Tang of the sea,
Billowing jib sails
   Took him from me.

Kimonos from Hongkong,
   Beads from Malay . . .
But ever he wandered
   Farther away.

Slowly but surely
   Years moved along,
Taking for toll
   A maiden's song.

And now while his parrot
   Profanely screams,
A lonely old sailor
   Mends broken dreams . . .

While another man splits
   My kindling wood,
And calls me his sweetheart—
   As a husband should.

But who shall be saying
   I am content,
With the heart of me still
   In the Orient?

JEAN STEPHEN JOHNSTON.

SECOND WIFE

I know that what you say is true, and yet,
If I could choose—of course I have no choice—
But still, if I could choose, I think I'd keep
Things just the way they are. I know you think
You're doing what is right to tell me this.
Oh, please forgive me . . . I am tired, I guess.
It's been a lonesome day to stay at home
Alone without him—and the baby gone
To school. The way she's grown! I hardly know
Or realize how big she really is.
Yes, she was four the year we married. Now
She's six and starting off to school, and still
I think of her as "baby". All the house
Has seemed so empty. I am glad you came;
It's hours yet before my baby comes
From school . . . I know you smile to hear me call
Her "mine"; and yet, I think of her as mine
And his . . . I never saw her mother. Though
I've heard him say she had her mother's eyes . . .
Of course he talks of her—I'd want him to . . .
Don't look so grieved. You act as if you thought
I'd never known he loved somebody else.
And yet you said yourself, just after you
Came in, that he had loved his first wife so . . .
I don't know why you said it—least of all
To me—for that was understood, and I'd
Not have it different, even if I could.

He loved her. Yes—I hope he always will,
At least the memory of her . . . Does that
Seem queer to you? Oh, how can I explain—
She was a part of his own life, as I
Am now. I do not mean I took her place;
I could not, even if I tried. You see,
She shaped his life as he was then. She helped
To make him as he is today, into
The man I love . . . I hadn't meant to tell
So much to you—or anyone. I had

Not even thought it out myself . . .
She put
The look of gentleness and peace within
His eyes. Her death had brought a sadness there
That only made me want to comfort him,
But not to take her place. I'd rather have
The place that's all my own . . . Can you see that?
Somehow I think perhaps she'd understand,
Be happier, too, to know the way I feel,
And know I love the baby as my own . . .
It's early yet . . . Don't go! The baby's still
At school, but *he'll* be coming soon . . . He's due.
. . . Oh, thank you for the things you said. I know
You meant to help—and I am glad to talk
It over, too, with you . . . Come back again . . .
I think I hear somebody coming now . . .
Is it? . . . But, oh, it is . . . He's coming home . . .
I see him smiling quite as if he knew
He'd find me waiting just inside the door.
(I wouldn't have had things different if I could.)

EMILY DAWSON CRAIN.

This is a true story . . . but aren't they all . . .

LINES WRITTEN FOR A WIFE

Within a little while he may forget
  Her wholly—I will wait, and trust, and pray.
If only he would not dream so, and yet
  I know a man his age must love the gay
Aprilian freshness of her hair and eyes,
And feel years younger, when they laugh together . . .
I do not blame him much (nor is it wise
  To blame her greatly, ignorant as to whether
She knew he had a wife and children here).
  Within a little while, perhaps tomorrow,
He may turn toward me, whispering "O my dear,"—
  So I will trust, and wait him through my sorrow.

ELAINE V. EMANS.

"Parting Is Such Sweet Sorrow . . .

Sometimes an actor forgets a few lines ... skips them ... goes on ...
and forever after he is haunted by the little raveled hole ... in the play
... romance can cry of unkissed kisses too ...

MIDSUMMER

You loved me for a little
  Who could not love me long;
You gave me wings of gladness
  And lent my spirit song.

You loved me for an hour
  But only with your eyes;
Your lips I could not capture
  By storm or by surprise.

Your mouth that I remember
  With rush of sudden pain
As one remembers starlight
  Or roses after rain ...

Out of a world of laughter
  Suddenly I am sad. ...
Day and night it haunts me,
  The kiss I never had.

SYDNEY KING RUSSELL.

One and one make two ... but two alone make Heaven ...

MEMORY

I had one small glimpse
At heaven
Thru an opening in the sky;
One tiny peek at paradise
To fashion my heart's dream by.
Perhaps if you had seen it too,
It might have opened wide,
And showered all its blessings through,
Or let us pass inside.
But you didn't,
And I guess I mustn't really mind it;
While one can lose a paradise,
There must be two to find it.

HELEN HOOPER.

Can you remember your first "heartbreak" at parting . . .

AT PARTING

This, then, is "Goodbye." This empty aching,
This feeling of despondency and loss
As if we two were walking, side by side,
And suddenly the earth had opened wide
And swallowed you. Or if, from deep sleep waking,
I stretched my hand to you, and in despair
Found only emptiness, and silence, there.

This is "Goodbye." Although my heart is breaking
I clasp your hand and smile into your eyes,
Then turn and go my way, as you go yours.
(Saving my tears to shed behind closed doors.)
Without a pause to see which road I'm taking,
Nor daring to look back, lest I should see
Love's silent ghost were keeping step with me.

E. PEARL DANCEY.

If one could only build a fire . . . and have no ashes left . . .

MEMORIAL IN FLAME

If I might write of you in flame
    So men might warm cold hands
Before the grate your love had lit!
    But, dear, my thought now stands
Beside the table where we two
Shared heaven, alone, chilled through.

I may not capture you, indeed,
    For others nor for me,
Yet in such pine cones as you brought
    To fill our grate I see
A glowing heart of flame, brought back,
From lost days, in an old gray sack.

FLORA S. RIVOLA.

193

Before the tall mirror of a well-stocked vanity ... cosmetics and lotions scattered about ... creams ... and lipstick ... eye shadow ... and perfume ...

THIS I REGRET

This I am sorry for—
This I regret:
Having the kind of heart
　He could forget,
Having the sort of soul
　He could misplace;
It is no comfort ...
　His knowing my face.

CURRY FEWELL.

So fine a line divides my mind's forgetting and recalling ...

EXCEPT ... SOMETIMES

I get along without you very well—
Of course I do ...
... Except ... sometimes ... when a summer breeze
Brings cool rain dripping from the trees
And this recalls the woods and mist
Where together we strolled one day and kissed.

But ... I get along without you very well,
Of course I do.

I really have forgotten you, you know,
Of course I have.
... Except ... sometimes ... when someone sings
And brings you back on memory's wings,
... Or when I hear a name
Like yours, or a voice that rings the same ...

I really have forgotten you ... almost ...
Of course I have,
　... Except ... sometimes.

VICTORIA ADELAIDE HARVEY.

*The moon does not always break with vivid brightness from behind a
cloud . . . the silver shower can tumble down . . . gradually grow . . . then
fade and go . . . leaving darkness . . . all around . . .*

FOOT NOTE TO EDEN

This I shall remember
  Beyond all time and space:
We owned one Spring together;
  And Eden was a place
With little knowing tables
  And candles blue and tall,
With cobwebs on the ceiling
  And shadows on the wall.

There is no gate to Eden
  Nor any threshold where
The wary hearted falter
  And wonder if they dare.
Though we were there I never knew
  Just how it came about—
Or how we happened on the place
  Where we came out.

Annette Patton Cornell.

MUTE

Some ever quiet thing
  I would that I could be,
A window through whose opening
  You look upon the sea—

Some inanimate bit
  You cherish day by day,
Having a constant need of it
  Forever in your way.

A song that makes you glad,
  A picture on your wall,
Some unfeeling thing that had
  No need of you at all.

Julia Van Norman.

*Driving down a country lane . . . the day and year and place has vanished
. . . but a sudden fragrance of sweet clover . . . I shall remember till I
die . . .*

I don't know how it happened: All I know
   Is there were many faces—then your face!
Out of the din of voices, yours . . . so low.
   Someone had said your name and mine. The place
That had spelled boredom was enchanted now,
   And we sought solitude where we could talk.
We left, but I cannot remember how
   We found ourselves together on the walk
That had been but a walk an hour ago,
   Or how we found our way to that far peak
Up where the stars are close, and clean winds blow,
   And Dawn sends forth her first pink-tinted streak.
I only know rain fell . . . and your hair curled . . .
Whose voice will haunt me far across the world.

NOVA DORNIN.

There are so many pictures on a road a mind remembers . . .

MAY ROAD

The road we followed led us to a hill.
Hands clasped, we mounted toward the morning sun;
And when the wooded summit had been won
We laughed together as young lovers will.
You drew me slowly close to you until
Our first kiss told what mischief had been done.
Pan prompted you but no Syrinx bade me run
To be a clump of reeds beside a rill.

My heart recalls the budding paw-paw tree;
The whistle that you whittled out for me.
The hill, the tree, the toy are lost for aye—
But always, darling, when the year brings May
I cross my heart, because we have arranged
Somehow, to keep the love that we exchanged.

ANNETTE PATTON CORNELL.

PLEDGE

There is a part of you that I shall keep
  When Time has softly hidden you from sight,
When I forget to wonder or to weep
  That you have crossed the boundary of night;
Though the grave candor of your searching gaze
  Elude me, and the magic of your voice
Return no more to gladden somber days,
  I shall discover reason to rejoice.

There is a memory that will not fade
  Though fugitive the years forever flee,
A glowing word you whispered unafraid
  That Time can never snatch away from me.
There is a part of you as frail as breath
  My heart shall proudly keep, even from death.

SYDNEY KING RUSSELL.

*Lush grass grows in a jungle forest . . . where no man's foot has ever
stepped . . . and no man knows . . .*

YOU WILL NOT MIND

You will not mind if, deep within my heart,
  I tend an altar fire that burns for you
And our lost love . . . if from the world apart
  I bow before the shrine in reverence true!
You will not mind if I should call your name
  Unconsciously—for habits are so strong . . .
If in my loneliness, I let the flame
  Blaze high, when dreary nights are long!
Nor mind my daily plans to earn your praise;
  My silent ritual with evening star . . .
It somehow helps to fill the empty days . . .
  And if I still should worship from afar
A sensitive soul that helped my own to grow,
You will not mind, for Dear, *you will not know.*

GRACE HARNER POFFENBERGER.

197

NO TIME

There is no time to say the things
Our hearts would say;
Regimented in a regimented day
Our thoughts are locked,
Our words are cut and weighed—
So much about the weather and the wars,
So much about the price of bread—
A copied word about the current play,
A sad word—ready-made, about the dead.

(I watch a sunset,
Yes, but watching me
There is a clock, inexorably paced—
My sunset watching is not free.
I sing a song,
But hearing me,
Some jealous duty turns a frowning face—
My singing is not done in liberty.)

But when an hour is unlocked from the chain
And given me to be with you,
Can my cramped wings, so used to being caged,
Lift me for just that hour into the blue?
Can I say then, with tongue that's free,
How beautiful you are—how dear
The little smile you sometimes give to me?
And that your voice is music that will ring
Throughout my darkest midnight? Can I sing
That being with you is release from pain,
And that rare health lies in your clasping hand?

No—I say it looks somewhat like rain,
But probably it's needed in the land.

EVA RIEHLE.

A termite in its tiny way is bent upon destruction . . .

ONE WORD

Which of us uttered it? And why?—
This little word that will not die.
Nothing has changed. No need to restore
That which is as it was before.
Now as ever your longings lean
To mine across the space between.
We talk and laugh; our intimate chat
Flutters mothlike from this to that.
As you were before, you are to me
And I to you. Yet suddenly
The simple gesture, smile and glance
Assume a sly significance,
And both of us know that into the room,
Like dank seamist, like breath from a tomb,
Has slithered the little ghost of a word
One of us uttered, and one of us heard.

MYRTLE ADAMS.

A recipe in a golden book may not resemble the cake in the oven . . .

PAPIER-MACHÉ

A woman likes a tall man,
A broad man and strong;

A woman likes a tweedy man
With keen eyes and blue.

You drew me like a magnet,
My heart it sang a song.

But, oh, a woman likes a brave man,
A kind man and true.

Looking deep within your eyes
I could not stay with you.

KATHRYN L. DROUGHT.

PRIDE PLAYS A PART IN MY HEART'S CONSTANCY

Take your dry crumbs that fall from love's table,
  Cast them aside, they are rubbish to me;
Give love's whole loaf, or else give me nothing,
  Pride plays a part in my heart's constancy.

Give love's dry crumbs to less passionate lovers
  Give them the dregs of love's cup that is drained,
But please do not proffer to me the leftovers,
  I must come first, if my love is regained.

I gave to you love's whole loaf unstinted,
  Gave you the nectar of love's sparkling wine,
Then take your crumbs, I spurn such small trifles,
  I must have all, else nothing is mine.

Keep your dry crumbs that fall from love's table;
  Love, heart and soul must be given to me,
Then I'll forever be yours for the asking—
  Pride plays a part in my heart's constancy.

BLANCHE CUMMINS PATTERSON.

BEREAVEMENT

I saw Love die! Not slowly, but at once.
  The world was changed to commonplace, and dull,
The one that yesterday had been so close,
  So near my heart; and I was worshipful.

Have other hearts known this bereavement too?
  Love did not let me know—I had no warning!
I see a stranger stare at me, instead.
  Is this a dream, and shall I wake at morning?

VIOLA BAILEY WILSON.

*If only six tall men could carry it away . . . and bury it forever . . . but
tomorrow and tomorrow will be Easter . . .*

MOURNING

Draw the shades across the window—
Place a wreath of flowers by.
Let there be no sound to mar it,
If a lovely thing must die.

Quiet—in the endless gloaming—
Let no worldly breath invade.
Time may heal the ache a little,
Memories, like flowers, fade.

Only let the scene be holy—
In the darkness kneel and pray;
Silently—, a prayer of sorrow,
For a heart has died today.

WILLA BLAKE.

"Humpty dumpty sat on a wall . . .

DOULEUR

Batter the doors of Heaven;
Fling the stars aside;
What is a door or star to one
Whose blithesome heart has died?

Reach for the copper moon;
Spread desire like wings;
How can love reach the utmost height
When the heart no longer sings?

Go to the depths of Hell;
Search through Satan's mart;
There in the cavern of despair
You will find a broken heart.

LULU BRUNT DAWSON.

201

FIELD OF HONOR

In truth, we might have known it from the start,
　　This path would have its turnings; there would be
　　No real alternative for you and me,
Fashioned of honest earth, except to part.
　　Whether the blow were mine to deal, or whether
Yours the swift blade by which this bond were sundered,
The hearts must bleed, because the feet have blundered
　　Into a way we may not walk together.

Rebuke me not, beloved, in that I
　　Perforce do quickly that which needs must be—
I am as one who fights because she fears
　　A darker wound, a deadlier agony
Than fronts her now.　And if I say goodbye,
　　Believe me that I say it through my tears!

I do beseech that you believe me true,
　　And cry your solace in a desperate need—
　　Belovedest, I had been false indeed,
If I did not this bitter thing I do!
Better a thousand times the anguish due,
　　The heart insolvent, but the conscience freed,
　　Than turn thus traitor to a certain creed,
Be faithless to myself, as well as you!

For it were surely treachery most base
　　To risk the sullying of so proud a shield;
To chance a single stain upon the face
　　Of what we bear in honor from the field,
Worthy to keep untarnished through the years,
Though polished daily with what meed of tears!

Strange paradox, my friend, that you and I,
  Who deemed our trusted strength so pure and sweet,
Should find ourselves stricken to earth thereby,
  Our swords turned sharply to our own defeat!
"Wisdom" writ large across the frozen breast
  Is doubtful comfort when the heart is breaking—
What final irony is manifest
  That we are scourged with thongs of our own making!

So I shall nevermore behold your face,
  Nor look for heaven at your finger-tips,
And all my ordered goings shall attest
  How I have set mine honor in its place—
Albeit by the wormwood on my lips,
  Albeit by the ashes in my breast!

                                        SARA HENDERSON HAY.

*A diplomat says yes ... meaning maybe ... and maybe ... meaning no
... but when he says no ... he isn't a diplomat ...
A lady says no ... meaning maybe ... maybe meaning yes ... but when
she says yes ... she isn't a lady ...*

STUPIDITY

  I said you'd better go away
    And forget you ever knew me,
  But women say such funny things,
    I thought you'd see right through me!

                                        MILDRED M. HOTT.

DREAM

You will be gone
  Like the wind and its blowing;
Love cannot go with you
  Where you are going.

Love fits his step
  To the man in the street;
You ask the wings of the
  World for your feet.

Love is the width
  Of a house and a bed;
Why must the sky alone
  Cover your head?

Yet who can say
  Which is wisest or best,
The dream in the heart,
  Or the dream possessed?

DOROTHY DAVIS.

Better have cookies . . . than a fallen cake . . .

PURCHASE

"It's better to have loved and lost . . ."
Were "quotes" I used too often.
I hadn't reckoned up the cost,
  Of a heart-shaped memory coffin!

RUTH D. McGINNIS.

204

THE WOMAN YOU USED TO LOVE

Did you ever go back to the woman you used to love, after it was all over—the heartaches, the self-conflict, the numbness, and all that—to find in her a friend who understood, whose spirit had grown sweeter, finer, truer than it used to be in the old days when you loved but did not understand how beautiful is such a friendship, and how rare? There is a tenderness between you, a sincerity of truth, a subtle bond of union infinitely greater in its strength and firmness than the old-time passion ever bore. It isn't love as the world sees it; it doesn't ruffle you or make you blind; there is no swift and frequent alteration of ecstacy and despair; no jealousy, or intoxication of the senses, but just peace and natural sympathy, and a subtle, quiet gladness of the soul. You never quite forget her, even though you meet another woman— which you always do—and marry her for love. There is always the fragrant memory of the other woman, whom you loved and lost, and found again in a friend who understood.

UNKNOWN.

"These Foolish Things . . . Remind Me of You . . .

And one is remembered by the magic of the day . . . another by the mystery of the night . . . but both are remembered . . .

NIGHT-BORN

You loved the wind at twilight, and the snow
   Clouding the uplands with its whirling white;
And you loved shadows in the east that go
   To mystery in the new moon's waning light;
Tide ebbing from a rocky headland; still
   Deep water flowing to a long lagoon;
Echoes at midnight from some distant hill;
   Showers at dusk or rainy nights in June.

What matter day's clear flashing wings, or sun
   Upon a hundred hills? The ecstasies
Of bird-notes ere the morning had begun,
   Spilling their careless silver sequences?
The bright, insistent brilliance of the day
   Too white and hard against your eyelids burned;
Wearied of light and sound you slipped away,
   Night-born, your spirit to the night returned.

And now no sudden gust may bring the fleet
   Wild rain at midnight but the echoes wake,
And bring a prescience of your passing feet
   In ways remembered for the old years' sake.
And never April starlight but has shaped
   Some memory of your smile that used to be
Before your spirit to the night escaped
   Beyond the door to which we have no key.

                   MARY LANIER MAGRUDER.

The wall of China has stood a thousand years . . . but it is crumbling . . .

MISUNDERSTANDING

Between us, stone on stone, we built a tall,
   Obstinate wall, intangible as pride;
And gardens prospered ill on either side
   With sunlight circumvented by the wall.

The wall was like a prison house that thrust
   Its stones against the sky; there seemed no way
To level it—until I tried to say
   "Forgive me, love," and lo the wall was dust!

                   MAY RICHSTONE.

FRAGMENTS

The way you slipped a ribbon in a book to hold your place,
Your toying with a wisp of hair while contemplating space,
The startled look that cymbals of a storm would always bring,
The way you left unfinished any song that you would sing;
The roguish wink when someone caught you pushing back a
      yawn,
Your serious demeanor when your chessmate took a pawn,
The way you one time marked the rug with pointed toe to tell
How far the maple stood between the arbor and the well;
Your plucking at my coat sleeve when a crippled urchin
      passed,
The way you helped a helpless bird into the longer grass,
The genuinely tragic look you tried so hard to hide
If I in earnest haste might push a vending hand aside;
The way I saw your lips press tight then gradually part
As you removed the tissue from a carmine-sugared heart—

All these are past and should grow dim with all such things
      in kind,
And yet their fragile fragments clog the traffic of my mind.

JESSIE FARNHAM.

ANY WIFE

It is the small familiar things that hurt—
   Your garden hat behind the kitchen door;
The muddied shoes still standing by the sill:
   Your old dog stretched full-length upon the floor.

Your gay disorder vexed me once, I know.
   But now if I could wipe that record clear,
I'd cancel out each small impatient frown
   And have you still as once I had you here,
   So faulty and so human, but so dear.

ALBERTINE H. MILLER.

WHEN YOU'RE AWAY

Each night,
I take your name,
And tuck it snugly around my heart,
One syllable at a time,
Then I place your laugh,
And funny way of holding a cigarette,
And crooked grin,
Carefully,
At the foot of the bed,
So I can go to sleep
Looking at them,
In the dark.

MARY LANIGAN HEALY.

I'm not at all sure . . . myself . . .

QUERY

Dear silent one—
What is your silence
But a cloud
Crossing the sun?

Can it be other—
Dear unanswering one—
Than a lost strip of darkness,
Lonely and high?
What of the silver edge?
What of the rays
Shot far
Into some distant sky?

What is this silence
Shadowing all my days—
Unless some lonely cloud
Fancies I shall forget
Your steadfast ways?

ELIZABETH STANTON LAY.

BITTERS

Why do I keep remembering—
Little things you said?
And the intimate way you said them?
Why do I cling . . . remembering . . .
To a thrill . . . I should have
Long ago forgotten?
Why do I close my eyes . . . seeking
To see you . . . as I beheld you . . . then?
So near . . . and yet, even as now . . .
So very far away . . .
You caressed me . . . adoring.
For a space I lost identity
In the oneness of our being.
And, not even our fingertips
So much as touched.
And . . . your lips . . .?
I can not even remember them.
Why . . . must I keep remembering . . .
At all . . . I . . . who have . . . so little
To remember?

ROSE PORTER.

But life is made of sterner stuff . . . than songs and frosted cakes . . .

LOVE

Surely, I thought, it must have wings
To soar above the homely things,
And lovely spirit seeking chance
To sway with April winds and dance.

And yet upon that day you came
I only swept the garden walk
And answered when the doorbell rang
And sat with you to talk.
And when you left, I thought your name
And thought it over and again
And baked a cake and sang.

MARY HENDERSON.

211

I LIKE

I like polka dots. And molasses. And Spanish antiques.
Perfumes. Spices. And mice!
Diamonds and sapphires. And silver, galore.
Beans. And butter. And rice!

I like maps. And garlic. And all furry things.
Music. And melons. And ham.
Color, and kittens. And fine intellect.
Circuses. And Cream. And lamb!

I like nature. And weeds. And an open fire.
Buckles and straps. And moonlight!
But best of all—and it's silly and small.
I like to hear crickets.
At night!

ESTHER WEBSTER SKILLMAN.

So why ask . . .

ALCHEMY

Ask me to remember and all that I could tell
Would be of night coming and how the dark fell
Silently and softly and the world seemed older
And a hill went to sleep with the moon on its shoulder.

Ask me if I loved you and I could only say,
There were three tall trees and the river lay
Dead and above us was a star-pricked patch of sky,
And once I was awakened by a night thing's cry.

I've long ago forgotten how the story goes,
But I still remember sharply how a cold wind rose
And the stars fled trembling and the moon dropped near
And the dawn came riding like a cavalcade of fear.

SARAH LITSEY.

You came last night
And stood by my chair as I sat
On the porch, smoking an old briar pipe,
And the heavy honeysuckle let through
Just enough light to make your face
Visible. And you sat on the arm of my
Rocker, and took my hand in yours, and the
Warm breeze, and the starlight
Twinkling through the black night made a
Heaven with you there beside me, and
Suddenly someone
Next door pressed a button and a porch light
Glared—and I reached out to
Touch you, but you were
Gone, and there was nothing but the
Honeysuckle where you had been, and then I
Realized that you were still a thousand
Miles away—but just the same
I knew you came last night
And stood by my chair as I sat
On the porch, smoking an old briar pipe.

SAM ANTHONY IVEY.

Oh, yeah . . .

ANGRY ADMONITION

Husband! I am just a woman!
Not your *mother!* Not an *angel!* Not a *cook!*
I haven't borne six rugged sons;
I haven't nourished them through school!
I'm not a cook-book prodigy,
I'm just a fool. . . .
So . . . be BIG, my love,
And let pass by
The "Devil's Food" I had to try,
Without your usual, "Dorothy!
You're sure you watched the recipe?"

DOROTHY JANE DEUELL.

This is utterly unfair to man . . . it shows the irresponsible prejudice of the female of the species . . . and anyway she told him it was fillet of haddock and there were no bones in it . . . and he simply swallowed this particular mouthful to indicate his original trust in her . . . the moral to this is "serve oysters" . . .

MAN PORTRAIT

"Look out!" she exclaimed,
    "There's a bone in your fish!"
D'ye think he said thanks,
    Laid it back on the dish!
"Mind your own business,
    I'll manage alone!"
And to show independence,
    He swallowed the bone.

MARION JUDD.

Applesauce . . .

EVEN EVE 'n' ADAM

Even Eve 'n' Adam
Had 'em,
    Those little quarrels that married people know.
Even Eve 'n' Adam
Had 'em,
    The battles and the makings-up.   And so—

Since even Eve 'n' Adam
Had 'em,
    And yet came through and managed pretty well;
If even Eve 'n' Adam
Had 'em,
    Those little between-heaven bits of hell;

Since even Eve 'n' Adam
Had 'em,
    And yet were fairly happy, as we hear;
Our quarrel—let us patch it;
Have a funeral for the hatchet,
    Till we fight again.   Come on and kiss me, dear.

MARY CAROLYN DAVIES.

214

But must my life be spent . . . with these for company . . . who'll light my candle of an evening . . . who'll point to pools . . . and sup my tea with me . . .

THINGS I LOVE

I love the winds that sing of roaring sails
    That go their spindrift way down trackless lanes—
And then again, I love the early glow
    Of candlelight against the dripping panes.

I love the door of home and glowing hearth,
    The solitude of hills—a whispering pine—
The fragrance of a rain-swept trail at dusk,
    And little pools where silver stars may shine.

A song when night comes groping over hills,
    The drowsy chirp of birds, and bits of blue
Between the grayish clouds that roof the moor—
    And little things that make me think of you!

CRISTEL HASTINGS.

A dangerous witness . . . to court . . .

SPELL

I remember lovely things
    That happened on a hill,
The swinging of a tall tree
    When the wind was still.

The blowing of a giant cloud
    Across the grass,
A small blue chicory
    He could not pass.

I remember lovely things
    In that upper air,
But mostly I remember you,
    Who never were there.

MARGARET MOORE MEUTTMAN.

215

It seems so long a time ... traveling the "thinking back" way ... to that far time ... before the war in China ... and yet I like that way the best because ... "thinking back" I'm sure to find again old Ming ... now sleeping with his ancestors ...

MEMORIES

Oriental courtesy, jades and cloisonne,
Tabourets and incense haze, colored lanterns gay—
Elephants of ebony, fragile porcelain rare,
Sprays of artificial flowers, prints beyond compare;
Pidgin English gutterals, lily bulbs and shawls,
Lacquer-ware and linens, paper parasols—
Writhing dragons cast in bronze, gleam of ivory,
Gorgeous peacock feather fans worth one's while to see;
Bland inscrutability, burnished copper bowls—
Tesselated cabinets, bracelets, beads and scrolls—
Carvings of Confucius, lapis-lazuli,
Chopsticks, trays and tassels, dolls both large and wee;
Saffron hands gesticulating, ancient temple-gongs,
Broidered slippers, Mand'rin coats, ginger jars and tongs—
All these I remember when I think of one named Ming,
Keeper of a certain little art shop in Nanking.

BERYL ELECTA MOSHER.

On a corner of Forty-second and Broadway ... I heard a laugh ring out ... my head whirled ... no one I knew stood near ... and yet the laugh ... if I could just remember ... whose laugh I thought it was ...

REMEMBRANCE

I had not noticed scarlet haw,
    Or copper leaf on elm or oak,
Until I crossed the dunes and saw
    The wild gold of the artichoke.

Strange how for just a moment's space
    The summer breeze that idled there,
Brought the lost beauty of her face,
    The wind-blown tangle of bright hair.

JOHN RICHARD MORELAND.

216

Or maybe it wasn't the laugh . . . that might have caught my attention
. . . just as someone lit a cigarette . . . and a trick of the mind . . .

PARTY

There was much zest
And sparkle, and the air was shrill
With laughter-stabbed inebriation.

I was gayer than the rest
Until
Somebody lit his cigarette
In your odd way—

And the wind of memory
Blowing across my animation,
Choked the thing
I was about to say.

RITA M. DRAGONETTE.

And though I have no things at all . . . not even foolish little things . . .
I too am reminded . . . and remember . . .

RAIN FELL LAST NIGHT

Rain fell last night—quiet, gentle rain
That tapped against my window pane
And called me back from troubled sleep
To soothe a heart too numb to weep.
My loneliness was deep and real,
And like a wound that will not heal,
It throbbed within me, and I knew
My arms were empty without you.
But as I listened to the sound
Of soft rain falling on the ground,
I heard your voice, tender and clear,
Call my name, and, oh, my dear,
I threw my window open wide
To let the sweet rain rush inside.
It kissed my lips, my eyes, my hair,
And, Love, I knew that you were there.
Tears that my heart could not release
Fell down from heaven, bringing peace.

Last night while grey clouds softly wept,
I held you in my arms and slept.

VIRGINIA DICKSON.

"Out Where the West Begins . . .

WINTER MIDNIGHT

The watchdogs bark from farm to slumbering farm
  Some coded message through the tranquil night.
  Across the level fields the moon shines bright
To aid that sharp, vociferous alarm.
With drowsy dread of some impending harm
  The henhouse stirs to undefined affright;
  And in his place the plow horse, sleeping light,
Is roused to misty snortings, moist and warm.

The rumor goes its round. The bayings cease.
  Our dog comes back to curl against the door.
  The barnyard hushes into rest once more.
  Through all the countryside good silence falls.
  Sleep bends above the land, the roofs, the stalls;
And every living thing returns to peace.

FRANCES HALL.

Stoppin' in the country hotel over night . . . goin' on tomorrow . . . maybe . . . we always say two trains a day . . . but we get that by countin' the one comin' in . . . and countin' it too goin' out . . .

TO A COUNTRY HOTEL TOWEL

I'll touch you not, you much abus-ed rag,
  Poor slave of all those epidermic rites
Performed by thousands who have come to drag
  Their cindery surface to this bowl's delights.
This tattered hem I vow shall thus remain,
  These holes shall grow not till another time.
You've had enough; that faint but lingering stain
  Shall take no fresh addition from my grime
Respected, honored, I will leave you here
  For others' service—or to join the dead.
Nay, more! That pair of holes have roused my fear!
  I'd better stow you here beneath the bed
Lest, rising in the dark, I do you hurt
Trying to don you for an undershirt.

ELMER C. ADAMS.

STRANGE TENDERNESS

He frightened me when Ben and I first came
To live in this remote home of his clan:
His shanty up beyond the sugar woods
Was like him, dirty, in a boastful way,
As if it, too, defiantly,
Was glad to be so far from godliness—
It smelled of salt pork and an old clay pipe.

Once Ben and I were walking by and heard him
Cursing God and man. I was a little scared and clung to Ben:
"Uncle Ozora's only odd—a sunstroke long ago—he's put out
Because that yellow birch is full of knots
And dulls his ax," said Ben.

Uncomfortably he balanced on our woodbox edge
And whittled matches on my Sunday floor—
"I didn't know but I should go up town
And help Ase Beals this fall and git my board,
But his damn kids is allus under foot."

Last summer when my child was born
And I was lying dazed and weak, I heard his voice,
Like Ben's hay wagon when the axle's dry—
"I went up our old place and fetched ye these,
    They growed in Grandmarm's gardin plot,—
It's three mile up the old Hale road, 'n' three mile back—
Gorram these gorrammed shoes."
Gingerly on the counterpane he laid
A bunch of drooping yellow roses:
But they were sweet, and smelled like cinnamon.

FRANCES ROGERS UPTON.

COUNTRY GIRL

There's spring of thick-set sod in her sure step,
 The sweep of wind-blown willows in her stride;
Her movements hint a surplus of cool strength,
 As, slim and trim, she travels by my side.

Her smile is bright as rain-washed evening skies,
 Her eyes as clear and innocent as dawn—
My country girl's the genius of the land
 Attired in soft and fluffy mists of lawn.

SAMUEL H. STUART.

White meat . . . wishbones . . . pulleybones . . . gizzards . . . wings . . .
necks . . . legs for the youngsters . . . who wants the back . . . nobody
. . . nobody . . . that's all right . . . mother eats it . . .

YOUR PICNICS

Your picnics were the best! They made
 Most other people's outings pale,
For when we sought the cool pine shade
 You took fried chicken without fail!

If we were with another crowd
 Who had meat loaf or roasted beef,
We almost had to cry out loud:
 "Of picnic thrills, you've skipped the chief!"

You gauged enjoyment's rare degrees
 With a discernment sure and nice;
You knew the piquancy of cheese
 And ham baked with alluring spice.

But more—you knew what children like
 To set a day to perfect rhyme—
And so, on picnic, trip or hike
 You took fried chicken every time!

FLORENCE WENNER.

THE OLD HITCHING POST

I discovered, one day, while taking a walk,
An old hitching post on a narrow back street,
When a bent little man that I happened to meet
Stopped me to talk.

He said, "See the house with the shutters closed tight?
Strange things happened there years ago;
Winter or summer, rain or snow—
Lights late at night.

"Never did see a horse at this post,
But when it was dark we would hear one neigh,
And hoofprints were found in the dust next day,
Faint like a ghost.

"Only a man lived there by himself,
Had a small blacksmith shop in the back yard;
Neighbors who watched him said he worked hard—
Was hoarding up pelf.

"They found him, one morning, dead by his door—
Coroner came and folks hurried in,
Ransacked the cupboard ('twas neat as a pin),
Tore up the floor.

"Nothing but paper there—wasn't it funny?
Paper with writin' in uneven lines
Lookin' like poetry.—There were no signs
He'd ever had money.

"But there was a boy who claimed to have seen
A horse with great wings mounting into the sky;
And his father whipped him for telling a lie—
Which I thought was mean—

"For I found in the shop a small silver shoe
That fitted a track near the old hitching post,
And I found a queer feather, so probably most
Of his story was true."

CONSTANCE ENTWISTLE HOAR.

223

A little girl named Bubbles has stumped me with the question . . . why they ever put a cover on the cover of a river . . .

COVERED BRIDGES

Does anyone build covered bridges now?
   They used to mark the country here and there,
   Not leaping streams, wide open to the air
With gallant masonry arched like a brow
Above the water's eye. You hushed, somehow,
   Your chatter as the horse-hoofs plodded in,
   Thumping the boards, all shadowy but for thin
Bright rays the loosened shingles might allow.
   A child could lean from out the carriage seat
   And see through ill-set floors the river's trend,
The shaken dust; knee-deep, a docile cow,
   Or, far ahead, a picture framed and neat;
   The sunny outer world at shadow's end—
Does anyone build covered bridges now?

JENNIE PENDLETON HALL.

It's a long way from Alaska . . . figuring miles . . . but if you really want to know how far away . . . take a thermometer . . . and figure it out by degrees . . .

ARIZONA SUMMER

If then at last this ordeal shall be done,
   This test by fire, these javelin lights that splinter
The delicate mind, I will abhor the sun.
   If ever I fell out of love with winter,
Now have I lived with summer to my fill,
   And I am heartsick for the orchid shadows
The hemlocks cast on a December hill,
   And for the snowdrifts on the river meadows.
When these, the desert and the drouth, are ended,
   I will go homeward to the frozen brooks.
By the still hearth the dazed mind shall be mended,
   And the long firelight play across my books.
Ah, then at last, the summer being over,
Winter will be more kind than any lover.

ELEANOR BALDWIN.

Say Glenn . . . is this the valley I lost up in New Hampshire . . . a few
miles north of the Old Man of the Mountain . . . someday I'm going back
to look for it . . .

LOST VALLEY

I found it on a morning when the wings
   Of song birds rose with music to the sun—
A small green valley gemmed with mountain springs
   And filled with sounds of brooks that through it run.
Its trees looked as if stars had nested there
   With birds whose notes came forth in starry song,
And fragrance of wild flowers filled the air,
   And morning lingered long.

There, from leaf shadows, came a dappled fawn
   To drink at that clear spring where I had stood;
A thrush shook dew upon me, and was gone
   On rapture drifting through a singing wood.
Trout arched their sudden rainbows in the pools
   And circles spread their silver at my feet—
Each time I think of it some magic cools
   My throat, the air grows sweet.

I have not found the way to it again
   But something of that valley still I keep—
I hear its music as I heard it then,
   Its fragrance sometimes lingers in my sleep.
It still is there—I have but lost the way
   And not the valley that I wandered through . . .
While I can feel it near—and while I may
   Share some of it with you.

GLENN WARD DRESBACH.

Scene from a car . . .

OLD BARN

On the edge of the town
  See the old barn sag
With a drop in its ridge
  Like a sway-backed nag,
And the shingles torn
  By the west wind's will
Fly from the skeleton rafters
  Until
You may count its starved ribs,
  One by one;
Old barn, old horse,
  Your day is done.

JANICE BLANCHARD.

Hello, neighbor . . . that's a good stand of corn you have there . . . if we get rain enough . . . and no cut worms . . . and no spindle worms . . . and no stalk borers . . . and no corn weevil or wire worms . . . you may make enough to pay the interest on the mortgage . . .

ILLINOIS FARMER

Between the fragrant rows of corn he strides,
  The cultivator handles steadily,
Pulling upon his arms; and as he guides
  His willing mare, a homely melody

Is rendered by the lines that saw
Across his denim-covered shoulders, gnaw
Of tugs on whippletree, and caw

Of scouting crows. The earth is young that slides
Beneath his cowhide shoes—fertility
That promises to fill the maw

Of granary and crib, come husking days.
Robust, assured, how fitly he portrays
Our native labor, there among the maize!

BEULAH JACKSON CHARMLEY.

CLEORA BECOMES A DAKOTAN

Cleora rose and shivered, looking out
Across the prairie where the cottonwoods
Whipped to the frenzied flapping of the wind.
"If only the wind would stop," she said. "Back east
In Saugatuck the dogwood is in bloom,
And in that riot of pink the rambling walls
Wander off to the haze, and over the earth
A blessed silence rests. Here the wind
Is never done with blowing, day or night.
I shall go crazy listening I think."

Old Man Martin shifted his fresh eggs
In their straw basket to the other knee,
And his quid of tobacco to the other cheek,
As the wind came tearing at the kitchen pane.
"Well," he said, "I heard 'em tellin' now
About a farm here in Dakoty once
Where the wind stopped blowin' a' sudden one summer's day
And all the chickens fell down, plumb flat. Yes, ma'am.
They leaned 'em up against the chicken shed
Till they got their stren'th and bearin's back, I guess.
Take me now. I grew up back east—Vermont;
But I lived here a long time and y'know
You don't hear the wind after while, or mind it much.
The Missus used to say them early years
It'd blowed every day but one since we folks come
And that was the day of the kite contest. Not one
Of them durned things'd get off the ground a mite."

Cleora laughed and paid for the fresh eggs.
And Old Man Martin hobbled off toward town
Fighting the streaming wind with every step.
"You don't hear the wind after while . . . or mind it . . .
    much" . . .

                        HARRIET SEYMOUR POPOWSKI.

The west is not a state of geography . . . but a state of mind . . . In Central Park . . .

LONELY? MAYBE

Yet, I was alone in a thousand
Of mortals, the same as I
Who proffered their synthetic pleasures
To those, who had money to buy.
But out in the grass of the pasture,
And around every bush and stone,
Were hundreds of laughs, for the laughing,
And somehow—I wasn't, alone.

CECIL PERKINS.

Pity the poverty of a Wall Street broker . . . who never can give his child a chance to help . . .

SMALL HELP

I knew you wouldn't mind if I sat upon the fence and watched
     you dig.
You didn't mind.
And when you clipped the hedge
I followed.
You explained about the shears
And answered all the many questions I could think of,
Mopping your brow with patience and a sigh when it was
     done.
Then I trailed you with a rake into the yard
And on the heap of leaves hopped up and down before you
     burnt them.
In the garden while you weeded, bending over,
I hunted bugs and brought the ones with pretty wings to show
     you.
Later when the tools were put away behind the door
Of the shed, remember
How I balanced the small hoe
Upon my hand
And had you look before it dropped?
Then as you dipped your face into some clear, cold water
And the towel was smudged with my wet hands,
Mother said, "Where have you been?"
"Helping daddy with the work," I said,
And saw you grin.

VERNA TOMLINSON.

228

MORNING SOLILOQUY OF ONE FARMER

Ho-hum—
There goes that rooster
Long before sun-up,
You'd think he had to plow and plant
Like me.
Poor wife, she's dead to the world,
I'll slip out and wash my face at the pump
To wake me up.
Gosh the air is sweet and fresh
As a bride's breath!
Makes me glad I'm livin';
Now where in thunderation did I leave
The milk pail?
Soo boss—soo boss—
Come on in critter,
I'm in no mood to wade dew to my knees;
Them silly doves on the ridge-pole
Bowing and scraping to each other—
Gosh the wheat's up fine,
Dear Lord, send rain so I can
Pay my taxes and
Buy a cradle.

HELEN REED.

THE MADONNA OF THE PLAINS

Bronzed by the western sun, and wind, she stood,
As firm, and strong, and sound, as seasoned wood,
Her strength, the strength of elemental things,
The fertile earth, the cool deep shadowed springs,
Long on the heights the sun's late splendor lies,
Its light, and warmth, were mirrored in her eyes,
The years, that traced their passage in her face,
Left peace, and patience, touched with dauntless grace.

HONORA CARROLL HURD.

229

MERRY-GO-ROUND

Men plow their fields, manure and plant,
Ward off crows, and puff and pant
All summer through with hard toil torn
And anxious thought, to raise good corn
To feed fat hogs to get red gold,
To buy more acres to the old,
To plow, manure, and plant and toil,
Redoubling last year's care and coil
To raise more corn to feed more hogs
To get more gold, that only clogs
Their coffers till they buy more fields
To plow, manure, and swell their yields
Tenfold, to feed more hogs, and spin
The seasons round to rebegin.
Land, corn, hogs, money, toil and trouble
(All empty as a child's blown bubble),
Then cease at length from all their labors,
Convoyed to rest by solemn neighbors,
And leave an heir to plow and plant,
Whose pride it is to moil and pant
The summers through for corn and gold
And land and hogs a hundredfold.
Or haply they may leave an heir
Who for such baubles has small care,
Who thinks his heritage more fit
For pleasure, and so squanders it
On dogs and horses, wine and women,
Plunging in seas too deep to swim in,
Until some neighbor with his gold
Hog-gotten, corn-born, as of old,
Redeems it from the prodigal,
Restores it, crib and sty and all,
To plow, manure, and plant and buy,
Harvest and kill, grow old and die,
And leave an heir in honor bound
To keep the hog-corn merry-go-round
Revolving in perpetuity
To honor the god of things that be.

JOHN WILLIAM SCHOLL.

TO A CITY MAN

You say you left the highway,
  The threat of hurrying cars,
And, following down a byway,
  Were stopped by pasture bars.

Now gates you well might reckon
  Were meant to shut you out,
But pasture railings beckon—
  Why, man, they fairly shout

To let them down, leap over
  The lowest bar and make
The kingdom of the clover
  Your own for beauty's sake:—

Your own the cattle sunning
  Their silken flanks at ease,
The little pathways running
  Wherever rabbits please.

That man must walk unfriended
  Even of the friendliest stars.
Who thinks a road has ended
  That leads to pasture bars.

MARY SINTON LEITCH.

And some years there are too many rainy days . . . and some years not enough . . . and you never know which it's going to be till it's been . . . and nobody ever did . . . and probably nobody ever will . . . but wet or dry we raise a good crop of boys . . . you betcha . . .

FARM BOY

Have you seen him
When he comes to town,
Farm boy, sturdy, slow, and brown?
He's come to spend the day.
Out their way
It's rained so much, you know,
Too wet to plow, or disk, or sow.

He's young, thirteen, perhaps.
He looks older.
His eyes are deep and clean, but sad.
Why should eyes be so somber
In so young a lad?

His hair, a chestnut thatch at home,
Is flattened down,
Slicked with water,
And a vigorous comb.
His skin is clear, cool,
His throat a hollowed pool
Where sun has lain.

His hands, if you chance to see them
Outside his trouser pockets,
Are large, bony, one knuckle red and raw
Where he barked it on the manger,
Or maybe 'twas on the saw,
When he whiled the time away in the woodshed,
On another rainy day.

O young farmer, earth-bred, shy,
City reared, I envy your heritage,
Your calm unhurried look.
In your striding walk
I see a running brook,
And in those steady eyes,
Solitary dawns, and clearing skies.

ALEXANDRA MERTES.

232

SUN-DOWN SONG

There's a shabby little shanty leaning tipsy on a hill
    With an early lighted lamp already blinking;
There's a fresh and starchy lady waiting on the clean door
        sill;
    And, looking on the fields, the lady's thinking:

"He has ploughed the live-long day and he has sweated in the
        sun;
    Soon my cool and eager kiss he will be taking;
And when all his chores are finished and the feeding has been
        done,
    He shall have the luscious pie I have been baking.

"O, he may be just a plowman and go plodding through his
        days;
    He may toil and struggle through the toughest weather;
In his shack he's always lord of all the region he surveys;
    In his shack a lord and lady live together!"

                                        JANIE SMITH RHYNE.

AUCTION

How much am I bid for a proud old wall
    That a forefather built in the long ago?
And how much for the acres, the reaching rods
    That climb the way that the tall winds know?

And what will they give for the rambling barn
    That brought and sheltered the new-born things
That knew his love, in their helplessness?
    And what is the price his silence brings?

And who will offer a worthwhile sum
    For a house that was never a house to me,
But a home? and what for a pasture gate
    And a spring, and the soul of a hemlock tree?

And how much for the road that searched the hill
    And led his feet to the setting sun
When his work was finished, his great hands still? . . .
    And what for a heart, when the sale is done?

                                        LEONE RICE GRELLE.

233

"They Mixed the Steel and Concrete Up with Little Rooms and Narrow Streets and Called the Thing— a City . . .

REMINDER

A city is a giant sound,
   A great continuous groan of power,
The terrible voice of mightiness
   Enjoying its Babylonian hour.

How easily we might forget
   Life has another softer key
Had we no sparrows in our parks
   To intimate tranquillity!

KAY BALLENBERG.

I don't mind a street number three flights up . . . but who wants a phone number three flights down . .

SONG AGAINST STREET NUMBERS

We live in a house
   On the top of a hill,
With sun for a carpet
   And flowers for the sill,
Our teakettle sings,
   Our forks and our spoons
Are made of the silver
   Of tender young moons;
And I turn my head,
   Pretend not to hear,
When neighbors insist,
   "She lives in the rear."
They staunchly deny
   Three stair-flights can be
The same as the top
   Of a green hill to me,
And only when stars
   Dip low in the night
Can I keep on saying
   "They're wrong and I'm right."

GLADYS MCKEE.

PLANTS IN AN ATTIC APARTMENT

Yes, we *are* a trifle crowded, our furniture lines the walls,
But that leaves window spaces, and the heart within me calls
For growing things, for greenery, for trailing, festooned vines,
For saucy home-grown blossoms, for even cactus spines
So jardiniere and fernery, and basket, pot and urn
Fill sill and spill rich chlorophyll just everywhere we turn;
True, some of the plants are pallid, a little inclined to mope,
But with plants, you know, as with people, as long as there's
    life there's hope.
I never can bear to part with one that shows a sign of a shoot,
And we'd live in a veritable jungle if half of the slips took
    root.

MAY ALLARD HENNEBERGER.

Park Avenue . . . at one hundred twentieth street . . .

CITY STREET

The old holder woman wears several skirts,
    And held by a great safety-pin
An apron of woolen, with pockets, begirts
    Her round waist, and under her chin
Is a muffler of plaid that she always ties twice;
    And just past the church with the steeple
Is the dark, jolly fellow who sells catnip mice
    To ever so many kind people.
And the old holder woman says "God bless ye, dear."
    And the catnip man's funny green hat
He takes off to ladies, and says, when they're near,
    "Here's a very fine mouse for your cat!"
But far down the street is a man who cries out
    "Pears!—Pears!" in a voice of despair
And the clerk in the store says he's always like that,
    But it's seldom a soul buys a pear.
And isn't it sad, when so many like mice
    And holders, that nobody cares
For the ragged old man who asks such a small price
    And calls never a word except—"Pears!"

GRACE MANSFIELD.

237

NEW TENANT

She led me to the second floor,
The room was dull and bare,
The light came dimly from without,
Gray dust was everywhere.

I felt an ill-concealed disgust,
But since my purse was thin,
And there was little choice I turned
Once more and looked within.

And crossing to the window-ledge
Peered through the murky pane
To where a slim white birch-tree
Stood singing in the rain.

With eager haste I wheeled and thrust
In her thick hand the fee;
She clumped away, and never guessed
She'd rented me a tree!

BERYL V. THOMPSON.

The doorman at the Waldorf-Astoria . . . puts on his underwear . . .

MY CASTLE

Last night I stood in the castle hall,
Where the candles cast their eerie light,
And saw the kings
And their ladies, fair
Cast their shadows into the passing night.
I closed my eyes, as in a dream,
Saw a young knight kneel to his queen;
She raised her eyes all starry and blue
That spoke untold messages
Kissed by love's dew.

The scene was changed,
The time was right,
The candles flickered, their work was done;
My cot in the garret was flooded with sun.

ALMA G. WALLACE.

238

This is an ugly hole ... but there are a lot of them in cities.

Forgive me for being reminded of a timid old gentleman standing before
the statue of "the thinker" questioning expectantly . . . "Give up" . . .

CHILDREN'S ROOM

This grimy cherub, lacking wings,
Leans to a printed page that sings

Of knights and wars and older days,
Of gallant times and gallant ways.

Laughter and chaos mingle here
To whisper glory in his ear;

He mixes life and death awry,
Sets earthly beings in the sky.

In his mind, peace and marching feet
Blend to a wonderment complete:

His eyes, his heart, are keen to all
The splendours which about him fall,

While, ignorant of time or scheme,
He gives allegiance to his dream.

RUTH E. McCOY.

Men do have dreams . . . even in a great city . . .

NIGHT SOLITUDE

Far down the dark avenue of trees
He watched the swaying street lights
Nod, like old heads just falling off
To sleep. The roadway's muddy span
Was patched with puddles, while on the air
The frogs' croak from a distant Pond
Belabored solo crickets nearer by.

Had he not felt the impulse of a wet
Lone leaf fly past his tired cheek—
He might have thought he dreamed—
And that the unlit sky, was but
The cardboard cover, on a box of paper
Toys. . . .

LOUISE LOUIS.

240

If Cyclops really runs the traffic . . . that explains why only Janus can cross Times Square safely . . .

TRAFFIC

The Cyclops blinks—his eye glows red,
And the scaly dragon up ahead
Falls into segments, severed clean
By furious worms that dash between . . .
Laboring elephantine,
Ponderous trucks clatter,
Horns stentorian . . .
—Nothing proud, nothing pompous
About their pace—
A business matter!
"Paper and furniture,
Scrap iron, ham—
Out of our way, there!
Scram, you,—*Scram!*"

The Cyclops blinks—his eye beams mellow,
And raucous hooters cease to bellow;
Brakes screech, and tortured tires scream . . .
Then curb to curb pedestrians stream,
Insolent—casual
Eyeing each chauffeur,
Drifting, hustling, whistling, giggling—
Ribbon of larvae
Lively wriggling . . .
Leisurely loafer,
Brisk tycoon,
Young romance,
Cross in the beam
Of that kindly glance.

The Cyclops blinks—his eye turns green,
And dragon-segments close between;
Bugs from the by-ways halt, permitting
The glittering length a closer knitting . . .
Shedding scales
At loop and corner,
Squawk at the vagrant
Furtive-threading, rambling rapt,

241

Skipping and dodging
Destruction-scorner!
Into the tunnels,
Forth from town
Crawl as the cool green
Eye looks down!

HAROLD WILLARD GLEASON.

Forty-second and Broadway ... New York City ... New York ...

SIEGE

Times Square is stone and bronze and glaze
And wheels on asphalt and a blaze
Of light where unseen pappi drift. . . .
Twin sumachs, finding lodgment, lift
A brick on Christopher Street. . . .

                      The phlox
Has withered in your window box
But through a crack in the court cement
A grass blade, meek and violent,
Lifts up pale green, sinks firm roots down. . . .
Relentless siege is on the town.
The prying surge against your piers
Floats bulbs and burrs and vital spears
Of rooted reeds. . . .

               The long attack
Will loose those rivets, will win back
Pre-empted soil, the smothered ground;
The steel-clinched clay shall be unbound.

(I know a still, New England wood
Where once a thrifty hamlet stood;
Where oaks and thickening maples stand.)
Concrete your shores and sheath your land
But still the acorn shall be peril
To all your towers, steel and sterile.
Build firmly!

         (Vines are matted on
What were the streets of Babylon.)

KILE CROOK.

242

MANHATTAN MALADY

Subway-streptococci
Tear through the entrails
Of Manhattan: the island
Shivers with sudden ague,
Trembles with intermittent fever;
Its epidermis breaks with strange protuberances—
Wen and blister, furuncle and papulai—
(Can it be possible there is need to mention
The Proud Flesh?)

Who will isolate this devastating
"Micro-organism of a genus of bacteria
Grouped in long chains and dividing in one plane,
Causing erysipelas, etc.," and restore
To the embarrassed lady her school-girl-complexion
That so intrigued an old roué named
Hendrik Hudson
At their first rendezvous,
(Chaperoned by eighteen Old Salts!)
On that long-gone September afternoon?

MARION DOYLE

"London Bridge is falling down . . .

FROM DUST THOU ART

And we shall build upon the earth
And cover grass-swept fields
With stone and brick and mortar.
Harnessed streams shall lend their strength
To men.

We shall replace with our creations
All that she has made to live and grow.
Oh, what conquerors we!

Yet, in our hearts we know
That we will succeed
Only so long as she decrees—
Until she claims not only what we have built,
But even us, its builders.

FRANCES WADDLE.

"Sing Me a Song of Social Significance . . .

A poem to a fat lady who counts her calories . . .

PRAYER FOR THE LITTLE'UN

I have dug a hole and put him in the ground
And put the red clay over him in a mound,
And fixed a purty trimmin' all around
With sody water bottles I brung from town.
I have done my do . . . the rest is up to You.

Lord, the little 'un never did git enough meat;
I used to swear his vittles went to his feet.
Him so little—and whitish and sort of sweet—
He's dead now—and never got enough to eat!

So, God, You need not take him up on Your knees,
And kiss him and give him toys and Christmas trees.
Just give him chicken and bread and cake and peas,
And let him git his belly full—just once, please.

I have dug a hole and put him in the ground,
And put the red clay over him in a mound,
And fixed a purty trimmin' all around
With sody water bottles I brung from town.
I have done my do . . . the rest is up to You.

PHYLLIS LIVINGSTON.

A mop lady at the Metropolitan comes early every night . . . she knows the operas . . . better than the "diamond horseshoe" . . .

WASHER-WOMAN

I am a washer-woman
Scrubbing, scrubbing—
In my heart
A white hand
Lengthens graceful fingers
Over black and ivory keys.

You are a poet
Dreaming, dreaming—
In your heart
Is there ever
A strong, red hand
Wiping toil's damp brow?

CONSTANCE CRANE.

246

CHARMAID

Silver slippers beckon me
Offering to climb the stair,
To forbidden everywhere.
Silver slippers? Ecstasy!
Fairyland for one like me!
In my clumsy rubber pair,
Made with zippers,
I scrub down the golden stair,
That other maids may find it fair,
To tread, in silver slippers.

MAUDE SMITH DELAVAN.

"Build me more stately mansions" . . . oh my dole . . .

BY MY OWN SWEAT

I'm a sober polyp in a coral prison,
  Tireless, until the slender spark is spent;
My work-gauge is measured with the same precision
  As his, and stirs the world to less comment.

I'm a puffing beaver by a demon driven,
  Grudging ordered days to dam and dyke and bar,
My wet nose is the muck, I may not glimpse heaven,
  Never, on raised haunches, bellow to a star.

I rear bridges, breastworks, delve in earth and water,
  And break heart and sinew to house homeless dreams
Of my kind. I'm hewer, smiter, heaver, carter;
  I swing iron tools to level heavy beams.

For I am of the earth, born to be its lever,
  A digger of dirt and filth till my muscles swell.
I bathe in my own sweat, swampborn like the beaver;
  Like the polyp, I can never leave my cell.

ALEX R. SCHMIDT.

247

SAN FRANCISCO BRIDGE

Slung from the stalwart necks of four steel towers,
Festoons of steel sweep wonderfully down,
Rock-anchored, many-stranded, strong enough
To lift a shining street across the water—
Graceful and confident over wide water.
  Watching the water, two men blow smoke over a railing:
  "Well, looks like they're almost done."
  "Sure does."
  "How much is it costing? Seventy-five million, they tell
  me."
  "Uh huh."
  "Would you look at the size of that tower with the ship
  going past it?
  Look at that little guy way up there on the catwalk,
  Waay up there.
  Geez, wouldn't that be a hell of a job ᶠor you?"
  "Sure would."
  "Biggest bridge in the world."
  "Yeah."

Gigantic through Embarcadero fog,
The legs of towers stand as square as doom,
Steel and concrete, impregnable, inhuman.
They carry a shining street, but we can't see it;
We are too close to see, and anyway
There is no room for beauty on these docks.
We only see the ships, and oily water
Lapping the stony feet of ignorant towers.
  "Hya, Joe, watcha doin'?"
  "Nothin' much."
  "Ever try the bridge, Joe?"
  "Yeah."
  "No soap, huh?"
  "No soap."
  "Christ, some guy must be makin' a lot of money outta that
  thing."
  "Yeah, some crook."
  "I'd like to work on that thing. It'd be swell to work on
  something like that."
  "Maybe."

From Telegraph Hill the bridge is bright and tiny.
(So many things are small from Telegraph Hill.)
Stretching from streets and docks to slow brown hills
A glittering wire, strung with delicate towers
Relieves the sunny smoothness of the Bay.

Mr. McFee, the artist
(That is, he writes stories)
Likes to sit on his Riviera terrace.
(Watch him, I betcha he's thinking up a story.)
"That bridge now, I might do a little thing about that.
Design, perfection, pattern.
Still, might sound like Civic Betterment.
How about the Communist angle; that's certainly being
done.
Progress, cooperation, comrades.
No, I'm afraid not.   H'mmm.
Don't cross your bridges before they're hatched; hch, heh,
heh.
Heh heh."

Between the monoliths of lower Market
The bridge is a sector of steel, half a festoon,
The gleaming tip of a tower, slender, confident.
"HOP Mokket, Mokket Cah,
CITY of Paris, shopping distRICT."
("Bus leaves for Chinatown, genuine Chinese joss-house.")
"HALLaway up Mokket!"
(The tubby gentleman approaches the car)
"Hey, 'Zaminaw, Krawnickle,
Pappy, misteh?"
(Oh I hope it isn't war; yes, I'll get one.)
BRITAIN DROPS SANCTIONS
LANDON STATES VIEWS
POPE HITS COMMUNISTS
HITLER HITS JEWS
(Always strikes, and trouble; why can't they tell more
    about the Bridge.   That's going to be a great thing for
    the city, what with the fair, and all.)
"AWRIGHT, STEP ABAWD!   STEP ABAWD!
Can't stand still here, mister.   HUP Mokket!"
(Risking his life, the gentleman swings aboard.)

Only at night the Bay is cool and quiet.
Gleaming from black infinity ascend
Square and serene, these monuments of stone.
Enormous corners, set with warning lights,
Glitter along the tips of silent ripples.
      What do you mean, incredible strength of stone,
      Built to remain when cities die in flames,
      Built to endure the end of this my city?
      Already guns (this is a violent city)
      And bayonets have licked the Embarcadero.
What do you mean, incredible arcs of steel,
Merciless incidental beauty of steel,
Built out of sweat and danger, touched by death—
Built from a plan, to speed our city's future.
Order and peace? It will be long I fear
Before the struggle dies on Market Street.
Order and peace? This is a lusty city.
      Watcher return. Neither the world nor you
      Will die tomorrow. Return, now is no time
      To stand by quiet water asking questions.
      Return to zeal and anarchy. . . . But first
      Discern the fearless tower, follow and see
      Against deep sky the curve of soaring steel,
      Graceful and confident over infinity.

HENRY MAY, JR.

Why not an orchid . . . and sleep in the streets . . .

HYACINTHS TO FEED THY SOUL

If of thy mortal goods thou art bereft,
And from thy slender store two loaves alone to thee are left,
Sell one, and with the dole
Buy hyacinths to feed thy soul.

MOSLIH EDDIN SAADI.

If God ever told you . . . it would strike you dead . . .

FAMINE ON A SCHEDULE

Hungry, little fellow?
Fathomless blue baby eyes dart about,
Reproachful with expectancy;
Little inimitable baby sounds
Gurgled between pink cramming fists
Alternately coax and scold;
You tempt me to break schedule,
But—
No, no, that fuzzy bite of blanket
Just won't do—
You will have to wait until
The clock strikes two.

God, what do all the mothers do
Who have nothing to give their children
When the clock strikes two?

HELEN HARDMAN.

*The Agricultural Department has a whole building of facts and figures
. . . and first one tries . . . and another tries . . . to make them total
something . . . but you can't add in the weather . . . and you can't get
an answer without it . . . so . . .*

BEET FARMER

It is not weariness that lines this face,
    Nor bitterness that surges from within,
But fear of drouth, deep dust upon this place,
    Of hailstones come to batter green crops in.
No bruising, crowding weight of years alone
    Has brought an early gray to this lean head;
Nor was it age that moulded skin to bone,
    But rather, reckonings that foster dread.
Such stiff dry winds as these have blown before
    And many times such thunderclouds were built
Against the northern sky. It is the lore
    Of past, of how some precious years were spilt,
By which reality may twist the heart
And tear a quiet courage all apart.

MARK MIRICH.

251

SONG OF THE HOP FIELDS

A harvest moon rose gracefully and rode the morning sky,
It chased the lonesome fog away and flung its banner high.
The fragrant peach, the purple grape, each heard the lustful
call;
The leaves curled up, the apples fell, the earth prepared for
Fall.
The hop fields offered rich, green balls that quickly turned to
gray
When stripped from vines that tumbled down upon the clods
and clay.
The tall, red kilns where growling beasts with yawning,
hungry jaws
That dried the hope and pressed the bales with heavy, iron
paws.
With dirty faces, clothes in rags and fingers stiff and sore,
The pickers cursed, they sweat and toiled, they laughed and
cursed some more.

You laugh like a vixen, you swear like a man,
Your body is dirty, your life without plan;
  Oh poor, little girl picking hops.
A tent is your shelter, the ground is your bed;
The sweetness of girlhood has somehow been shed;
Your parents are fruit-tramps who slave for mere bread,
  Oh, poor, little girl, picking hops.

Hey, Wop, what's the reason for this sudden mirth;
This song that comes lilting across the hot earth,
  A musical, rollicking tune?
With white teeth and red lips and black, curling hair;
Spaghetti and garlic and devil-may-care,
The hop fields will miss you when you are not there,
  With musical, rollicking tune.

What queer trick of fate turned this scholar to toil,
Whose mind is a store house that nothing can spoil,
  Old man with the peering, blue eyes?

He quotes from great masters and strips the long vines;
He speaks of the Romans, of Burns and his lines;
Of Buddha and Darwin and modern assigns;
Old man with the peering, blue eyes.

Your skin is like copper, your hair blackest night;
Your breasts ready fountains, your eyes pools of light;
Big squaw with the sober papoose.
Your waist line is missing, your garments are torn;
Your colors are brilliant, your face dull and worn;
But five hundred pounds of ripe hops you have shorn
Big squaw with the sober papoose.

A harvest moon rose gracefully and touched the world with
    gold;
The trampled vines, the huddled tents, the pickers, young and
    old.
The campfires gleamed, the mists crept in to camouflage the
    dirt.
The Wop sang on, the old man read, the girl nursed hands that
    hurt.
The great kilns tainted all the air with sulphured, drying hops,
Where dawn revealed a wall of green the night found string
    and props.
                                        INA DRAPER DEFOE.

A pawn shop dealer told me . . . he bought a wedding ring from a penniless old couple . . . so they could eat . . . they were starving . . . and within an hour sold it to a reckless young couple . . . so they could marry . . . and they were penniless . . .

WEDDING FEAST

Just one more bride has passed before
The altar and out the old church door.
Her friends flung rice, her laugh was gay,
And merrily she was whisked away.

Then a brooding quiet settled down
On the dusty street in the little town;
And out from a nearby house there stole
A shabby old couple with broom and bowl.
They swept up the rice while their grateful faces
Blessed the bride in her silks and laces.
                                        AMY BOWER.

FROM THE TRAIN WINDOW

Lost children, and hurt dogs, and begging hands,
    All these to pity—
But O, the furtive men who roam at dawn
    The great dumps of the city!

GRACE MANSFIELD.

A song of hate . . . not yet too late . . .

LIGHT

What of the World,
Whose centuries have hurled
To death the faith and trust of men!
Our nations' hopes and glories die,
The wilderness has claimed us now,
Under a threatening sky.

What of the Light,
First born, that put to flight
And split the black primeval mist
To drive the skulking darkness back!
Blinded by lust of man-made power
We follow the running pack.

Iron and steel!
Monsters that strike and deal
Their blows like beasts and wreak their spite,
Plunging their mighty hulk, they stride,
Cracking our bones like forest boughs,
Seeking blood as they ride.

Shall evil smite
To quench the ancient Light?
Chant high, O spirit of sage and priest,
Purge us of pride through heart and state,
Kindle the beacon! We yet may see!
Teach us to hate our hate.

ADELENE KISSAM WATT.

254

TO WHOM IT MAY CONCERN

How big is your heart?
Have you seen these?

    Low hovels built from tin and scraps and cardboard
      Squatting in a tin can littered Hell,
    Where slow Death crawls, and with impartial finger,
      Lays hand on old and young and sick and well;
    Dull heat, and babes inert and sick with hunger,
      Swelled throats and parched dry lips that dream of ice,
    Death lies in eyes that vainly seek for shadow,
      And cracked red earth and hot sun must suffice;
    Strong men whose bodies and whose minds are twisted
      Upon the lathe of Life and worn too thin,
    And women who sit stupid by the bedsides
      Of their children and watch slow Death creeping in,
    Or have you seen low hovels in a snowstorm,
      Or starving bodies lean against the wind
    Like lean ribbed foolish cattle in a blizzard,
      With burlap, rags, and papers round them pinned?
    Have you ever cowered foodless in a corner,
      While the wind brings in pneumonia where you lie,
    And with purple face and pinched cold-brittle fingers
      Wait and weep and plead and pray to die?

Have you seen these?
How big is your heart!

LOLA AOLA SEERY.

*The hop fields . . . here is an interesting study in the sharp contrast
with which two poets approach the same subject . . . neither aware of
the other's treatment . . . one writes with a pen of flame . . . the other
pipes a song . . .*

MARG'RET MAY O'BRIEN

Marg'ret May O'Brien,
    The froth of summer seas,
Blew into the hop field
    A leaf upon the breeze . . .
And thru that migratory crew
    A fairy child, she slips,
While all their quaint old country names
    Are music on her lips:

        "Juan Francisco"—his eyes shine—
        "Might a gringo share your vine?"

Marg'ret May O'Brien
    Speaks English of the street;
Her voice is old harp music,
    Her young lips curved and sweet;
With eyes like blue-black shadows
    Where laughter loves to stray
For the sun is far less sweltering
    When everyone is gay.

        The Scotch field-boss she turns to greet:
        "Tired, Big Chief? Have my seat!"

Marg'ret May O'Brien
    Croons softly as she goes
And haunting airs of Erin
    Drift down the dusty rows
Where weary pickers listen
    While nimble fingers fly,
And Hindu, Swede, and Indian
    O'er Erin's sorrows sigh.

        "Abdullah!" she stops to say,
        "How are tricks in Mandalay?"

Marg'ret May O'Brien
  Has bridged the East and West
With frame-work cunningly designed
  Of sympathy and jest.
  Around her basket fairies draw
  A magic laughter ring,
For not one chuckling jibe or jeer
  As ever left a sting.

> "Greetings, Ito, Busy Man!"
> Erin smiles on old Japan.

JOY O'HARA.

*And Bubbles asked me this morning . . . what was the Civil War . . .
what all happened . . . and it suddenly occurred to me nobody knows
yet . . .*

SONG OF DESOLATION

All de chillens am growed up an gone an lef de place.
  De missis laid to res long time ago.
De winds ob many years hab laid der fingers on ma face.
  Where de lusty health ob springtime used to glow.
De snow am sifted thru de hairs upon ma haid.
  Ma eyes cant see de stars up in de sky.
All dat i can do is sit beside ma door.
  An watch de mississippi ribber flowin by.

De hoe am in de corner, cant use it any mo.
  Cant see to pull de suckers from de cawn.
De weeds an grass am boun to take de place i know.
  Since ma strength an will to conquer dem is gone.
De barrows standin desolate against de cabin wall,
  Ma tools am rustin where i lef dem lie.
And de moonlight shimmers in a raident silver glow.
  On de waters ob de ribber flowin by.

Oh dat mity ribber has a place in all ma dreams.
  It nussed me on its bosom all ma days.
As i watch its rippling water, to me it always seems.
  To voice its lilting laughter many ways.
Sometimes it laughs in gladness, sometimes it cries in pain;
  It has been ma sorrow an ma joy.
Sometimes its mity current goes ragin to de sea.
  Den what it cant take along, it will destroy.

JUST JOHNSON.

ANOTHER MAN'S POISON

I squander dollars while you save the pence.
I'm in the fight, while you're upon the fence.
I eat and run the while you masticate
The contents of your neatly grooved blue plate.
My books are dog-eared, yours are seldom read.
My dog's a mutt. Yours is a thoroughbred.
I never wear my rubbers when it rains.
You do, and get neuralgia for your pains.
You think my friend is common, but he's kind.
Yours is a cad, however much refined!
It may be true that opposites attract,
But not for long. This ends our little pact.
Deliberate, as always, my dear boy.
For once I have. I hope it gives you joy
That I at length have taken your advice
"To look before I leap." To be precise,
I cannot change this cherished dearth of mine
For horn of plenty filled with iodine!

CONSTANCE MILTON.

FREE TO CHOOSE

Depressions, wars—spring from greed.
A world perplexed? Its only need
The lowly Galilean's creed
Be lived today.

Men boast their might has brought them wealth,
The creature comforts, fame and health.
Then all is gone as though by stealth.
Do they forget

"That man lives not by bread alone"?
Through fallen nations this was shown.
And though today it still be known,
We blunder on.

GERTRUDE SHISLER DUPPER.

LUXURY'S CHILDREN

If they could view us now, that steadfast throng
   Who dared the perils of an unblazed trail
And, following their dream, slow-hewed their long
   Crude progress toward their goal, pitting their frail
And shrinking flesh against the wilderness—
   That band whom hunger's pain could not dispel
Whose vision would permit of no regress,
   Whom fear or raiding savage could not quell—
They who advanced to meet the frontier's dare,
   Staked comfort, life, and loved ones on their win,
And left for us the unearned, safer share—
   What would they think to see their issued kin
Tossing aside the torch they held aloft
   To reach for hand-outs, whining, growing soft!

ELAINE PIERCE MCCRELESS.

YOU SHOULD LISTEN CLOSELY, GOD

How many voices must be echoing in Heaven, God;
How many sounds must beat upon your ears!
While I hear one man pouring out his fears,
The sorrowful chorus of the world is sung to You.

While I hear one bell tolling through the quiet night,
Millions of bells are clamoring on high,
Billions of people shouting, "When?" "Where?" "Why?"
All day, each day, they scream their frenzied ravings at You.

Though the ceaseless noise of my small world seems deafen-
    ing,
A universal din to You is raised;
With banging, clanging noise You must be dazed
As the whirling wheels of Time rush through the centuries.

But You should listen closely, God;
   You should bend your head,
And hear the hungry children
   Whimpering, "Father, bread!"

MARTHA A. M. THOMS.

"Six Days Shalt Thou Labor . . .

PRAYER FROM A WORKING GIRL

Dear God,
I wonder if you've time
To listen
To this thing
I'd like to ask.

Perhaps a prayer
Seems kinda funny
In a place like this,
That's roaring with machines,
And jammed with desks,
And filled with men
All yelling orders—
(Or just hanging 'round
To try and get
Some girl to make a date—)
And yet it seems
As if we girls
Need praying more
In such a place
Than in a church that's still—
And safe—And so I'm praying,
God, and if you've got
The answers, I wish
You'd shoot 'em straight.

They say girls work
Because they like it, God—
Because they're keen
On money or careers,
Well, maybe so, but as for me,
What I want most is not
Those things at all—
What I want most
Is just Your help

262

To stay a woman
In this world
Of working men
The kind of woman
That my mother was
So sweet and gentle
That you never guessed
How brave and strong she was
Beneath her quiet ways.

Help me be soft like she was—
Soft, in spite of all the brawls
A working girl must face—
And square, like she was—
Square, in spite of all the tricks
A working girl might use
To hold her place—And honest,
Though I know it may not pay—
And cheerful though the job
Goes wrong all day.
Help me to stay a woman
And to keep
The dreams I used to have
At seventeen—
Kid dreams of kneeling
In the fairy sheen
Of wedding satin
Trailing white—And sweet,
Half-frightened dreams
Of my own husband
Coming home at night to me
And our new baby—
Oh, please help me keep
Those dreams
In spite of all
The work and worry,
And the times
When things seem
Too horribly hard
For any girl to take.
For, honest, God,

It certainly is tough
When you are only getting
Half enough
To keep yourself alive—
Say, maybe fifteen bucks—
And sleeping where you can,
In some cheap dump
And wearing rags,
That make you look a frump
And all the time afraid
You'll get the air
Because the boss may think
That you don't care
About your looks—
Why, then, it isn't easy
To pretend you're mad
If some rich guy should say
He'd like to lend
You something
Toward a new Spring hat,
Or maybe hint
About a furnished flat
In some nice street,
Or ask you—"Baby,
When do we two eat?"

Believe me, God,
It certainly is tough
For girls to go on
Being good
When things are rough
Like that—
And so I'm asking—
Help me hang on hard
To my kid dreams—
Help me stay clean
And pure,
The way my Mother stayed,
Until I find my man—
And then, dear God,
Please fix it so I can

Quit work—
And just do nothing
All the time
But love my man
And make his home
And have his babies, God.

That's what I pray—
And now I've got to quit—
The boss is yelling—
But you'll not
Forget the thing
I've asked for,
Will you, God?
Amen.

ELSIE ROBINSON.

After the plowing . . . harrowing . . . planting . . . cultivating . . .
cutting . . . shocking . . . and thrashing . . . then man learns if it's
acres of diamonds . . . or acres of dust . . .

THIS LONELY ACRE

This lonely acre given me, O God,
  So hard I've tried to till these long, lean years.
Day in, day out, I've worked the barren sod;
  Now all I have is loneliness and tears.
I'm not complaining, God, but this bleak field
  Has mocked me since the day I first began
To tread its lonely rows, and if the yield
  Is over small, remember me a man,
And weak as man is weak. So long I've tried
  To wrest from this bleak earth an offering
To honor Thee, but I have been denied
  And forced to bear a cross of sorrowing.

But I shall plow until my shares are rust,
And this lone acre shall return to dust.

                              BERT HENDERSON.

Seven days . . . and seven nights . . . in the homes by the seven seas . . .

VIGIL

Wind is a fool tonight . . . fierce . . . unfed . . .
Better you boys take to your bed;
(A stormy night and a stormy day)
Egan and Lars . . . be off, I say!

Wind is a fool tonight. What goes there
Beyond the lantern's fretting care?
For one long moment I thought a boat
Bewitched on the rocks of Dead Man's Throat!

Wind is a fool tonight. Egan and Lars
To bed, I say! Nor moon . . . nor stars
To mark the eve of your father's going . . .
A lonely heart and a fool wind blowing!

I shall keep watch the night and through;
No telling what a fool will do!

                         CLAIRE AVEN THOMSON.

266

One of several agricultural problems . . .

THE HINT BEYOND

He and the wilder part of earth
were secret allies from his birth.

He hates to plant a sloping field
which last year had a mustard-yield.

Hawkweed and paintbrush on his land
you'd think he'd sown with his own hand.

And as for blue vetch flanking hay,
he'd stand and stare at it all day

nor lift a scythe to buttercup
that might as well be down as up.

His hired man says that he was hired
to work, and he is getting tired

of waiting while the farmer looks
at brown-eyed susans by the brooks,

of being told to mow around
a patch of colored haying-ground.

He and the wilder part of earth
were secret allies from his birth:

that may be why his eyes behold
a hint of blue, a ghost of gold.

FRANCES FROST.

*Artists . . . painters . . . sculptors . . . simple carvers on a wood block
or linoleum . . . days and days . . . so many ways . . .*

CRAFTSMAN

I'm carving lilies on the Cross.
I clean our house and cook our meals,
And plant Swiss-chard and Irish moss;
I bathe the baby, mend our clothes.
I darn enormous gaps in heels,
And tend to little Bobby's nose.
I'm carving lilies on the Cross.

EDNA BENDIG.

267

FARM WOMAN

The children finally in bed, each bare
Foot scrubbed and dried before it climbed the stair,
The milk pails washed and set up in a row,
The day's unending toil at last runs low,
And she may rest a moment on the seat
Out underneath the elm, her slow heartbeat
The only effort now that weary strength
Need make; and as the twilight's blue-gray length
Unfolds across the fields, her tired eyes
Look off to where, pale gold, a crescent lies
Above the western hills. The stars appear
And bring their friendly high still silence near.
At last up through the darkening yard she goes
To join her man in sleep's well-earned repose.

BERNICE CAREY FITCH.

INVITATION TO A HUSBAND

I need to go away with you, my dear,
    Where all the cares of every day that press
Our love to earth and weight it down with fear
    Are merely background for our happiness.
I am a slave to your small tyrant sons!
    They fill the heart and soul and life of me,
And yet they are the very guilty ones
    Who have destroyed our certain ecstasy.
The woven web of daily life displayed
    Too closely to our eyes has lost some charm.
The pattern seems a little dim and frayed—
    I view the situation with alarm.

My dear, together, we must go away
And be just lovers for a whole long day!

ANNETTE PATTON CORNELL.

Residential districts . . . bungalows . . . two-story colonials . . . old
English models . . . homes . . . homemakers . . .

DOMESTICITY

In this secluded, sheltered life
Of domesticity,
In the simple, humdrum tasks
Of sweeping, dusting, making beds,
Of washing dishes by the million,
There is the same serenity
That lies upon a deep pool
Caught in a river's bend,
While the swift current
Sweeps its channel to one side
And leaves unruffled a smooth surface.

ELEANOR GOODSON MITCHELL.

Spring and fall cleaning . . . a million mothers in a million homes
cleaning out the grime . . .

GRIME

You might have paled Bernhardt's Camille
    Or Shakespeare's greenwood tree,
Drowned out Shelly's skylark or
    The Chimes of Normandy.

But you are beating parlor rugs
    And scraping kitchen soot,
And washing window glass with grime
    Bound to you hand and foot.

You might have walked in marble courts,
    Stood under frescoed domes;
You might have climbed the Eiffel Tower
    And plumbed the catacombs.

But you are bandaging stubbed toes
    And poulticing bee stings,
And drying smudgy tears with grime
    Tied to your apron strings.

And if it should touch your lips
    More bright than any chime,
Or lark or flower or greenwood tree
    Is grime.

ANNE HARLEY AVILA.

269

TASKS

I thought I'd catch up with my tasks today,
The little things that needed mending;
A sweater, socks, and toys with broken parts;
A picture needed framing.

I'd planned to clean the attic,
Throw away the old, make way for more;
Old souvenirs that needed dusting.
Oh, the musty smell of memories dying
When I opened wide the door!

My diary there, long since neglected,
With such reproachful air,—
The day I met you,
The night you kissed me
By the stair.

We promised not to make our life a task,
But days of joy.
I remember now, the dreams we dreamed,
The gladness in your eyes
When you beheld our boy.

I felt so worried over work undone,
Trudging up those stairs with weary dread,
Thinking I'd catch up with my tasks today.
Perhaps you noticed when you came home tonight,
I caught up with my dreams instead!

IRMA LOUISE EHRENSBERGER.

THE STRANGER

A tall, dark stranger
Came into my breakfast room this morning
With a faint grunt of greeting
And fell upon his food and newspaper,
Preoccupied and inarticulate.

I looked about me furtively
At the yellow curtains and potted hyacinths.
I rearranged the daffodils in the blue bowl,
Reached up with a nervous finger tip
To see if that ridiculous curl
Stuck up as usual in the middle of my forehead
Hoping it didn't . . . wondered if the cream
In Grandmother's squatty old pitcher
Was rich enough to suit him.

There was no word spoken
Except once when I said, "I wonder if spring
Isn't nearly here!"
The stranger answered vaguely,
"Huh? Uh-huh, I guess so."

I choked a little
On the last bite of waffle
As the stranger rose and threw down his napkin
Stalked into the hall, put on his hat and rubbers
And left for the office.

The breeze ruffled the yellow curtains,
Or was it a sigh?
There was strange dew on the daffodils
As I bent over them
Remembering how I had carried daffodils,
An armful of gold,
When I married the stranger
Seven years ago!

WRIGHT FIELD.

271

FINESSE

He came in just at 5:15
   The same as any other day,
But after that he didn't do
   A single thing his usual way.

He never even gave the news
   A hurried glance. His eye on me
He hid a package in the desk
   And I pretended not to see.

He straightened up a book or two
   And placed the reading lamp "just so"
(I'd cleaned and dusted thoroughly,
   But then, of course, he wouldn't know.)

There came a knock, yes, just at eight,
   Then "Happy Birthday" and "Surprise."
My hand flew upward to my throat
   I glanced at him and he looked wise.

I laughed and stammered, blinked my eyes
   To hide a *faithful* mist of tears.
(Why shouldn't I appear surprised?
   I've practiced at it twenty years!)

RUBY E. BOLTON.

MOTHER LOVE

Some said his sins surpassed belief,
   Some that he was devoid of sense;
They called him coward, fool and thief,
   And damned him for his insolence.

But she, employing all the proud
   Defenses of her woman's art,
Preserved him from the hostile crowd
   Behind the bulwark of her heart.

DOROTHY DAVIS.

NO TIME TO DIE

Dear Lord, I must not leave this earth
In spring, when hyacinths come to birth
   And winds are heavenly sweet!
And, oh, in summer ruby cherries,
Amber plums and garnet berries
   Provide a nectared treat.
Then autumn's tranquil, turquoise sky,
Deep coral leaves, pirouetting by,
   Wind symphonies in the field—
A winter roof's icicled frieze,
Frost's lacy ferns, and tinseled trees
   Make life so hard to yield.

Lord, *Thy* will be done, for I
Can find no fitting time to die!

SUDIE STUART HAGER.

"And the Seventh Shalt Thou Rest . . .

*Rest . . . rest . . . but there is no rest . . . after the work and the waiting
for . . . then when it comes . . . is it rest . . .*

THE MOTHER

Since the black winter night when John was born,
I never knew a night's unbroken sleep.
When John was two and less a care at night,
Mary was born. Then Paul and Ernest came
And there were four. I often thought, those years,
If I could get but one night's sleep, just one,
Without a break, I might not be so tired,
Always so tired. But that night never came.
I heard their call the second it began
And breathless, shivering with cold, I reached
Their bed before the cry was still.
Or, if I heard no cry, I rose to see
That things were well, and covers tight and warm.
The house was small those years, four rooms for all
The six of us. I thought I never could
Find place for half the things we needed there.

Our house is larger now, with seven rooms,
And there are two of us to live in them.
Nothing remains to break my sleep at night,
But now I find I can no longer sleep.
A sound, a cry, awakens me, and in my mind,
Breathless and shivering with cold, I stand
Inside their door. And then, remembering,
I stop, and look on empty beds.

HELEN PEAVY WASHBURN.

Rest is made of so many things . . . an old, old house is sometimes full
of it . . . so full there's only room for one . . .

COMFORT

She is alone in the fine old home.
Though they wished to remain,
Though she clung to their hands,
One by one they were gone;
No blade of grass knew
They had crossed the wide lawn.

"Why does she stay there . . .
She can't use the space?
Isn't she lonely in the old place?"
Well meaning words . . . she alone understands
That rooms packed with memories
Of smiles and tears,
Of voices and faces, have no room for fears.
She isn't frightened by sounds and squeaks,
She knows the language the old house speaks
To the wind and the rain.
Nothing is strange . . . through each window and door
Is the same friendly view
That her mother's eyes knew.
The carpet's deep plush holds her steps in embrace,
She hears the gay greeting from the tall clock's face.

Though they have gone . . . and with them laughter,
Home things hold comfort until she follows after.

RAMONA DUNNING SPRINGALL.

Everything in all the world gets tired ... the trees get tired of holding leaves ... the grass gets tired of growing ... the tide gets tired of coming in ... the winter tires of snowing ... everything in all the world ... and maybe far beyond ...

A TIRED PRAYER

Father:—
The way is hard, and I am torn by doubt,
Confused by theories, dulled by the long grind
Of work and worry, loneliness and grief.
God, can You hear above this dust and din?
They say You once were man, and knew man's pain—
Can you remember that far agony,
And, out of pity, grant this prayer to me?

Grant me a quiet spot within my soul—
Like a green refuge in the forest's heart—
Walled round with silence, dim and sweet and cool—
Where I can hide myself, sometimes, away
From all the heat and clamor of my life.
A quiet spot, where memories may come
As dappled deer come down the forest aisles,
Drifting like shadows through the sun-shot gloom—
So may my memories pass, without a pang,
Leaving me quickened by their loveliness.

Then, as a weary traveler slips within
The still green crystal of some forest pool,
So may I slip within a pool of peace
And cleanse myself of all the dust and strife
And hate and greed and prickling conceit.
And then lie still—forgetful for a while
Of my sick self and all its noisy doubt.

So, dreaming, may I slowly come to feel
Your friendly Presence, brooding all about—
And catch some shining glimpse of Your great plan,
And, for an instant, feel my hand in Yours.

Because You were a man and knew man's pain,
Because You were a man and knew man's fear,
And all man's tire and loneliness and grief,
Give me this secret space where I may rest—
Then, having rested, help me go once more
To face the challenge of this thing called life,
And make as good a showing as I may
In those hard tasks You've given me to do.
This is my prayer—Grant it, I pray, oh God—
For once, they tell me, you were tired too.

ELSIE ROBINSON.

And where shall one rest . . . on the seventh . . .

THE CHAPEL ROAD

The chapel road is wise and still,
   And pious people say,
That every flower that blossoms there
   Has learned the way to pray.

So holy is the chapel road,
   The old folk tell the young,
That every tree bows down its head
   When Angelus is rung.

The pagan roads dance into town,
   A laugh in every sod.
The chapel road is still and wise,
   It knows the way to God.

MARY C. HAUGHEY.

REMEMBERED HANDS

My father's hands were long, palms finely lined,
Showing the thinker, teacher, lover of truth.
Yet they were strong and large,
Hands accustomed to toil.
They had milked cows, could handle horses well,
For they were masterful, but kind.

In my earliest childhood they led me gently
And strongly lifted me.
One incident so plainly etched in memory
A young girl unused to pain,
With my hand in his it could be bourne
His suffering was as mine.

Down through the years that handclasp was for me,
Something to tie to.
And to others friendship, honesty, and strength.

At last his earthly work was finished.
As he approached the valley where each must go alone,
His hand through days and sleepless nights
Still clung to mine,
As mine had clung to his in infancy.

And now though months have passed,
When night brings dreams to bless,
I feel his hand in mine.

WINIFRED UPTON McCAIG.

"Before we too into the Dust descend;
Dust into Dust, and under Dust, to lie . . .
Sans Wine, sans Song, sans Singer, and—sans End." . . .

SO IS HE MADE

Beneath the hill, athwart the stream,
The mind of man pursues its dream,

Burrowing, building to erase
Nature from earth's eternal face,

To seal her mouth and close her eyes
With what he may himself devise.

The temporal shadow on his heart
His stubborn will must thrust apart

The everlasting land and seed
The waiting furrow with his need.

With hands no larger than a leaf
He brings a forest down to grief;

Troubles the air with metal wings
And prowls between the roots of things.

Clearly he sees the strength of stone
In mountains yet he'll match his bone

Against it and the mountains bend
Their terrible backs to shape his end.

* * *

Whatever he may hew or hack
He knows that time will take it back;

That his swift mind may not outrun
Earth's patient cycle round the sun.

And yet so urgent is he made,
So transient and so unafraid,

Who now before our mortal eyes
Conquers the deathless thing and dies.

SARAH LITSEY.

281

"Ready . . . Aim . . . Murder . . .

Casualty Recorder, please include . . . War Industry Board, please consider . . . Historian, please remember . . .

THE WASTE OF WAR

We are the songs that were never sung,
Pictures that never will be;
We are the ghosts of the stately ships,
That never will sail the sea.
We are the wraiths of a million babes,
That will never, never be born,
And we are the shadowy whispering rows
Of unplanted fields of corn.
We are the thousand glorious things,
That *living* hands would have done—
But we perished there on the battle field,
Between a sun and a sun.

Viola Perry Wanger.

Give this space . . . to that tragic soul . . . whose song would have sung a world to peace . . . his lips were closed with gas . . .

AND THE GREATEST OF THESE

Unknown—Chateau-Thierry.

THE UNKNOWN SOLDIER SPEAKS

You lay your wreath above me tenderly,
    Why can't you wait till I have had my say?
The cry of every heart resounds in me,
    In every tongue since Babel speaks my clay:
Dear God, it matters not that here I lie
    Unknown to anyone save Thee and me.
Earth's crust is full of mold of such as I,
    And such as I shall yet be born, as free
To breathe Earth's air, warm in her sun, exult
    In love of life as once I did. But why
Such wanton waste of wealth of youth? No cult
    Of barbarism wasted more! If my
Full powers had, unmolested, given birth
    To all potential promise, would not man
In time have been more truly helped, would earth
    Have not been much more richly blest? How can
Mere clay be of more value than myself
    Pulsing with dreams constructive? Let me lie
Thruout all time unknown, if some sweet elf
    Can touch the heart strings of you passers-by
And bid you claim me kin, and for my sake
    Proclaim this holy mission: Not again
Shall man lead fellow man to this mistake,
    Colossal, stupid slaughter, not of man
Alone, but of ideals, and growth of soul,
    Material progress, science, art! Release
For me can only come when once the whole
    Wide world re-echoes madly, gladly, "PEACE!"

IRENE COLE MACARTHUR.

Make room for a poem never written . . . by a French soldier from Calais . . . at the academy they said he was a new Villon . . . he was blown to pieces by a German shell . . .

JE T'AIME

UNIDENTIFIED AT VERDUN.

Make a space for a poem by an American doughboy . . . he didn't write it but if he had lived he was destined to have eclipsed the works of Shakespeare . . .

TERROR IS A GREAT TEMPTATION

CRUSHED FENDER

It happened in Milan one summer night,
    While we were driving down a narrow street.
A fender crashed—the brakes froze to a stop
    Beneath the pressure of the driver's feet.
I hurled my ire against the guilty one:
    "You should be taught to signal as you turn!
At least put out your arm!" I cried at him.
    "You could have caused our car to overturn!"
At first the man was silent, then he spoke:
    "Sorry." he said, "to cause you such alarm.
You did not see it, for the night is dark,
    But as I turned, *I did* put out my arm.
Please take my license number and my name—
    I hope you will forgive and understand.
I was a soldier once somewhere in France . . .
    My left arm is a stub. I have no hand."

I could not speak. The words choked in my throat.
    I did not take his number, nor his name—
I turned the car against the dull-black night,
    My face averted to conceal my shame.

ROSA ZAGNONI MARINONI.

288

RELICS

To say,
  Don't cry. Your father doesn't mean it when
  He scolds. We have to remember, always we have to
      remember.
  For he—
  He's not to blame that he can't see;

To say,
  Isn't it lucky the government taught him a new trade?
  Oh, yes, we live quite nicely now.
  We get along.
  It's wonderful, isn't it, how much work a man can still do
  Without his legs?

To say,
  I don't seem to know you any more
  Since you've come back.
  You act so strange.
  You go
  Off to some ghastly distant place where I can't follow you
  At all;
  Can't find you
  Ever;

To set the plates for supper,
Then to know
That you have one plate too many;
To go
Slowly, and put it back;

These things are war, long after war is done.

HELEN PEAVY WASHBURN.

289

SCRAP IRON . . . FOR THE YEN MARU

Scrap-iron! Tons of twisted scrap-iron!—
Writhing, ugly, rust-red tangle—
Destined for Japan, for shrapnel . . .
Loading, on the Yen Maru!
Standing on the bridge, we watch them—
Modern cranes and gear for loading . . .
   Scrap-iron, soon to feed the guns
   That slaughter Chinese Mothers' sons!

From the river-towns, in barges,
From our city streets, by junk-men:
Rusted stoves and twisted fenders,
Broken wheels—a baby carriage! . . .

Scrap-iron, in a moving tangle,—
With one purpose—sent to mangle
Mothers' sons across the waters!
(Mothers, scorning puny daughters.)

Little mothers of Japan,
Working in swift relays, can
(And their War-lord says they must)
Clear the hold of scrap-iron-rust . . .

Plough-shares, beaten to a sword!—
Mercy on their souls, oh Lord!
Scrap-iron, in a rust-red tangle!—
Manhood, in a flesh-blood mangle!

Scrap-iron, waiting on the dock!
(God forgive us!) You but mock
All our boast that "Wars must cease!"—
Re-crucify the Prince of Peace! . . .

From the river-towns, in barges,
From our city-streets, by junk-men—
Penny-sales, by me, and you!—
Writhing, ugly, rust-red tangle,
Destined for Japan, for shrapnel . . .
Loading, on the Yen Maru!
      Standing by, we watch the loading . . .
      Scrap-iron . . . for the Yen Maru.
BLANCHE DEGOOD LOFTON.

Shame, shame . . . of course he joined to see the world . . . and international diplomacy required gunboats in a foreign port . . . true it wasn't our war . . . but after all when the boat was bombed . . . our government protested . . . and when they bomb again . . . don't think we won't protest . . .

STARDUST

I loved a lad with summer eyes,
   A sailor lad in blue.
He sailed away one winter day;
   Now what am I to do?

He wrote to me from Singapore,
   From Peiping and Shanghai;
And now the moon that covers him
   Sits in a frosty sky

And watches pillaging and death
   Oh, can he be the same—
My sailor lad who loved me
   And now is but a name . . .

Grant me one boon, O crystal moon,
   In the land of By-and-By,
Will you carry a message (of stars) for me
   To a lad in far Shanghai?
ALICE WILBUR.

HIS LAST LETTER

He wrote it, sitting with his back against
A blasted tree—its leaves were crushed into
The sodden earth. He did not write of war
But of the things at home he'd known . . . before.

He said he knew that spring had come, back home;
He mentioned flying skates on sun-flecked walks
And small boys' kites, and tulips in a row;
Plum blossoms floating down, like scented snow;

The worn place in the rug before the fire,
Where, in the evenings, his old dog would lie;
He asked if there were cookies in the jar
And if I still wished on the night's first star.

He tried so gallantly to hide his fear;
He joked, and said this might be his "swan song."
It was as though he turned and waved his hand,
Then blithely started into No Man's Land.

ESTHER WEAKLEY.

*Let the white cane of peace . . . remind the world . . . of its blind hate
. . . in war . . .*

THE WHITE CANE

He jostled her a little in the crowd,
    And she had said, "Look out where you are going!"
She had not meant her voice to be so loud,
    And she had seen the white cane, without knowing
Its meaning . . . He replied, "I wish I could—"
    And she looked up to find his face was drawn
With sudden pain, and then she understood—
    "The last I saw was stars at Meuse-Argonne!"

She could not think of anything to say,
    Shame gripped her throat and would not let her speak;
She bowed her head and hurried on her way—
    When she had kissed him softly on the cheek.
And when she sees a white cane she will know
    Its meaning—lost horizons, vanished dawn—
And hear a voice, deliberate and slow—
    "The last I saw was stars at Meuse-Argonne!"

GLENN WARD DRESBACH.

After the grasses of centuries cover the crosses . . . after the eternal flame has burned out . . . after the Arch of Triumph has crumbled like the pyramids . . . what shall survive . . .

SURVIVAL

A thousand years from this tonight
　　When Orion climbs the sky,
The same swift snow will still the roofs,
　　The same mad stars run by.

And who will know of China's war,
　　Or poison gas in Spain?
The dead, . . . they'll be forgotten, lost,
　　Whether they lose or gain.

Of all the brilliant strategies
　　Of war-lords now alive,
Perhaps a Chinese iris vase
　　Of porcelain may survive...

Perhaps a prayer, perhaps a song,
　　Fashioned of love and tears,
But only beauty, . . . only truth
　　Will last a thousand years.

MARGARET MOORE MEUTTMAN.

293

Season's Greetings . . .

Why do the crowds surge through Times Square . . . why do they scream and shout and blow their horns . . . what are they trying to drown out . . . the death rattle of the old year . . . or the first baby wail of the new . .

NEW YEAR'S EVE

New Year's Eve—it's raining—
  The streets and buildings are wet—
The old year in agony dying—
  Breaks forth in a deathly sweat.

ELEANOR VEE SCHNEIDER.

Transition . . . winter giving way to spring . . . false spring that always comes too soon . . . and even fools the orchards . . .

QUATRAINS

"Winter"

Limbs abare, icy stare . . .
Brazenly wanton in Its crudity;
With lowering frown the Sky sends down
A fleecy white blanket to cover Its nudity.

"Night Wind"

So soft you sigh as you pass by,
My window wide I ope to see
You boldly seek my brow and cheek
And steal a good-night kiss from me.

"Spring Song"

Spring came liltingly along . . .
I caught the echo of a song;
Swift flash of blue-bird homeward winging . . .
Was it my own heart I heard singing?

ROSE KATTERHENRY.

A warm night . . . so early in the year . . . and suddenly . . . the whole world comes to life . . .the trains are bringing spring . . .

SPRING NIGHT

The train's whistle blats impatiently through the still air.
Its noise draws nearer—nearer.
It sounds like a hundred million feet
Clad in straw sandals
Running down a ramp. Suddenly I am conscious
That only the echo is running—
Now only a sullen roar, with the persistent moo of the iron
      beast
Lingering—lingering.

Someone's voice calls out "Fine time. See you soon." A car
      turns the corner,
Its gears shrieking like the prolonged scream of a man
Upon a rack.

Spring scent enters the open window.
Not the lush, round, velvet scent of magnolias,
Nor the slender stab of ecstasy that is honeysuckle,
But a misty green-violet one—the new green-grass smell, first
      crocus, hyacinth sweet, daffodil pure—

I feel myself floating in the center of a white tulip.
I look out and see the pale quarter of the yellow
Dryad of the sky.
Silver beams slide down the lip-smooth sides.
Sway, dip—dip, sway—in undulated movement.

The train still mutters distantly;
My eyelids close.
Blue night holds me close.
Sway, dip—
I sleep while spring in satin slippers moves
Along the earth.

ELISABETH GOOLD.

297

Old wives out west . . . point to a robin . . . sign of spring . . . here in the city hurdy gurdies . . . do their best . . . sing of spring . . .

HURDY-GURDY

Hurry, little laughing girls
With flying skirts and dancing curls.
Grip moist pennies in your hands
Where the hurdy-gurdy stands.
Run, you boys, with laugh and shout—
See the monkey dance about,
With his red cap perching high
Over one sagacious eye,
Holding out his cup of tin.
Hear the pennies jingle in!
Hear the tunes that you will hear
New springs whisper in your ear
Long years after—while you wonder
What lost window they are under!
Watch the merry breeze that blows
Franco's winged mustachios
While he grinds, with far-off eyes—
On what blue Italian skies!
Let two lovers pass this way,
Pleased with all their words can say,
Still more pleased that something draws
More than words, until they pause
Silent, gazing in surprise—
Springtime in each other's eyes!
Windows open to the notes—
Some forgotten fragrance floats
Inward, and the curtains stir
As if changed to gossamer . . .
Now so many people stand
Gripping pennies in the hand,
Hearing, very far away,
Other hurdy-gurdies play.

GLENN WARD DRESBACH.

Spring thaws in the mountains . . . creek rising . . . no danger here . . .
wouldn't want to live in the lowlands this spring . . . heavy snows . . .
lots of water . . . lots of water . . .

FLOOD CONTROL

You should have seen the flooded creek today,
  So changed you wouldn't know it, running strong
With the strength of little streams escaping clay
  For a while, and frothing, but doing nothing wrong.
Creeks need to go on a tear, reviewing a way
  Of flowing they haven't known for ever so long.
Though they run wild they will be back by May
  With broader banks, singing a better song,
Reserving a place for weeds and frogs in their seasons,
Conceding them life nor questioning their reasons.

Louis Stoddard.

After the flood . . . after the drouth . . . things still grow . . .

Once in a fog
  I came on a bog—
  'Twas cold and chilly;
I passed it on
  And from it anon
  Grew a lily.

Petaled perfection,
  Fragrant afar,
Earth-born flower,
  Fit bride for a star.

But my lily died—
  As lilies do—ere
  Came frost to nip her;
And earth and air
  Gave next, I swear,
  A lady's slipper.

White against black,
  From muck, a flower;
Story of creation
  Retold every hour.

Jay Huskins.

*Floods in the lowlands ... Ohio ... Tennessee ... over their banks ...
Mississippi rising ... folks going back to their homes in the lowlands
... old man river left his mark ...*

HIGH WATER MARK

The March winds howl and the gusts of rain
  Blow into the barn on the heifer calf;
The corncrib tilts and the hens complain
  Of their sodden roosts and the moldy chaff;
A plow horse slips on an oozy ramp
  And the cows go back to their muddy stalls
Sniffing the mangers where the damp
    Ensilage clings; and along the walls
      Rafter-shadowed, a line of dark—
    The umber and sepia high-water mark.

The kitten washes a chilly paw,
  The baby whimpers upon the bed;
I've coddled the fire—it's beginning to draw—
  The sides of the rusty stove turn red;
I am back in my home again tonight,
  Windows washed and the buckled floor
Scraped and scrubbed to a splintery white ...
    Oh, it is good to be home once more
      Though the yard is buried in silt and sand
      And the house has a coppery high-water band.

ALMA L. GRAY.

She didn't raise her cone to be a Christmas tree ...

FIRST MATERNITY

Out of my window the woods are a-flutter,
  A starchy birch nurse stalks importantly by,
The patriarch oaks squeek, "Tut-tut!" and mutter,
  Matronly beeches nudge them and sigh.
Spinsterly cedars primp envious and mocking,
  Dogwood gossips whisper and groan
At a bright-eyed needle-pine, crooning and rocking,
  Parading her first young cone.

KATHARINE BROWN BURT.

Spring kneels down . . .

REVERENCE

The Spring this year, as other years,
 Ran through a breathless night
That shook a thousand violets down
 The hill and out of sight.

The Spring this year, as other years,
 Knelt on her narrow knees,
And talked with God, in drops of warm
 Blue rain on apple trees.

And I who bend above a crib
 In the lighted, noisy town,
And tuck a little elbow in,
 I know why Spring kneels down.

MARGARET MOORE MEUTTMAN.

Tear another sheet off the calendar . . . see the flock of birds flying north . . .

NORTHWARD FLIGHT AT DAWN

Now, fly the sturdy squadrons of the sky,
 Impelled by some primeval urge to wing
Aloft, while wastelands brood in reverie
 And farms' neat squares of land lie slumbering.
Above mute villages where one lone light
 Glows like an earth-bound star before the dawn,
High over cities hushed in muffling night,
 The gallant wayfarers adventure on.

Their deep toned calls arouse the race of men
 As lusty prophecy of nascent earth.
Long-stifled dreams revive, hope breathes again,
 Forgotten aspirations have rebirth:
Man feels new faith, when those strong wings beat by,
 Which follow Spring across the purple sky.

GAIL BROOK BURKET.

CONCEPTION

God's need for beauty must have been immense
  Because he made the world so beautiful.
His need for love a passion so intense
  No man escapes its influential pull.
His soul and song, I think, are synonyms;
  That dirge we hear along the ocean's shore
Is God's voice weeping mighty requiems
  To beauties that are lost forevermore.
The exultation that we feel in spring,
  The sweet deliciousness of yielding ground,
As though God walked before us, reckoning—
  He seems to pause and listen to the sound
Of earth renewing—then we hear his words
Straight from the sky, straight from the throats of birds!

Grace Phillips.

SPRING CLEANING

The wind of March blows clean; it prunes
  All dead wood from the trees; it sweeps
Across the sea, and shapes the dunes
  Into well-ordered mounds and heaps,
Burying all the mouldered store
  Of rotting leaves beneath the sand.
And now I fling the sagging door
  Of my heart wide, with eager hand.
Sing through each winter-darkened room,
  Winnow the dusty fears I've sinned,
Then bury all the doubt and gloom
  In shining golden dreams, March Wind!
Only a sloven would be caught
In April, cluttered with wintry thought.

Winona Montgomery Gilliland.

SPRING

The willows' celadon aigrets
    And the robin bantlings warn
Snails to erect antenna—
    So the carnival be on!

Bambino swallows dartle
    On gracile, facile wing:
The world's again a'startle
    To the rigmarole of Spring.

The air resounds with chit-chat,
    For revelry is rife;
And we smile, as we remember
    That Spring's an antic life!

HARRIET DAYTON BELL.

APRIL

In billowy bloom the apple trees wave
Along the April sky,
Where white clouds toss in the joyous wind
Like pirate ships at play.
In the emerald grass the violets
A royal carpet have spread,
And over the hedge the lilacs nod
Their plumy, perfumed heads.

Oh, why in this world of warmth and sun
Do your tears fall, my pretty one?

ANNE WOLF,

MAY

O the wonder of living while May is here giving
Ten thousand new dreams. Who unfurled
New blue in the sky, new gold in the vale
New bonnets, new scarlet, new caps
For the blossom, the bud and the bush;
New songs for the singers in forest and dale;
New marvels of love for the world.

I laugh with her madness, her joy and her gladness
For they leap from the earth as I look;
I laugh with the sweetness of her as I listen
To bleat of the sheep from the woods;
To new waters that click crystal heels
On stony descents—I thrill as I christen
Each naked new dream in the brook.

ERIS GOFF.

Second Sunday in May . . . 'cross the way . . .

NOT EVEN A MEMORY

Today is Mother's Day.
   You wear red for your mother,
I wear white for mine
   Just like many another.

The years have filled me with longing,
   And hope and longing again
Until hope . . . and longing . . . and hope . . .
   Have changed to hunger and pain.

No one ever remembers
   The one in whom hope is dead;
I have not even a memory
   Of a nestling baby head.

VICTORIA ADELAIDE HARVEY.

MOTHER'S DAY

With hosiery, gloves, and bright bouquet
They shower her on Mother's Day—

Then for three-hundred and sixty-four
Days, remember her no more.

Things, for her who would rather see
Them drop in once a month for tea.

BERYL V. THOMPSON.

The first flower I ever used . . . to play the petal game . . . she loves me
. . . she loves me not . . . was a funny . . . floppy sunflower . . . she loved
me not . . .

A MOUNTAIN-GIRDED GARDEN AT ASHEVILLE

I love the tiers of wooded mountains
Encircling this garden;
And the swift flight
Of birds, towards the light
That scallops their rim.
Above gay colors, here,
Sun-flowers flaunt their note of cheer
And of a lady testify
Who planted gold petals
Against a gray sky.

LAVINIA R. CLARK.

June . . . when flowers blossom and romance blooms . . . and fragrant
nights bring memories . . .

ONCE WHEN ARCTURUS SHONE

Only the young can say
  How things befall,
Having philosophies
  That cover all.

I could dissect a rose,
  Identify
Song of a lark or thrush—
  Vega descry,

But could not bring again
  Something we lost
Once when Arcturus shone,
  Rimmed with the frost.

You have forgotten,
  But never could I,
With June and the Lance-bearer
  Trailing the sky.

MABEL POSEGATE.

UNDER A GARDEN STONE

Blue light and rancid slate is this strange soil
Where pigmied valleys trace their cribbled way
Along alluvian rims where ant eggs lay
Intaglio. Here lambent blood worms coil
And silver slugs with what symmetric toil
Escape the summer sun's relentless ray;
Red-eyed and tentacled, what queer shapes flay
The light of day, till secret terrors foil
The curious hand. Down falls the lifted stone
Precipitate; and yet not swift enough
To stay the silent flight of glowing mould—
The fabric of another world undone,
Fashioned of fragile, jewelled, fire drake stuff,
That nothing but a garden stone can hold.

CLARA HYDE.

Just a plain old fashioned quart jar . . .

GLADIOLI

If I should wish to hold and neatly phrase
Gladioli, I would not haste to seek
A Dresden vase or one whose oval cheek
Was shaven smooth and cool with potter's glaze;
But I would search each hidden nook and maze
Until I found an empty jar, whose bleak
And bald contours would match the virile streak
In blooms leashed to a sword to pierce my gaze.

And thus I would envision the bright glance
Of a rainbow from keen blades; yet meet the frank
And open fragrance of the garden's yield
Restrained in earthen molds by circumstance,
Yet spilling on the cellar's must and dank,
The essence of a spring still not congealed.

ANN BRYANT.

307

HOW WISE ARE FLOWERS!

How wise are flowers!
  No rebels, these,
Insisting on
   Strange liberties.

Never has
  The mignonette
Been jealous of
  A tulip yet.

Nor hollyhock
  Stepped on the toes
Of a lily,
  Or a rose.

From budding, till
  Its petals fall,
Each,
  An individual,

Contented through
  Its brief bright hours
To be itself.
  How wise are flowers!

             ETHEL ROMIG FULLER.

GARDEN RELIEF

Did you ever carry water
  To a truck patch on a hill—
On a hot summer evening
  When all the earth was still?

Could you hear the faintest crackling
  As you poured it on late peas—
As though the parched plants thanked you
  Upon their bended knees?

            MARGARET PITCAIRN STRACHAN.

August . . . record-breaking heat wave . . . local showers expected in the late afternoon . . .

SUMMER AFTERNOON

The Day, quite overcome with heat,
Weary with being on her feet,
Threw herself down across the lake
Fagged utterly—too tired to make
A swarm of drowsy, drony bees
Lie down and nap with yawning breeze.
She fell asleep immediately
And so, of course, she failed to see

The marsh-grass wading out knee-deep,
The sentry-crane drop off to sleep,
A palm, half-naked, kneel to view
Her shapeless form in breathless blue,
A loafer-lizard's stupored strength
Bend low the leaf that bore its length.

The Day stirred—roused by sudden shove
Of objects being moved, above!
Could she have slept? In shocked surprise
She dashed cold cloud-rags to her eyes!
Refreshed, she shook the dream-drunk breeze,
And bidding him rouse nodding trees,
Looked down on limply-hanging stocks—
On multitudes of rough-dried phlox

Dipping gay fingers in a cloud
To sprinkle them, she laughed aloud!

MAY HOWARD McEACHERN.

Autumn strolls in . . . taking September by the hand and running off toward winter . . .

REQUITAL

A fortnight ago, a thief plundered my zinnias,
    Robbing their gold and their scarlet at will.
Today, I found all of the gay, flaming color
    Spilled on the maples that brighten the hill,

RUTH INSCHO.

309

THE WHITE BIRCH

The young white birch was slender and frail—
So slight a tree, in so fierce a gale!—
And I, through the window, sheltered warm,
Watched her writhe in the screaming storm;
Through the pounding gray, saw a flash of white,
Tortured and twisted, yet holding tight,
'Til I longed to open my window—wide—
And coax the little white birch inside.

Her leaves were small, and their edges curled;
Far too small to be tossed and whirled
In a wind that twisted them all awry—
Delicate leaves, that would bruise and die
If a bird, asleep in their branches, dreamed—
So pale, so fragile, so young they seemed.

Yet she flaunted them forth in a saucy way,
And only seven were blown astray.
She clung to the rest with a stubborn pride,
However the blustering storm-winds cried,
And however harsh the threatening blast—
Her little twig-fingers held them fast.
Then a telephone call, and an errand to go,
And what happened to her I shall never know . . .
Whether broken and conquered she fell, at last,
Or rose, head-up, when the storm went past.
I'll never be sure, and I wish I knew,
But this, at least, was certainly true:
That a slim white stem, on the wind rode high—
Splashing her leaves at the sky.

GLADYS GUILFORD SCOTT.

ALL DAY RAIN

I had forgotten it could rain like this.
After the ominous dramatic dark,
Suspension; all things listening; then, hark!
The torrents come; the storm portended, is

Obliterating downpour. What a day
To rummage in old trunks beneath the eaves,
Or by the fire, turning yellow leaves,
Muse on the long ago and far away.

Here is a little interlude in time.
No weather, this, for brisk accomplishment;
But from the outer world far, far aloof,
Lulled by the rain and some old poet's rhyme,
To feel within a shelter snug content—
Primeval exultation in a roof.

LARRY GOULD.

And still it rains . . . the neighbor's children have gone home . . . the
shrill excited laughter . . . childish screams . . . no more . . . and still
it rains . . . the puddle getting deeper by the door . . .

RAINY NIGHT

This is a night for long rememberings,
    Light up the fire and watch each ripening spark
Drift like a firefly where the chimney sings
    With all the purple mystery of dark.
This is a night for books. Turn to a page
    That throbs with Aprils that were lost, go deep
In folded letters yellowing with age;
    A night of rain is not a night for sleep.
Pile up the hearth with cedar boughs and listen
    To silver music flashing on the pane;
Speak long forgotten words, and they will glisten
    Wrapped in their vanished Glory once again.
Turn back the clock, and till the break of dawn
Your heart will beat with hours that are gone.

DANIEL WHITEHEAD HICKY.

OCTOBER CAME AGAIN

My pattern made for life was good to see,
  With every glowing color well in place.
My threads were singing words that came to me
  Before the marks of sorrow left my face.
I said: To strive to love and help mankind
  (Forgetting wistful dreams for self alone)
Could liberate the lonely heart and mind;
  That we are owned by what we choose to own!

I broke the pattern with my tears today;
  The leaves were rose, and gold, and amethyst;
Each autumn tree was like a huge bouquet,
  And one who loved October was at rest.
I will be brave again when leaves are tossed
  To beds of brown, and silver white with frost.

AVIS TURNER FRENCH.

*The birds flew north . . . the birds fly south . . . old nature has a
calendar . . .*

WILD GEESE GO OVER

Along dim lanes lit only by the stars
  These catapults of nature volley on.
Beneath night's far flung, tenuous cloud-bars
  They breast the north wind, racing with the dawn.
With sibilant, rhythmic swish of mighty wings,
  In splendid solitude the gray geese go.
Hurtling triumphant over earth-bound things,
  Seeking a haven which they only know.

Far overhead, a phantom, fading wedge,
  Their gong-like notes beating against the sky,
They hasten to the distant reeds and sedge,
  The cloistered lake, the sheltering hills nearby.
    Like galleons which drift into a bay,
    They gently drop to rest at break of day.

EDWIN CARLILE LITSEY.

312

Leaves . . . leaves . . . in the spring I remember the first buds . . . then bending . . . blowing . . . bouquets of brightest green . . . and now red and gold russet brown . . . tumbling down . . . leaves . . .

LEAF BURNING

I swept the fallen leaves up yesterday
   And touched them with slow fire;
And as I saw smoke rise and drift away
   I knew a keen desire

To sweep my mind of old things lying there,
   Dreams long since dead . . .
Hopes that have clung like leaves on boughs now bare,
   And tears that I have shed . . .

I longed to gather every little grief
   Left scattered round,
Small doubts and fears and lay them in a sheaf
   On fire, smoke crowned,

Then stir the embers so a wind might find
   And lift the ashes of old praise or blame
And bear them far away, leaving my mind
   Clean as if swept with flame.

VIRGINIA EATON.

Do your Christmas shopping early . . . close your eyes and wrap the packages . . . tie your hands with ribbons too . . . or this might happen to you . . .

COUP D'ETAT

I wrap each gift in cellophane
  And seal it with a sigh,
The selfish urge has come again
  To keep the things I buy.

These candlesticks would look so dear
  Each side the ingle place,
The Scotty book-ends lend such cheer,
  I love this Chinese vase.

The boudoir lamp I really need,
  And new books, what a fate,
I vow next year to curb my greed
  By giving things I hate!

DOROTHY HOWELLS WALKER.

And the funny thing is . . . a fir is full of needles . . . while a peach is smooth and luscious . . .

WINTER — PRO AND CON

The fir tree snuggles in Winter clothes,
  Gladly cold weather she'll greet;
While the peach tree shivers with bare, bare limbs,
  Her clothes crumpled up at her feet.

O. M. L. DETTY.

314

BEDTIME IN GALILEE

When the little Jesus had been fed
And warmly covered in His bed,
I wonder, if like other folks,
His mother told Him little jokes.

Or if she washed His little shirt,
All soiled from playing in the dirt,
And smoothed it out with loving care
Before she hung it on a chair.

Then, after she had fixed the latch,
Sat quietly and sewed a patch.
Perhaps she tiptoed with the lamp
To see if Jesus' curls were damp.

I wonder if she knelt and prayed
About the bills that were unpaid.

* * *

These precious bedtimes Mary had
Before she lost her little lad.

BERENICE RICE.

The old year burns to ashes . . . in a searing silver flare of Frozen Fire . . .

FROZEN FIRE

I

The air is full of diamond dust tonight,
Cold glittering sparks between us and the snow:
The hills are ragged etchings, black and white, pointed with
      stars;
The crowding spruces go,
A still black army, down to the curving shore.
The frost lights glitter on every twig and brier
Till we set intruding feet on the jewelled floor
And shatter the cranberry bushes' frozen fire.

II

The still cold sharpens as the sun goes down;
The frost-fog thickens;
Plumes of white smoke stand
Straight up from every chimney.
Near at hand
A husky lifts a wailing quivering cry;
The low hills hold the sound
Answered, repeated, till from all around
The husky chorus swells to the winter sky.

III

Against the blue of spruces, and the grey
Of bare-boughed poplar, suddenly
As though a snowdrift burst in scattering fragments,
Ptarmigan rise with heavy whir of wings,
Show for a moment clear among the branches,
Then disappear,
White lost on white again.

IV

The northern sky
Is pale transparent green
Where one lost star
Has climbed the snowy peak, to see
The world.

316

V

No whisper stirs the valley
Where blue dusk already lies;
But where that sunset-reddened tusk
Stabs the cold skies,
The air is lashed and torn,
As great winds blow
Across the peak, to lift the frozen snow
In gleaming haze,
Till streaming snow plumes fly
Above the valley in the sunset sky.

VI

The hills are changed today,
The white mist shows
Ravines unseen before.
The bare peaks stand
Separate; as though last night
They moved apart, and pausing now
Exchange slow stare for stare,
Like grey old men
With ragged shawls tight-drawn.

VII

The pines stand dark against the sky,
Northern Lights are streaming high,
Far along the snowy trail
Sounds the prowling wolf-pack's wail;
Cold and swift the night comes down:
How bitter black that trail to town!

FLORIS CLARK McLAREN.

"Grow Old Along With Me . . .
The Best Is Yet to Be . . .

*What are the days you will recall ... relive ... when you grow old ...
who are the people you will see in memory ... where are the places that
your heart will go ...*

FROM MOUNT MANSFIELD
(In Vermont)

I shall recall this day when I am old.
And though my brain be dull with weight of years,
And my heart's blood run thin by life's long tears,
I shall have this my spirit to uphold;
I shall have this to cloak me from the cold.
As Death the intermediary nears,
I shall remember Mansfield and my fears
Will vanish then into the mind's stronghold.

Today I stood on Mansfield's upturned face—
An atom of a god whose vision spied
Into infinity through finite space;
And narrow is the world, but very wide
The mystic reaches of that other place
Where we are one with earth and wind and tide.

BETTIE MARGOT CASSIE.

*Sleep — mm — sleep — mm — You wait Francis when the time really
comes this is what will happen ...*

WHEN SUNSET OVERTAKES ME

When sunset overtakes me
    On roads too dim to scan,
Then I shall leave at evening's door
    The moving caravan.

I'll put my gypsy shoes away,
    Say my prayers thrice over,
Slip an emerald nightgown on
    And button it with clover.

MARY ELIZABETH JONES.

320

Now here is a lady who would like to serve a little tea ... when you get
old ... and the coffee gets cold ... she might unpack her tea set ...

THE CHINA TEA SET

A China tea set—just to own,
   A China tea set was her dream—
Dear fragile cup, quaint little bowl,
   A cunning pitcher for the cream!

So graciously she'd pour the tea,
   Her friends would chatter bright and gay,
"Such perfect tea! Such lovely cups!
   I'm glad I happened in today!"

But he to whom her life was joined
   Thought money would be better spent
For land, for implements and stock—
   And to his will her will was bent.

His toil and gain were all for her—
   And when the two were old and gray,
That she might have no wish denied
   He brought the tea things home one day.

Dear fragile cups, quaint little bowl—
   She thanked him with her patient smile.
She placed them in a shining row,
   Admired them a little while,
Then packed them all away, you see,
No friends were left to drink the tea.

B. Y. WILLIAMS.

Well I don't like to mention it . . . but gout and rheumatism aren't the only things . . . There comes a time when elevators are a necessity . . .

APARTMENT PARTNERS

Tidy apartment
Airy and high,
Up a tall tower—
An ideal nest
For love and rest.

Joyfully working
She hummed and sang
Never tiring—
'Cause, newly wed,
Her heart's love-fed.

Proudfully content
He lounged and read
Books galore—
Saying ever
He'd make life easier.

Now she needs more rouge
And wonders why
Her darling boy
Without effort
Is so short of breath.

FRANCIS M. BOTELHO.

Tut . . . tut . . . you know your rheumatism won't let you be an old gadabout . . .

IT'S THE GYPSY IN ME

When I am old I hope to sit up nights
And drink black coffee while the city lights
Drop out, and stars I had not seen before
Peer through the sky, and call me to the door—
And lure me out upon deserted streets
Away from home and comfortable sheets
To follow after dreams while yet awake—
And take no chance on that which sleep might take.

FRANCES BRAGAN RICHMAN.

Be careful about unpacking an old tea set . . . it can lead to complications . . .

LATE LOVE

Serene and calm they were,
   As only the old can be—
The little old man in his visiting clothes
   And the little old lady at tea.

A romance here, a love affair,
   That was plain to see—
The look he gave his hostess
   As she handed him his tea.

"Does love come so late—thus—in the fall?"
   Yet void her voice of doubt, of fear.
He answered, his head bent close,
   "Of course. What better time, my dear?"

LORNA TALLENT KIDWELL.

Just let this be a gentle reminder . . .

THE PRIEST IS COME AND THE CANDLES BURN

The white moth is wooing his chosen mate,
   The birds have a nest in the weed and fern,
But, love, you knock at my heart too late,
   The priest is come and the candles burn.

Where were you, love, when the morning was heavy with
     mating?
   And in life's noonday before vivid dreams had departed?
Why did you tarry when twilight was heavy with mating?
   Now, it is midnight . . . pale sleeptime . . . And I am chill
     hearted!

The moonflower bends with the moth's frail weight,
   The birds are asleep in the grass and fern,
But, love, you knock at my heart too late,
   The priest is come and the candles burn.

JOHN RICHARD MORELAND.

323

OLD-FASHIONED VALENTINE

Larkspur and mignonette! Well does she know
The florist brought them, scarce an hour ago—
This blue sheaf in the modernistic jar,
From which each spur lifts high a fragile star
In pale pastel or deeper violet
Against the fragrant cloud of mignonette,
While on the card, in letters bold and clear,
Is scrawled, "A valentine, for grandma dear!"

She knows they're hot-house grown—that winter snow
Drifts deep outside—yet, closing dim old eyes,
She walks where scent of mignonette hangs sweet
On an old garden of the long ago,
While tall blue larkspur, under sunlit skies,
Drops fragile bits of heaven at her feet.

Jessie Wilmore Murton.

Silver threads . . . among the gold . . .

MISER

I have seen many things,
    Too beautiful for words;
Twilight tremulous with mist—
    Birds.

I have heard music
    That was to me
Soft as the clinging fingers
    Of the sea.

I have known many things
    Now I am old—
I am a miser
    Counting my gold.

Harold Vinal.

PERSPECTIVE

So many things to learn and see—
So many things to do and be—
We are encompassed and imbued
With limitless infinitude.

So many years—behind—ahead—
The vast unborn—the countless dead—
Interminable sky and sea
And undefined eternity.

Innumerable nights and noons,
A billion stars—recurring moons—
The central sun's revolving light—
The miracles of sound and sight.

The astral planets set in space
And each in its appointed place;
The cross, the crown, the rule, the rod—
The answer can be only—*God!*

LOUISE MOSS MONTGOMERY.

And taller than a pillar . . . and stronger than granite . . .

MEMORIAL

The forest rears no tombstone for its dead,
    But builds a soft brown floor of fallen leaves.
And where torn logs remember glories fled,
    Only the night-wind grieves.

The towered lords of yesterday still give
    Their substance for tomorrow's bud and shoot;
Ten thousand murmurous generations live
    Within each thrusting root.

And this the monument the woods bestow
    On the great oak, cloven and rent apart:
That a green seedling, after years, will grow
    Out of its crumbled heart.

STANTON A. COBLENTZ.

325

No hurry Thelma . . . glance back through the Album and read the last poem in . . . "Listen my children" . . .

MATURITY

One day I shall like a quiet room
    With dark window shades drawn down,
And never go where violets bloom
    In sunny fields beyond the town.
I shall kneel in a crowded church
    And feel real close to God;
I shall listen to great orators
    And neither yawn nor nod.
March winds will not stir my soul;
    April showers cease to thrill;
I shall wear much heavy coats
    For winds will thaw and chill.
I will learn to like little words,
    An evening by a fireside,
Big books, and most of all,
    An early hour to retire.
I shall bend over solemn ledgers
    And never think to run away,
Swimming pools will cease to charm,
    I'll like things painted grey;
As to whether I'll be satisfied,
    Perhaps I shan't say . . .
But, oh, I'll know deep down inside
    That old has come to stay!

THELMA HOFFMANN.

On the south lawn of the Old Folks Home . . .

SHADOWY OUTLINE

She paid small fee to generosity
    During her eighty years and more of breath,
And clutches life with grim ferocity,
    When faced with the unwonted signs of death.

Her jewelled fingers had the will of steel
    That binds the ligaments of lofty towers,
But now, benumbed and gnarled, unfit to feel
    Their way through life, they grasp its withered flowers.

HELEN M. FIRTH.

COMMUNION

It may be that he sits so still.
(Men of ninety often will
In a corner warm with sun,
Knowing that their work is done.)

Or because within his eyes
There is something sweet and wise,
As if God, Himself, had spread
On the ground these bits of bread.

However it may be, things come
Creeping, flying for a crumb.
Chipmonk, squirrel and catbird dare
To gather largesse round his chair.

Perhaps his tongue that halts on words
Of mortals, now, can speak with birds,
And kindly eyes so nearly blind
To books, can read a red squirrel's mind.

DOROTHY P. ALBAUGH.

RECONNAISSANCE

There lies the far horizon
   And here am I;
Between me and its blueness
   What furlongs lie.

And, like the blue horizon,
   My dreams lie far—
Obscured by the commonplace,
   How dimmed they are.

But who would want the sky-line
   A breath away,
Or have one's dreams belong
   To everyday?

EDNA BECKER.

Only the old are wise ... and know these things ... listen to the young ones chatter ... the old are wise and silent ...

INARTICULATE

There are no words,
The sunset symphony,
The eucalyptus choir,
The paean of the stars,
The hymns of ancient seas,
Are harmonies too vast
For our poor tongues.

Grass,
Earth, and the smell of earth,
Small winds and ragged bits of fog,
New-born rivulets,
Tall cliffs—
No words—

There are no words to tell of these,
Nor of the pull of mountains
Or of morning
Or of love
Or death
Or anything that matters.

I stand before a redwood tree—
I, and a grey squat stone.

EVA RIEHLE.

To some people ... old age comes like a breath of autumn ... to some a blast of winter ...

RESIGNATION

Her tragedies she always keeps alive,
    She wears a wornout sorrow as the oak,
Retains marcescent leaves; the winds revive
    The monody by sobbing through its cloak
    Through the silently falling snow.

It's better to imitate the naked beech:
    It gladly surrenders all to winter's cold,
It's only its foot that ever tries to reach
    For all its fallen leaves that slowly mold
    Under the white covering of the snow.

EMILY ANN COFFMAN.

328

There is no end . . . and no beginning . . . and nothing can stop the in-
between . . .

CONTINUANCE

We cannot die who live on in our seed,
  Nor need it be the product of our flesh.
Just as a child survives, so may a deed
  Capture the soul within a vital mesh,
To live forever in the minds of men.
  Blood of our blood, the written word may be
Closer than children. Sometimes with the pen
  We can create a living entity.

The tree we plant lives on when we are not;
  The house we build, the sentences we say
Mark out on earth their own especial spot,
  A part of us, who sped them on their way.
To propagate itself is each soul's need;
  We do not die who live on in our seed.

Dorothy Quick.

Do . . . re . . . mi . . . fa . . . sol . . . la . . . ti . . . that is all there is
in a Beethoven symphony . . . or a mother's lullaby . . . do . . . ti . . .
la . . . sol . . . fa . . . mi . . . re . . . the song is in your heart . . .

ALWAYS WITH SONG

How sweet to softly-cushioned baby ears
Are lullabies, slow-winged and lingering
As unstirred clouds that float through lazy Spring.
A few years pass and then youth perseveres
Through strident voice to utter songs he hears;
Then time brings love with pulses quickening
To strains caressing, tender, whispering;
Then age . . . and songs to comfort waiting years.

Always man lives with song, with rhythms low
And tender made for love and lovers' ways;
Or fast and stirring notes to make hearts strong,
Or music made for dusk when deep clouds blow;—
Man's pulses pound to rhythm; darkest days
Are made endurable always with song.

Mary B. Ward.

Wrinkles in a face...shadows in a country...age they call it...
growing old ...

SHADOWS

White-capped waves and shimmering sands
Sailboats dancing in the sun,
But on across the sea
The clouds are gathering
And planes are dropping bombs.

The wheat that ripened golden in the field is garnered in the
      bin.
The waving corn that whispered, whispered peace and plenty,
Stands waiting in a myriad row,
But in the world somewhere, somewhere,
The children starve and cry for bread.

On four-lane highways smooth as silver
The care-free millions swiftly glide,
While armies all accoutered
Sternly guard the distant frontiers
And nations wait—for what—for what—

The skies are sapphire blue and tranquil;
The dew-wet dawn renews the day;
The crescent moon hangs up her bow;
The heavens are constant and eternal
But shadows—shadows—come—and go.

Maude S. Rea.

Am I to understand this is the best . . . this ever vacillating life . . . this never ending ever blending . . . shading . . . changing all around . . .

TRANSITION

What though a dream reached reality and paused,
   Shall I return to hum-drum things forevermore,
And count my life as over, regard all beauty lost,
   Not clinging to the future, but what has gone before?
Shall failure once, remove all taste for living
   And make of me an empty, lifeless shell,
Or shall I seek again, the dreams that life is giving
   And call the present mood a breathing-spell?

For now I know that steadfast is a word
   That cannot be applied to earthly things,
And changeless is its synonym; absurd
   To build a hope on loveliness with wings,
This being so, it must be true that grief
   Will also pass, and longing, too, is brief.

VIRGINIA SPARKES.

Where is the best that's yet to be . . . I'm growing old . . . I'm growing old . . .

BEYOND GRIEF

Man is amazed with sin and sick with terror,
   Traveling the earth-roads bleak with wind and stone.
To him each fellow face becomes a mirror
   Sealed with the long gray sorrow of his own.
He stands heart-leaden by the flowering way,
   His debt defaulted to the God he owes.
He walks with blind eyes and deaf ears by day,
   Unstirred by wild-bloom, birds or singing snows.

But let him cup a leaf between his fingers
   And listen to the orioles' outcry.
There is a core of love within him deep,
   Greater than the depression of its sleep,
That will awake to see that beauty lingers
   Beyond his grief, across the lupine sky.

RICHARD LEON SPAIN.

331

*When evening comes . . . work done . . . time to talk . . . time to talk . . .
and no one to talk to . . . no one who wants to know what you have to
say . . . when evening comes . . .*

BUT I DON'T KNOW

Woman, they say, are lonelier than men,
But I don't know . . . today I saw again
The same bright hunger in an old man's eyes,
And knobby hands hold fast, as if a prize
Too great for measuring, the simple boon
Of friendly talk, over too soon, too soon.

DELOVA DURNFORD.

*Then is it all worth it . . . for the great . . . perhaps . . . their names
. . . their deeds will live through time . . . but what of us . . . of you . . .
of me . . . you write a poem . . . I build a book . . . both will perish tomorrow . . . what of the millions more like us . . . the millions and millions
and millions . . .*

THESE HAVE GONE DOWN

These have gone down in unremembered time,—
    The still small offerings of hearts that knew
Rejection, yet would sooner cease to beat
    Than cease to give as was their wont to do.

The sacrifices where no eye has been
    A witness to the glory of the deed,
Nor eased the burden of too silent pain
    With sympathy in answer to the need.

And noble thoughts unshared, inspired words
    That perished with the breath that failed to give
Them utterance; and likewise all the dreams
    That vanished ere they could be made to live.

These have gone down in unremembered time,
    Unknown, unseen, unshared, a silent host;
But marching close to man's immortal soul,
    They have their life in him, they are not lost!

PAULA S. VOGELSANG.

*But oh the agony of tearless eyes ... the dry eyed pain ... the bound up
bosom yet unburdened ...*

TEARS ARE BUT SPINDRIFT

When little leaves are leaning to the light,
   Tears are but spindrift, blown along the dark.
Who hopes to hug his heart-break, has the night;
   But when the dawn spills silver, and the lark
Spills music, and the languid lips of leaves
   Loosen to let out laughter, there is less
Than shadow, even, of the thing that grieves,
   Skirting our lost horizon of distress.

The heart, however faithful to its pain,
   Has found no armor to withstand the way
Of each new morning coming back again,
   As though it were the world's initial day,
Weighted with wonder woe cannot dismiss.
   Tears are but spindrift in the face of this.

HELEN FRAZEE-BOWER.

*Grow old ... grow old ... grow old along with me ... the best is yet to
be ...*

WHO WALKS WITH BEAUTY

Who walks with Beauty has no need of fear;
   The sun and moon and stars keep pace with him;
Invisible hands restore the ruined year,
   And time itself grows beautifully dim.
One hill will keep the footprints of the moon
   That came and went a hushed and secret hour;
One star at dusk will yield the lasting boon;
   Remembered beauty's white immortal flower.

Who takes of Beauty wine and daily bread
   Will know no lack when bitter years are lean;
The brimming cup is by, the feast is spread;
   The sun and moon and stars his eyes have seen
Are for his hunger and the thirst he slakes:
   The wine of Beauty and the bread he breaks.

DAVID MORTON.

"And Memories Vague of Half Forgotten Things . . .

THE CLOSED ROOM

Here, time that was dim years away,
　　Upon a mouldy loom,
Rewove a story lost in dreams
　　Left sleeping in the room.

Remembering, the old walls leaned
　　To hear a lullaby;
But as to this, there is no one
　　Who could so testify.

The toys turned from their dusty past,
　　Marched down a thoroughfare
Of days almost forgotten now,
　　Worn faded and threadbare.

No sound, yet in that silence
　　Where little ghosts had slept,
A childish laughter sang again;
　　A lonely woman wept.

I vow no voice had spoken there,
　　No step had crossed the floor,
No hand had opened it that day
　　Nor closed the rusty door.

MARY PEASLEE ROOT.

Christmas tinsel . . . an old glove . . . an automobile horn . . . a wisp of melody . . . a fragrant perfume . . . a child's toy . . .

PIRATE DOLL

Come, tattered little pirate doll without an arm,
  Forsake your own stark shell, mute-steeped and grim.
To live again just one brief hour with me,
  This hour—in memory of him.
Let us bring forth the blue-checked spread,
  His coverlet, your wind-flung sea,
Let us forget that throbbing, aching dread
  Clutched at our hearts, that pain clung in his eyes.
Only the buccaneering hours shall we recall,
  The victories, pirate doll, the cache of gems so rare,
Hidden in stealthy darkness under tropic skies,
  When you were sailor bold, conqueror of all,
And he a pained, pretending boy with yellow hair.

Speak, tattered little pirate doll without an arm,
  From the tight lips which he gave life;
Tell me if you do feel those gentle finger tips,
  His hands, still guiding you through foam and strife?
Or is it only haunting, taunting memory
  That brings the brief, bright laughter of his lips,
His hair against my face, his call for me?
  Oh, pirate doll, you lived just while he lived, and now
You lie at peace, inert as ashes lie
  Once leaping flames have left the last bright ember.
But I—ah, I am living on, not knowing why or how,
  Fighting the barren anguished thoughts that never die
For always while I live I shall remember.

MERRY WIGGS.

Between awake . . . and sound asleep . . . there is an interval . . . that memory can't capture . . . only a vague and vanishing recollection . . . of something always haunting . . .

KNIFE OF NOSTALGIA

I wish that I had been awake last night
　　When that little wind wandered to my window;
But I was drowsy and it went with the light
　　Of dawn, brushing the wet wisteria below.

I am sure now that it came up from home . . .
　　Perhaps across her grave, in that tangle-garden's
River-chill.　It seemed that something of south-loam
　　Was left to my nostrils; and that old grief that hardens

Like hail in the heart was with me, again;
　　The gray memory of our old meadow-fence flung
A thin knife of nostalgia at my brain,
　　And silence, as of sleeping years, stilled my tongue.

AVANELLE WILMETH BLAIR.

There are several reasons I can think of . . . she might have a job in Boston now . . . or she might have married that college boy you introduced one night . . .

SPRING IN MANHATTAN

I wish that I could trade this spring for one
　　In which you played an all-important part,
Before our strange, erratic course was run
　　And you became a legend of my heart.
I wish that I could brush the months away
　　And find again the path that leads to you,
And hear your voice as challenging and gay
　　As were your eyes at tables set for two;
For, from the loot of love, this much remains . . .
　　The soft, persuasive glamor of the inn,
A moon that spilled its silver on the lanes . . .
　　And memories of a half-forgotten sin;
I wonder . . . as these old ghosts stir anew,
　　Why spring should bring *them* back . . . instead of *you.*

DON WAHN.

Tricky memory . . . all that I did on a certain day that you might name
a month ago . . . is gone.
Where were you on August twelfth, nineteen hundred thirty-eight . . .
yet I can recall the breakfast food . . . one morning seventeen years
ago . . .

WITH SUCH DETAIL

The mind with such minute detail
    Can summon back the past;
One half forgets that time grows pale
    And living does not last.

So vividly I walked today
    Beside a certain stream,
I could not send the waves away,
    Nor waken them from dream.

I walked a minted mile or more
    Along the water's rim,
Fishing for fish I'd caught before,
    Talking with Brother Jim.

JOHN ROBERT QUINN.

The Memories that I like most . . . are those few that amuse me . . .

FIRELIGHT

Tonight a picture haunts my blazing fire . . .
    A vivid memory of long ago . . .
    The merry flames, splashing a ruddy glow
Across the polished flooring, dance up higher
And I can see again a burning pyre
    Of letters, turning ashes . . . feel the woe
    And desolation only youth can know
When life has lost its hope and heart's desire.

I knelt, a tearful girl so young, unlearned,
    That I despaired of finding love again.
With trembling hands I crushed my dreams and burned
    His letters . . . watched them flame. I hated men!
. . . And now I smile to think I felt that way:
I would not have him as a gift . . . today.

MARGARET RUSH.

PATTERNS IN OUR HEARTS

Purple evenings and gray dawns
Have traced patterns in our hearts.

Evenings when the earth is wet
  We have dreamed beside a fire,
Dreamed of yesterdays—and yet—
  We have looked ahead and higher;
Hoping—lest the fading day
  Close our eyes to purple light,
Lest it steal away the magic
  Of the evening—leaving night.

Gray dawns when the world is still
  We have known and forgotten a sorrow,
Hardly a scar is left of the ill,
  And it will vanish tomorrow;
Fade like the shadows of dawn on the hill
  When thoughts of the future sing,
Deep in our hearts, our dreams and our wills
  And we can but remember the spring;

When purple evenings and gray dawns
Traced their patterns in our hearts.

KATHRYNE COLE.

INVITATION TO TEA

Some day when I am old and tired and grey,
  And my dull life is almost at an end,
When time has rendered me so passionless,
  That I can yawn and calmly call you friend;
Then shall I ask you in to sup with me
  And murmur, with a smile behind my hand,
How once my tender heart I let you hold
  And how 'twas dropped and trodden in the sand;
And then I'll light the lamps and pour your tea,
  I'll hum and tell you that I loved you so
Long years went past before I smiled again,
  And after tea I'll wish that you would go!

MYRNA ST. JOHN.

There was a big gray house across the prairie . . . folks said it was haunted . . . summer evenings . . . neighbor children would tell and retell the story . . . I couldn't sleep those nights . . .

HAUNTED HOUSE

I don't know why I came; it haunts me so!
    But something always draws me back again;
Oh, it's just a foolish dream, I know,
    But something of me always will remain
Within these walls; see how the shutters blow
    Cold and lonely by the window pane.
We planted flowers here, a little row
    Of stiff and shining zinnias, tall and plain;
And on the picket fence a lonesome crow
    Would always come and watch for scattered grain.
Here by this window I would sit and sew,
    And lay her dresses on the counterpane;
Such little things of lace and calico,
    I wondered if she ever would be vain.
It's growing dark; she was afraid to go
    Upstairs to bed whenever it would rain,
Then I would set the lamp so it would show
    Right up the steps; somehow, I can't explain,
The things about this place that haunt me so!

EDYTHE HOPE GENEE.

If one could choose . . .

LET ME FORGET

Let me forget how quickly
Twilight gathers
When days are done,
Let me forget the cold,
Gray rain a bitter wind brings,
Let me forget how shadows
Sometimes cover
The staying stars.
But let me remember forever
The little victories—
Forgetting the scars.

OMA CARLYLE ANDERSON.

"Now I Lay Me Down to Sleep . . .

Bubbles at her bedside . . . might have spoken these words . . . but when she learned that her mother had braids . . . and ribbons . . . and all before she had Bubbles . . . Bubbles was reconciled . . .

A SMALL GIRL'S PRAYER

Dear Lord, I'm not complaining,
  At least, I hope, not much;
But since you've made the crippled walk
  Without the aid of crutch:—
And given sight unto the blind—
  Well, I've a small request!
It means so very much to me;
  I'm sure it's for the best.
But couldn't you just let me have—
  (You can't, I'm so afraid!)
A lovely, long and shining curl,
  In place of this old braid?

BERYL SCOUTEN HOLGREN.

Mose was a religious old darky . . . he'd walk seven miles to a revival meeting . . . he couldn't read the Bible . . . but my how he could quote it . . . Mose was never any trouble . . . and now he's dead . . .

A MILLION COTTON BLOSSOMS

A million cotton blossoms dot the sky
  Toward the east as though swift fingers spread,
Ecstatically, their fluffiness.—God I
  Knew surely it was false that he was dead . . .
My dark-skinned Mose . . . You're comforting his soul
  With field work, such as he has ever known,
Easing transition. When night's vespers toll,
  My heart knows well, You'll greet him there, alone,
At the last turning of the homeward lane
  To lessen any strangeness he may know
With, "Mose, it's good to hear your step again."—
  O God, don't leave him for he needs You so!
But—should an angel wish new duties, see,
Please God, if he would come to comfort me.

GRACE STILLMAN MINCK.

344

PRAYER FOR A GIRL NO LONGER YOUNG

Autumn, be kind to her, slow your arrival;
Summer, be good to her, let the revival
Of Spring in her body be passionate, heady,
Love may yet come to her, let her be ready.

Chilled were desires in the Spring's mating season,
Shadows pursued her without a good reason.
Lately I noticed her after fresh grooming,
Almost, she's pretty now, wistfully blooming.

Let her have blossom time, white petals flying,
Making a bridal bed smooth for her lying.
Spring, with your magic touch lulling the senses,
Stay, while she joyfully hurdles Love's fences.

INA DRAPER DEFOE.

I ASK BUT THIS

For that small heart that beats beneath my own,
  I ask but this, in earth's chaotic blare:
Not fame or riches, when it beats alone—
  Save as they come—but may it be aware
Of those high moments that a life can give,
  And hold them precious as they come and go;
That life may be a joyous thing to live:
  To reap, without regret, what it may sow.
Let tang of Autumn, mornings in the Spring,
  Touch deep the soul, bring yearnings and despair;
And may the sea's soft utterances bring
  The call, resistless, leading none knows where.
You whom I bear into a world of strife,
  O, be aware of beauty, and love life!

NOVA DORNIN.

PRAYER WHILE DUSTING

Often, when she dusted, she would change
    The placing of a picture or a chair
And wait his grave consideration, hoping
    He would say: "Yes, it's better, there."

He said she had a way of bringing beauty
    To the barest place; and however much
Of loveliness a room might claim, it gained
    In warmth and sweetness, from her tender touch.

But now ... she hasn't made a change in months—
    Each chair and book keeps its accustomed place;
For she has left only the echo of his words,
    Only a memory of his face.

Perhaps she errs, but who is there to say?
    For time and time again, she breathes a prayer
That soon she'll see his smile and hear him say
    That Heaven is lovelier, because she's there.

VIOLA DOWNEN.

Let me be the inspiration
    I promised him I'd be.
Let him see the culmination
    Of all his dreams in me.
Let me be of material aid,
By his love, I'll be repaid:
Let him be patient, with me, wise,
And teach me tolerance thru his eyes.
Let us continue to discover
We are good for one another.

ELEANOR VINCENT PRICER.

Did you ever wake up in the midst of a dream . . . and try to go back to sleep . . . and hope that somehow the play would go on . . . is there someone somewhere who sorts out the dreams . . .

PROPOSED PACT

Last night, dear Lord, he dreamed that he was tall,
  And oh, dear Lord, you should have seen his face
When telling me; you wouldn't guess at all
  That he had shriveled legs or wore a brace,
For he sat up so straight, dear Lord, his eyes
  Were like blue crystals in a velvet mask,
As he told how he stretched his legs to rise
  To his new height; and so, Dear Lord, I ask
A favor; You may smile at my request,
  I've thought the whole thing through; can You arrange
With him who deals out dreams at Your behest—
  For my lad's broken dreams this fair exchange:
Let dark dreams fall to me, I'll take them all,
But give him back the dream that he was tall!

JESSIE FARNHAM.

Hymn for a million modern girls . . . by one . . . who meant it . . .

PRAYER

For still indulging this unruly child
  Sparing the rod,
And treating her with Jesus' mercy mild—
  God bless you, God.

For keeping her from looking very old
  From pain and fraud,
From death by violence and catching cold—
  God bless you, God.

For understanding that a girl may tire
  And entertain an impious desire
And still not visiting her with your righteous ire—
  God bless you, God!

ANNEMARIE EWING.

SAINT AND SINNER

My sister was a sinner:
  She wore a crimson cloak;
She slept against her lover's breast
  Beneath the meadow oak.

The oak spread friendly boughs apart
  To let the stars look in—
And not a single star was shocked
  To see those lovers sin.

My sister was a sinner:
  She walked in silver shoes;
She danced and kissed the nights away
  With any lad she'd choose.

My sister died at twenty-one—
  They say: "The good die young"—
They, that strange perennial race
  With lies upon the tongue.

I, who am conscientious
  And meekly go the way
My mother and the parson taught,
  Respectable in gray
With sturdy patterns dun or black
  That never learned the ways
Of winding paths through starlit woods
  Or a cotillion maze;
I, no doubt, shall live to see
  My full three-score-and-ten—
Still wondering what life's about—
  Who? What? How? Where? and When?

MARION DOYLE.

348

*Do you remember the English teachers you had in school . . . let's see
. . . I had a Miss Hill . . . and Miss Grimes . . . and Miss Hudspeth . . .
and Prof. Harvey . . . good old "Prof" . . . he'll check on Gabriel's gram-
mar . . . when he goes . . .*

MY ENGLISH TEACHER COMES TO THEE

She dealt out English with a master hand,
Especially the poets. Such a noble band
Of bards tripped from her tongue. And now,
Whatever school she keeps, if you'll allow,
Dear God, give her a little class of cherubs to teach,
With heavenly notebooks and never-ending pens. Let each
Have wonder in his eye. She loved her students so—
She won't feel right without her class, I know.
And in the golden afternoons, when school is done,
Let her favorites come calling, one by one:
Keats and Milton, Chaucer, Dryden, and Pope,
And Alfred Tennyson. Please, gracious Lord, I hope
You'll tame down Byron and Shelley, when they call.
She was so gentle, and she loved them all.
For her sake, let there be many glorious days
To meet the Bard of Avon, and discuss his plays.
And now and then, kind Father, let her be
Deeply glorified—have the Brownings come to tea.
Ah, what a jewel-filled harvest she will glean
In answer to: "Tell me, Mr. B., what did you mean?"
Let her converse of foot and meter, day by day,
With rare Ben Jonson, Spencer, and Thomas Gray.
And if the authors sometimes forget just what they wrote,
In these discussions, have them be silent, let her quote
Those grand old masters of the magic pen;
For even they will learn from her, angels and men.
After she, knowing their work, has known their souls—why
    then
Some day—please let me slip into her class again.
Prim lipped and smiling eyed, "Now, child, you're late,"
She'll say. "Who wrote De Gustibus? Give name and date.
By the way, I noted and understood your absence. Therefore,
Be seated, please. I'm glad to see you back in class, once
    more."

RUTH SCHENLEY.

PRAYER FOR A DAMPENED SPIRIT

Let me close my lids
  And dream beneath the stars;
Let sleep convey me where she bids—
  But move those ugly bars

Whose barriers enclose
  A flame that is a god,
The spark restrained which in me flows
  Like static choked in sod.

Let me lose at length
  This strange humility,
The while I bolster high my strength
  To pass futility.

If I shape my wings
  And turn towards Desire,
This night I learn a line that sings—
  Fire alone stirs fire!

GRACE M. GRAVES.

With all the tasks the Lord must have . . . must He too be domestic . . .

SPIKENARD

Today I took a silken rag
  Dipped in a bit of oil,
And quickly cleared a table-top
  Of all unsightly soil.

Tonight I wear a silken gown,
  They say I look so smart;
Yet when they look they do not see
  The dust upon my heart.

Dear Lord, please take a silken rag,
  Anoint it with Thine oil,
And daily cleanse my wayward heart
  Of all its petty soil.

FRANCES MENDENHALL.

PRAYER FOR A BOY WITH A KITE

If he could only stay a little boy
To whom the sky is but a place for kites
And winging birds not men, destruction-bound.
Dear God, please keep him safely on the ground.

What is he thinking when he looks away
Into the blue? I want his dreams to reach
Vast heights, but not his body, God. So far
He has seen nothing falling but a star.

He knows his precious kite can only soar
The cord-length of the spool within his hands.
But war departments cannot hold a string.
Among the Missing is a dreadful thing.

DOROTHY P. ALBAUGH.

ANODYNE

When I was young I learned to minimize
My crooked back and strive for self-control
When someone pitied me. I played the role
Of fair-haired princess under curious eyes,
And if at times there were heart-breaking cries
Within me, I drew close the velvet stole
Of courage loaned me by the sightless mole
And thought that pain had made me strong and wise.

But now I am besieged with trembling fear,
For yesterday my daughter looked at me
With shrinking wonder. God, please compensate
Her dawning consciousness when children jeer
And as an anodyne for agony
Oh let her realize my soul is straight.

HARRIET GRAY BLACKWELL.

351

A little story to promote a better understanding between living fathers and their sons . . .

A SON'S LETTER TO HIS DEAD FATHER

Dear Dad:

I am writing this to you, though you have been dead for thirty years. From your seat in the Place Beyond I hope you can see these lines. I feel I must say something to you, things I didn't know when I was a boy in your house, things I was too stupid to say. It's only now, after passing through the long, hard school of years; only now when my own hair is gray that I understand how you felt. I must have been a bitter trial to you. I was such a fool. I believed my own petty wisdom and I know how ridiculous it was compared to that calm, ripe, wholesome wisdom of yours. Most of all I want to confess my worst sin against you. It was the feeling that I had that you "did not understand—." When I look back over it now, I know that you did understand—you understood me better than I did myself. Your wisdom flowed around mine like the ocean around an island—and how patient you were with me! How full of long suffering and kindness and how pathetic were your efforts to get close to me to win my confidence, to be my pal.

I wouldn't let you, I couldn't—what was it held me aloof? I don't know. But it was tragic—that wall that rises between a boy and his father, and their frantic attempts to see through it and climb over it.

I wish you were here across the table from me, for an hour so that I could tell you how there's no wall any more; I understand you now, Dad, how I love you and how I wish I could go back to be your boy again. I know now how you felt. Well, it won't be long, Dad, 'til I am over and I believe you'll be the first to take me by the hand and take me up the further slope. And I'll put in the first thousand years or so making you realize that not one pang or yearning on your part was wasted. It took a good many years for this prodigal son— and all sons are in a measure prodigal—to come to himself, but I've come. I see it all now.

I know that the richest, most priceless things on earth, and the thing least understood, is that mighty love and tenderness and craving to help, which a father feels toward his boy. For I have a boy of my own.

And it is he that makes me want to go back to you and get down on my knees to you.

Up there somewhere in the Silence, hear me, Dad, and believe me.

Sincerely,

UNKNOWN.

"And hath made of one blood all nations of men for to dwell on all the face of the earth...

A HALF-CASTE PRAYS

"Forgive, O God, the occidental anger
    Fomenting through these veins, a seething flood,
Which vies with cool of oriental languor
    To form a bristling murk in mongrel blood.

The East and West, though twain, in me commingle,
    Yet each reviles me and I brood alone—
The earth affords no corner for my ingle,
    No pillow for my head but hatred's stone!

Why must this body white as any mortal's
    Forever be forsworn by eyes that slant?
Why must this heart-bird dash convention's portals,
    Foredoomed as any sea-mad cormorant?

Forgive, O All-Wise Father, if I wonder
    Why You Who made of one blood humankind,
Predestined me to be a living blunder
    In whom two separate bloods war fiercely blind.

Oh Christian God, I'd hail this hybrid chrism
    As one whom cleansing tongues of fire baptize,
If You would only halt this vengeful schism—
    Subdue my soul to match these almond eyes!"

GORDON LECLAIRE.

353

When you have finished reading this next poem . . . pause for a moment and listen . . . the tiny sounds . . . the distant voices . . . radio . . . street cars . . . automobiles . . . the crackle of wood . . . sounds that crowd out silence . . . little sounds . . . listen . . .

RELIEF

How great a song is Silence! When the ear
Is dulled and sated, surfeited with sound
Of radio programs, chatter on the ground,
Raucous broadcastings from afar and near,
It makes one wish him anywhere but here . . .
    Here where loud-speakers, crooners, gongs abound
    And pressure salesmen mouth their talk around
The inescapable clamor of the year!

Anathemas are futile. Earth is filled
    Full of man's tin distractions, yammerings, noise,
His pandemoniums past all sane belief.
Songful indeed were silence, once instilled
    Even briefly in a world so out of poise . . .
Grant us, ye gods, one hour, this sure relief!

WALTER JOHN COATES.

Prayer for enlightenment . . .

WAS THIS THE TASK?

To hear the wind whistling
    In the straw-thatched eaves,
To watch the ass bristling
    In the cold, cold sheaves—
To see the stars shooting
    Their bright, sharp light,
And hear the owl hooting
    In the dead of night—

Pray, was this the task
    Of a God-King helpless cradled,
    Who had made, though all poorly stabled,
For Herod damask and wine red flask?
Was this the task, I pray—
Or that Herod might see—one day?

MARIE AUSTIN MAJOR.

354

It has always intrigued me that one people . . . out of reverence . . . never wear a hat in church . . . while another for the same reason . . . never remove it . . .

DIVINE INFORMALITY

Dear God, you seem so near, so close to me
  I find it hard to call you "Thee" and "Thou"
As though the greatness of all your majesty
  Had placed you far beyond my reach somehow!
I think you would be sad if everyone
  Exalted you and stood, in awe apart . . .
And I believe, when all is said and done,
  You'd give your throne for just one loving heart!

At times you must grow very lonely, Lord,
  Though well-trained choirs sing your careful praise—
Lonely at man's perfunctoriness—and bored
  Receiving pleas from sinners all your days.
I am a sinner, too, and yet I pray
  For nothing, God, except to be your friend!
I see no reason you should take away
  The woes that are my folly's dividend.

It is enough for me to know you stand
  In readiness to give me strength in need,
In willingness to take my silly hand
  And let me love you by my personal creed . . .
I know you'll understand if I discard
  The formal "Thou", the reverential "Thee"—
With you I find formality so hard,
  Dear God, you seem so near, so close to me!

MADELINE SLADE.

A PRAYER FOR EVERY DAY

Make me too brave to lie or be unkind.
Make me too understanding, too, to mind
The little hurts companions give, and friends,
And careless hurts that no one quite intends.
Make me too thoughtful to hurt others so.
Help me to know
The inmost hearts of those for whom I care,
Their secret wishes, all the loads they bear,
That I may add my courage to their own.
May I make lonely folks feel less alone,
And happy ones a little happier yet.
May I forget
What ought to be forgotten; and recall
Unfailing, all
That ought to be recalled, each kindly thing,
Forgetting what might sting.
To all upon my way,
Day after day,
Let me be joy, be hope! Let my life sing!

MARY CAROLYN DAVIES.

A PRAYER

Let me do my work each day;
And if the darkened hours of despair overcome me,
May I not forget the strength that comforted me
In the desolation of other times.
May I still remember the bright hours that found me
Walking over the silent hills of my childhood,
Or dreaming on the margin of the quiet river,
When a light glowed within me,
And I promised my early God to have courage
Amid the tempests of the changing years.
Spare me from bitterness
And from the sharp passions of unguarded moments.
May I not forget that poverty and riches are of the spirit.
Though the world know me not,
May my thoughts and actions be such
As shall keep me friendly with myself.
Lift my eyes from the earth,
And let me not forget the uses of the stars.
Forbid that I should judge others,
Lest I condemn myself.
Let me not follow the clamor of the world,
But walk calmly in my path.
Give me a few friends who will love me for what I am;
And keep ever burning before my vagrant steps
The kindly light of hope.
And though age and infirmity overtake me,
And I come not within sight of the castle of my dreams,
Teach me still to be thankful for life,
And for time's olden memories that are good and sweet;
And may the evening's twilight find me gentle still.

MAX EHRMANN.

Amen . . . Amen . . . Amen . . .

357

"The Great Adventure . . .

TO ONE WHO DIED YOUNG

You believed with childhood's magnitude,
And all was well. You never saw the feud
When old ideals encounter world's demands
And come to dust. Your artless, chubby hands
Will never strangle hope, nor nurture greed.
You'll never know the time the gods recede.

How good a thing it is, those candid eyes
That saw a truth as truth and lies as lies
Will never see the taint of compromise.
You'll never be a part of sorrow's pact ...
Here rests a dream, here rests a faith intact.

LOLLY WILLIAMS.

FOR PHILLIP
WHO WOULD BE SIX YEARS OLD TODAY

For all of us the world's a stage,
Each with his part to play,
But Phillip just walked on and off
Without a line to say.

HELEN DOREMUS.

THESPIAN

Small Phillip played a part sublime
Before his Curtain Call;
He did each act in pantomime—
The greatest art of all!

MARION F. LEWIS.

PRAYER FOR A VERY NEW ANGEL

God, God, be lenient her first night there.
   The crib she slept in was so near my bed;
Her blue-and-white wool blanket was so soft,
   Her pillow hollowed so to fit her head.

Teach me that she'll not want small rooms or me
When she has You and Heaven's immensity!

I always left a light out in the hall.
   I hoped to make her fearless in the dark;
And yet, she was so small—one little light,
   Not in the room, it scarcely mattered. Hark!

No, no; she seldom cried! God, not too far
For her to see, this first night, light a star!

And in the morning, when she first woke up,
   I always kissed her on her left cheek where
The dimple was. And oh, I wet the brush.
   It made it easier to curl her hair.

Just, just tomorrow morning, God, I pray,
When she wakes up, do things for her my way!

VIOLET ALLEYN STOREY.

THE COMFORTING

I would not have you back on earth,
   Your body racked with pain—
I know that longing for your mirth—
   Your comradeship, is vain.

And yet, when I sit wondering,
   As night is merged with day,
It seems your spirit comes to bring
   The words you cannot say.

MARGARET E. BRUNER.

"Sustained and soothed by an unfaltering trust ... lies down to pleasant dreams . . .

FOR ONE WHO WAS LOVELY

Lilacs of springtime,
Dew-wet with morning,
   She who was lovelier still than your bloom,
Slumbers. Now lend us
Beauty and fragrance.
   These be the tributes we bring to her tomb.

Songbird of summer,
Spilling your rapture
   Over the valley beyond the green hill,
Lend us your music,
Requiem singing
   For her whose sweet voice forever is still.

Bright leaves of autumn,
Borne by the breezes,
   While you dance lightly her feet are at rest.
Spread a gay carpet
Scarlet and golden
   Over the pathways her footsteps have pressed.

White snows of winter,
Falling in silence,
   Weave a soft coverlet spotless and deep;
Fold it about her—
Gently, ah, gently—
   She who was lovely has fallen asleep.

B. Y. WILLIAMS.

There is no louder roar in all our lives . . . than death's last whisper . . .

THE LOUD SILENCE

His noise disturbed me—I could not abide
    The thrilling of his horn, the rush of feet,
    The slam of doors, and many sounds unsweet,
But these I hear no more for he has died.

The quiet breaks my heart—it haunts my dreams,
    For, since no sound from him can break the air,
    I only think and think with dumb despair,
How loud, how very loud the silence seems.

                        SUSIE M. BEST.

And what shall one say of a son gone on . . .

SO LONG

He was so smiling and so debonair
    That last gay night,
And going with a brief,—"So long!"
    He passed from sight.

Death must have loved his eager, dancing eyes,
    His spun-gold hair,
Death must be weary of drab forms,
    Dull-eyed with care.

Still innocent and smiling to the last
    He took her hand,
And with unwavering trust he faced
    A strange, new land.

And now each casual word he said, becomes
    A precious thing,
Each deed has rich import, with love
    Remembering.

"So long!" He called so merrily that night . . .
    So long the years
For her who loved him, and was left
    Alone with tears.

                     NELL GRIFFITH WILSON.

Bombs in China are so far away . . . unemployment stalks all day . . .
down Sixth Avenue . . .

THE EXPLORER

There was no bread the night he left,
    But he was better off by far
Than he who labored, dreamed and wept.
    He saw a star
Blaze forth in all its radiance;
    And, child-like, followed it too far
To even think of coming back
    To where we are.

LLOYD DAY.

A doorway is after all . . . only a doorway . . . and those who wish can
sit in separate rooms . . . yet live and think and work and play together
. . . knowing the doorway can never be closed . . .

MY FATHER

Even as I used to rumple his gray hair—
    Tempering its dignity—so, now, I strew
    His sombre grave with heliotrope's fair hue
And drape with clover chains the headstone bare.
Then, in the tall, lush grass above him there
    I sprawl and talk with him an hour or two,
    Planning the many things I hope to do,
Placing my heart's rich treasure in his care.

Small comfort mine, you think? So think all those
    Who walk beside a father, hear his voice,
And know his full affection. They suppose
    That only those so favored can rejoice.

At this we smile in secret, Dad and I;
We know that fathers never really die.

HELEN WOLFE DAVIES.

But none are lame or blind or sick . . . when they start the "great adventure" . . .

MESSAGE TO MY FATHER

Once, on a long-gone evening, you and I
   Walked quietly beneath the cinnabars,
Orchids and lapis of a sunset sky,
   And watched the lighting, one by one, of stars.
A score of childish questions brought a smile
   Upon your Pan-like mouth that rarely smiled,
And lifting me upon the broken stile,
   Your mind went questing words to suit a child:
You said, "The stars are stepping stones to God,
   And this, our little world that seems so great,
Is just another—one that must be trod
   And left for others' footing—soon or late—"

"But stars seem far apart for stepping stones!
   I think we'll need the Giant's seven-league boots."

"Yes.   Seven-league boots—and all your father owns
   Are something less than Average Size computes."

Ten years you've journeyed, and I have no way
   Of knowing how time's measured where you are;
Whether you've passed Orion and Er Rai
   Or stand upon some yet undreamed-of star;
Wherever you are, I send this word to you
   By wind or passing meteor or flame:
The ignorant child who begged the planets' story
   Has learned, at last, your wistful allegory,
And has no doubt you've kept each rendezvous
   Punctually, despite your being—lame.

MARION DOYLE.

365

A MONUMENT TO LOVE

Where are you, darling?
Was it yesterday you died,
Or have long ages passed
Since you went from my side
And left me here, alone?

How strange life is!
We who have buried
Half our hearts
Must live two lives
In one.

One part of me
Lives here—
Works, plays, loves, laughs,
As if it knew
No other life but this.
Yet, all the while
Unseen by those who watch,
My secret self
Goes groping on your trail;
Goes calling—calling.
Do you ever hear?
Or, hearing, know
How I still love you, dear!

How can I tell you
That our love goes on
Unchanged?
How prove to all the world
That love is worth
All that it costs in pain?
Easy enough to raise
A monument to grief.
But how shall one
Build monuments to joy?
Erect a shaft
To pride and gratitude?

Show, by some symbol
Or heroic act,
All that love meant
In those lost years—and now?

A slab of stone?
No; stone's too cold
And dead.
Your body died
And, with it, half my heart,
But not one throb
Of our warm love has cooled.
It burns as brightly
As before you passed.
Why mark a living love
With piles of cold, dead stone?

A wreath of flowers?
But funeral flowers are sad.
Cut off, they wither
And their sweetness fades.
If I should grieve,
Wear withered flowers
On my aching heart,
Then all the world would say,
"She's sorry that she loved;
"She mourns her own lost joy.
"Love spoils a life, sometimes.
"Be careful how you love!"

Cold stones
And faded flowers?
No. Such things betray
And shut you out;
Make death seem final;
Seem to say
That love's not worth
The price one has to pay.

Not stones and flowers.
Then what can I do
To show the world, and you,

That love goes on triumphant;
That love always pays?
DEAR, I CAN LIVE!
OF MY OWN LIFE
I'LL BUILD YOUR MONUMENT!

Poor stuff, my life;
For in myself
I'm neither brave, nor good,
Nor kind, nor wise.
But love can turn
My weakness into strength,
Cleanse me of lies,
And teach me tenderness,
And keep me patient
Through the cruelest pain.
Yes, love can work
That shining miracle;
AND MY STRONG LIFE
SHALL BE YOUR MONUMENT!

Elsie Robinson.

Flame ... yes flame ... that's it ... flame always flings its fullest flare ... toward there ... toward there ...

FLAME

Lips too red;
   Hair like a crow's wing.
She is dead;
   I will pray no more!

I will not implore
   Unto God
For that which I hid
   Under sod.

When the fire is cold,
   Ashes, left.
Flame, they could not hold,
   Gone to God.

E. L. F. Van Dyke.

THE RETURN

He sailed upon the misted sea,
  Upon the sea as night came down.
He saw the curving line of cliffs
  Beyond the distant lights of town.

She watched upon that fading shore
  The ship's lights vanish, one by one.
Unmindful of the dark, she watched
  An empty sea till night was done.

Ships came and went. No sail was his.
  The memory of his boat grew dim;
But still she kept her patient watch
  And waited through the years for him.

"She's mad!" the thoughtless townfolk cried.
  "The storms have claimed him. He is dead."
She heard the careless speech and smiled.
  "He will come home again," she said.

One moonless night, the townfolk saw
  An ancient ship within the bay.
Dank seaweed draped her shattered masts;
  Her rotted sails were torn away.

A moment seen, then lost in mist,
  Strange visitor from unknown lands.
At dawn they found the woman dead,
  Her arms outstretched across the sands.

ELIZABETH S. NOBLE.

CHAMELEON

Trembling in a doorway
Drenched with rain, the sharp
And desperate urge for you
Held me in its falcon grip.
And oh the lost enchantment over
Common things. . . .

Red and purple asters
On our garden-walk, the willow
Tree brooding over a passive pool
Holding gently its nearer love
The white and fragrant water-lily.

Pale blue clouds acting out
Charades against a brilliant
Salmon "drope" of sky; grass scents
After rain . . . after rain . . .
Oh that was what you used to say!

That all this brave enduring Beauty
Death must *leave* untouched—
To rise and woo my every grief
In your dear name . . .

LOUISE LOUIS.

The old country doctor could feel the pulse and tell . . .

THE WINDOW

Even the clump of soil on coffin lid
    Did not bespeak finality to her.
Her mind, beneath its false acceptance, hid
    The thought that he would presently bestir

His quiet limbs. In such wise she beguiled
    Her heart, nor bound too great a pain in breath
Till once she tried to think how he had smiled,
    And could not. Then she yielded him to death.

ELLA BRODY.

That's the wonderful thing about it . . . no matter how tied down . . .
how earthbound . . . all of us . . . everyone . . . gets to go on the "great
adventure" . . .

HEAVEN

I am too little for a grand eternity.
I want in my tomorrow, things I see
And things I've seen—that faded all too soon.
Instead of angels' voices, I would hear a spoon
Beating upon a table; seeing a laughing face
Warm glowing, living—without please God—
Death's cold, set trace.
Instead of golden streets, I'd stand within
A doorway I know well. Is this a sin
To want my kitchen door, sagging of stoop;
To want instead of Heaven's Host, a group
Of little folk, all hot and tired from play?
If so, please pardon me, Dear God, but
Short was yesterday!

I am too earth-bound for a grand eternity.
Sometimes I almost laugh at plans I make...
I see myself in Heaven wearing apron, checked;
I see the sky above the barn, cloud flecked;
The chickens strutting proudly in the yard,
Then—little folks around me; hungry, tired—
How their small careless touches
My heart fired.
Again at Heaven's bedtime I would see
All that made Heaven pale by earth
Turning to me.
Small buttons, lisping prayers, the big frog's cry
I want those—more world things
Past stars and sky.

I want to end my days beyond as I did here,
Tired from hard work for all I held most dear;
In Heaven's night to bend above small beds,
To straighten covers, look on tangled heads—
A foolish woman, I, perhaps but mine
I would the way
I traveled, loved and lost in a
Too short yesterday!

KATHARINE HAVILAND TAYLOR.

And how shall a mother write of her daughter ...

LETTER TO SAINT PETER

Most Reverend Saint:

I have been told you keep the gates of Heaven (If I am being overbold, I pray to be forgiven.)—And knowing well how busy you must be, I shall be brief. (My hand's unsteady as an aspen leaf.)

When Sheila comes—(You'll know her by her smile, her dusky hair touched with the bloom one finds on purple plums.)—Her gay "Hello!" may take you unaware; but I assure she means no disrespect: Sixteen, you know, can seldom recollect the rules of tongue. Sixteen's so young! And if her halo tilts a bit, worn at a seemingly frivolous angle, please keep in mind, she is not used to it, that time will set the shining bangle more sedately on her hair, and give her dignity to wear.

For your compassion, Sainted Brother, the gratitude of
Sheila's mother.

MARION DOYLE.

And life is only the corner ... which mankind turns in his day ...

BACK HOME

To live is to go on a journey,
  To die is to come back home.
My shoe soles are thin with wandering,
  Sticky with clay and loam,
There are marks of stones and of brambles,
  The leather is scuffed and torn,
And I must not have walked quite straight, I think,
  For the heels are unevenly worn.
I shall take off my shoes and sleep and rest ...
  If I dream, shall I dream that I roam?
To live is to go on a journey,
  To die is to come back home.

MAY WILLIAMS WARD.

What shall we take on the "great adventure" . . . since we really leave nothing behind . . .

LAST INCIDENT

In coma now—
    With no apparent breath,
Well on her way
    To keep the faith with death,

Past need of food,
    Past knowledge of caress,
She seemed to lie
    In awful loneliness.

But when one stroked her hand
    In comforting,
Her fingers closed
    To keep her wedding ring.

GRACE MANSFIELD.

Some explorers require all manner of scientific paraphernalia before confident of the success of an expedition . . . some set out to surround the world with only a song on their lips . . .

BEYOND THE ATOM

A myriad charged electrons coursing around
    Their nuclear suns: This is my study table;
The very wood of it, I mean, as found
    In yours, and mine, and theirs, and theirs; a fable
More preposterous than dreams, yet true.
    My hand feels an inert surface, weight is supported,
Vision of things beyond is blocked; still through
    My senses I am deceived, fact is distorted.

If then my scientific mind cries out:
    "There is no God—I cannot see Him, hear Him,
Touch His face"; shall this be cause for doubt?
    Always the troubled, seeking heart draws near Him,
Finding in things unseen the evidence
    Of super-sensory Intelligence.

JANICE BLANCHARD.

What more could one wish to be . . .

QUERY ULTIMA

Soon now I shall crumble into dust
And utterly pass,
The crumbling dust
That slips through the fingers of time,
And leave not a trace
There on the grass
Yellow and sere,
Of what came after
The laughter
Of time's shortest year.
But O my dear,
What am I here,
And what will I be
Hereafter,
But the love I give to you
And the love you give back to me?

CORINNE THOMAS.

And if I may choose a melody . . . a theme though not a threnody . . .
Auld Lang Syne . . .

AN HOUR

I ask
But an hour of music
When I die,
No service, sermon, prayer,
Nor sad goodbye.
It is enough
That I should go,
Armed with a song
Sung soft and low.

DOROTHY CURRAN.

PRAYER FOR LAUGHTER

Dear Lord, to preserve my sanity
Midst chaos which threatens to swallow me,
Help me, no matter what ill fate brings,
To look for the funny side of things!
Help me, above all else, to keep
My sense of humor when I would weep.
Let not my fellow-men cause distress;
Lord, make me to realize their funniness!
Help me to find the humor in pain
That throbs all day in my tired brain—
(To keep me constantly well aware
Of the brain's oft-doubted presence there!)
Send me a hearty laugh to calm
My quivering nerves with its magic balm . . .
And when Death comes, with lugubrious mien,
O Lord, may I chuckle with mirth serene
That a dour old spook as dread as he
Should be the means of releasing me!

MADELINE SLADE.

Too Late to Be Included
Too Good to Be Excluded

You know how it is ... after everything is all over ... then ... you think of the remark you would like to have made ... well it's that way with books too ... this book officially closed two pages back ... this is a section of after thoughts ...

On the car this mornin'
I heard a woman talkin'—
She was on her way to make a speech
On Sir Walter Scott to a woman's club;
She made her livin' givin' talks on authors!
Such clean work!
How I wished I'd got some education
So's I could make a livin' that way 'stead of
Scrubbin' other folks' bathrooms,
Cleanin' after other folks' parties,
Washin' after other folks' children—
But all the education in my family went to
     Julia,
My eldest sister. She was the smartest, an'
     my father said
He'd educate her and she could educate the
     rest of us.

We sold off one of the four cows,
The speckled heifer,
To pay her tuition in Miss Willard's seminary.
Once I walked five white miles in a stingin' blizzard
To borrow a dollar to send her
When her groceries give out.
We picked berries all summer an' sold 'em
To lay up her graduatin' money.
Well, she graduated,
But she never taught me anything.
She jes' set around home an' grieved.
The boys she would have wouldn't have her.
An' them that would have her she wouldn't have
Finally, she died, an old maid—
An' I never did git no education!

Jes' think of it—
Makin' a livin' givin' talks on authors,
Such nice, refined work,
Such clean work!

UNKNOWN.

If we all had the faith . . . of a little child . . .

THE FURNACE MAN

God has a house three streets away,
And every Sunday, rain or shine,
My nurse goes there her prayers to say;
She's told me of the candles fine
That burning all night long they keep
Because God never goes to sleep,
Then there's a steeple of bells;
All through the dark the time it tells,
I like to hear it in the night
And think about those candles bright—
I wonder if God stays awake
For kindness, like the furnace man
Who comes before it's day, to make
Our house as pleasant as he can—
I like to watch the sky grow blue
And think, perhaps, the whole world through
No one's awake but just us three—
God, and the furnace man, and me.

AMELIA J. BURR.

For someone somewhere who will never know . . .

ONO NO YOSHIKI

My love
    Is like the grasses
Hidden in the deep mountain;
    Though its abundance increases,
There is none that knows.

JAPANESE.

mm—m—m—m—m—m . . . there doesn't seem to be anything appropriate to say . . . in spite of all the things I'm thinking of . . .

FIRST KISS

Kissed before? My memory replies;
    "A dozen times or more."
But my throbbing singing heart denies;
    "No, not ever . . . really . . . kissed before."

CHRISTIE LUND.

379

If you don't find a dog that suits you . . . I have some very nice kittens for sale on page . . . ninety-eight . . .

DOG WANTED

I don't want a dog that is wee and effeminate,
Fluffy and peevish and coyly discriminate;
Yapping his wants in a querulous tone,
Preferring a cake to a good honest bone.

I don't want a beast that is simply enormous,
Making me feel as obscure as a dormouse
Whenever he hurtles with jubilant paws
On my shoulders, and rips with his powerful claws
My sturdiest frocks; the kind of a mammal
That fits in a parlor as well as a camel,
That makes the floor shake underfoot when he treads,
And bumps into tables and bounds over beds.

The sort of a pet that I have in my mind
Is a dog of the portable, washable kind;
Not huge and unwieldly, not frilly and silly,
Not sleek and not fuzzy, not fawning, not chilly—
A merry, straight forward, affectionate creature
Who likes me as playmate, respects me as teacher,
And thumps with his tail when he sees me come near
As gladly as if I'd been gone for a year;
Whose eyes, when I praise him, grow warm with elation;
Whose tail droops in shame at my disapprobation;
No pedigreed plaything to win me a cup—
Just a portable, washable, lovable pup!

MARGARET MACKPRANG MACKAY.

But what about the men, my dear . . . I'd like to bet . . .

CAPRICE

When I think of all the men I might have married—and
regret,
I breathe a thankful little prayer I haven't married—yet.

ROSE MARIE.

Somehow this always makes me think of an August afternoon . . . the day the news came of the death of Will Rogers . . .

INDESTRUCTIBLE

Is that you, Death? Hello, old skate!
Whatever you do, you have come too late!
I've had a life brimful of joy—
Good luck as a man, good luck as a boy.
It's been all right with me from the first;
I've had more'n my share, so do your worst!
Go down in the west; or the silver sheen
Of a starlit lake; or the mating call
Of a drowning bird when the shadows fall.
You can't snatch from me the soft love-light
Of my mother's eyes, or the blessed sight
Of a child of mine in his romping play;
Or my wife's sweet lips at the close of day;
Or the meals I've had; or the restful sleep;
Or the joys of health which have thrilled so deep.

I laugh at you, you blamed old skate,
Whatever you do, you've come too late!

H. STANLEY HASKINS.

This kitten is not for sale . . .

BUNKY

With a crumpled ear and a crooked tail
And a striped coat, like they wear in jail,
I may not amount to so very much
But still I'd like to make it clear:
I've earned *my* bed and board for life;
I caught a mouse . . . last year!

BILLIE MARIE CRABB.

MARIGOLD PENDULUM

I

Dear, with this tawny marigold
I send you Ophir.

I send you Spain,
high galleons from Peru
wallowing slow in parrot green water.

I send you the gold house of Nero on the Aventine,
the throne of Baur, the bed of Semiramis.
I send you the dromedaries of Zenobia,
the beryl jaguars of Domitian,
the yellow desert beyond Baalbek,
fresh minted drachmae of Heliopolis,
rugs of Sultanabad, amber and green.

Love, look with favor on the gift
and the rest of my wealth shall be yours
by the next caravan.

II

Will no one deliver me from the haunted moon?
When I lie abed thinking chaste thoughts
she crosses the floor, slips under the sheet,
and cuddles her icy flanks against mine.
If I move to another room she is there before me.
If I flee to the other side of the house
she looks at me from a neighbor's window
or stands on a rain barrel to wink at me.
Now I am always listening for her step.
On dark nights I fancy her hiding in the garret.
In the cellar I look to find her flushed and tipsy,
sitting cross-legged on a claret cask,
She is faithful as an unloved wife.
Once when her scattered hair lay on my pillow
I threatened to kill her. In derision

she drew a cloud over her breasts
and hid in the water jug on my washstand.
My thirsty knife severed only a long tress.
For a week now I have not seen her.
One of these summer nights I must find the way
to slip a knotted cord under ears.

III

All night the wind ran around the house
hugging her sides with laughter.
Thunder tramped clumsily to and fro in the garret
dragging trunks and old bookcases over the ceiling.
The women folk pattered upstairs and down,
closing draughty doors, seeking each other's beds
to mix their long undone hair,
and gibber like bats in the cavernous twilight
when lightning thrust a yellow paw
in at the window.
I alone was glad of the tumult,
glad of the storm that kept me awake
to put my arm around the lightning's neck,
and clasping her tawny leopard against me,
to hear once more overhead,
through the hiss and cackle of the rain
on the smouldering world,
the apple tree's gnarled hands
caressing the weathered shingles on a night
when I held in the circle of two arms
all the sun's hoarded gold.

IV

Who tethered that white balloon
to the hilltop of grainfield?
How it swings and tugs,
whipping the guy ropes,
bending the oak tree pegs,
swelling rounded and higher,
crowding the very swallows out of heaven.

383

Kneedeep in the hayrick
the sun at rest on his pitchfork,
in overalls stitched from a double breadth
of blue sky denim,
watches the glistening bag of silk
that fills and fills
with mounting vapour of ripe meadows.

Oh, love, to climb with you
into the wicket of the wheatfield.
Oh, to loose the twisted sunlight
that ties the white cloud to the hillcrest,
and rise and sail
dazzling over houses and steeples,
to see red barns and zigzag fences,
pastures shouldering green elm parasols,
rumbling carts that yellow dust clouds lope behind,
dangling thirsty tongues,
chugging engines that pant
sweating up long hills in nodding bonnets
of curled ostrich or aigrette,
snaky rivers striped with bridges
writhing across the haze of level plains
till the sea sets an icy green heel
on their envenomed heads,
while swarming houses run to crowd the wharves
and dabble their toes in the surf,
where the sailing ships
clap shining hands on the horizon
and steamers toss dark windy hair.

Then at evening to rise yet higher,
rung after rung up the laddered atmosphere,
through emptiness like a hollow dish
to the highest shelf of thunder,
and there above cockcrow, above cannon,
peeping over the world's tanned shoulder
down the pale abyss where the sun stables at night
to brighten his rusting harness,
and the stars polish their silver cups by day,
to loose a pigeon of lightning
from a hamper of storm.

V

On the barn's peak the moon sits washing her whiskers.
Now she blinks a green eye, slowly arches her back,
and walking along the gable on satin pads
glares at me hungrily.
All day she looks so demure.
When I lay on my back in the deep grass,
watching her prowl the sky eaves, and leap
over fences of blue
I never guessed she could show so thirsty a tooth.
Tonight I am afraid of her.
I wish she could not see me here at the window
observing her antics.
She is not nearly so attractive as by day,
sly creature, rusted with mange,
and one ear gone, I see, in the fight she had
with the orange leopard that owns the morning.

VI

Thunder hops on the garret roof,
rain scampers over the shingles,
old father God with a flash of his testy eye
slams the gold window of Paradise,
pulls a torn shade across the eternal splendour
on these rotted silks
where the moth's scissors slashed and snipped,
the years have wiped their yellow brushes.
Fold them away, dear, with the wasp-waisted spoons
in their flannel dressing gowns.
Let us wonder no more to whom they belonged
It is enough to remember they will still be here
when we and our love are dust.
But let us sit with an open book on our knees
turning pages the pedantic worms have annotated
with crabbed wisdom and obscure geometry,
where mildew inscribes with a blue pencil
poems in forgotten alphabets,
and when the storm pauses
to shake the dank hair from his eyes
and resin the bow of his fiddle,

385

we shall hear the green humming of the rain
as it lays a cold cheek on the cobwebbed glass,
all those curious noises that the dust makes
gently settling
on the cracked furniture of discarded lives.

VII

Summer's gold pendulum slowlier swinging
gleams through the fog-dimmed glass
of the year's tall clock.
Come with me, love, wrap your bright shoulders
warm in the swallow's cloak, and fly with me
over the brown stubble of reaped fields,
to rest side by side on the telephone wire
watching the loaded hay carts crawl important
like fat caterpillars down a leafblade of road,
of still pools where the sunset holds
long and long
the print of our wing tips,
till we find a lost blue key
that winds the intricate spring
behind a red pumpkin moon
and a nipped marigold sun.

VIII

They are all yours:
images plucked with the wild Turk's-cap lily
in deep reddy meadows guarded
by the darting regiment
of dragonflies in burnished cuirass.

Yours the songs I make
when weary with searching
I come with the tang of salt winds on my lips
and the beating of moth wings in my blood,
to hold my joy in the blue leaping world
and the tall dancing sun with yellow hair
against the wheel of my mind.
as the Greek cutter wrought
In the hard translucence
of sard or of jasper
the body of Eros.

Yours because all loveliness
Is a polished shield in whose hollow
I see your eyes.

And my poems are a fire
lighted on the brink of death
where I hurl like driftwood
moon, stars, and sun,
kingdoms, galleons, caravans,
with Hell and God and the four Archangels,
the better to see your face.

DUDLEY POORE.

You might be surprised how true this is ... I know an old dog that shuffled into the front room every evening a few minutes before his master's program ... he always raised his head and listened ... and the puzzled stare was always there ...

RADIO

All afternoon wind and rain
Swept the valley . . but with the night
Came peace and a great golden moon
Above the highest hill—full and bright.
Surely you remember . . and then your voice
Broke the stillness of dim spaces—O son of mine!
Within this little house your presence glowed once more;
It was as though you stepped, in all your youth divine
Through my open waiting door
And came to me . . You sang the old, old song
My mother sang long years ago,
The song I crooned to you within the valley dusk,
With tall hills listening in a row;
O son of mine—each note, each dear familiar word,
Came ringing from across a distant sea
And traced themselves indelibly, through miles of night
Upon the mother's heart of me . . .

Jim, your dog, came close and softly cried,
Within his old dim eyes a wondering stare—
Then ran with eager labored step
And brought your slippers to your chair.

DOROTHY BEEDY.

If you want an earlier chapter in this story . . . skip back to page two hundred twenty-seven . . .

DRIED OUT

This place was the first home we ever had,
And I was sick of farming for other folks—
First in Wisconsin and then in Dakota.
It looked so pretty when he broke sod that day.
There wa'n't only three sides to the house,
But what did I care!
There was sunlight and wet rain and a coulee full of
        springtime where the children could play.
Seven full years, says the Book, and seven lean—
And we come in at the end of the seven full ones, I guess.
There ain't no crops where they's no rain.
And the stock died in the big blizzard:
So now we're goin'
Back to Dakota to farm for other folks.

Oh, God, the nice white ranch house with a floor
We was to have! The roses by the door!

GWENDOLYN HASTE.

A bunny cotton tale . . .

LINES TO A LATE LAMENTED RABBIT

You lie,
Not where in madcap youth, you ran and played;
Nor where the mighty forest monarchs cast their shade
Nearby, some limpid pool or sylvan glade
Beneath the sky.

You do not sleep beneath a bloodred moon
Nor, brittle, bleached and white, are your bones strewn
Upon some grassy hummock;

You mix
And mingle with the corn and beans,
The salad, gravy, and sardines;
Asparagus and tangerines,
The pickles, pie, and mustard greens,
In my protesting stomach!

BILLIE MARIE CRABB.

I shall wonder as long as I live . . . what kind of a bug it was . . .

MY BUG AMOS

I done it . . . I killed 'im
   Poor Amos . . . he's gone . . .
Jus' choked 'im
   Tha's whut I done.
Know why?
   Mom's allus preachin' . . .
Tain't bein' a genelmun
To hit back . . . 'specially girls,
   'At's her teachin'.
Next time . . . I will sock 'em . . .
   It 'uz Poll's fault . . . she kicked my shin . . .
'N I dug my hand in my pocket,
   'N I gripped it 'n' 'en . . .
Poor Amos . . . he 'us tame . . .
   It 'uz her fault . . . my land,
How'd I know when I squeezed
   My fingers . . . 'at Amos 'us in my hand?

VIRGINIA ELLIS.

Poetry is like this too . . . it's the heirs of the poets . . . who reap the dividends . . . and don't think they don't . . .

RÉSUMÉ

She lived her life unnoticed, tucked away
Among the cobwebs on a dingy street
Where neighbors shunned her alien retreat,
And called her odd, and children paused in play
To scan her withered countenance, still gay
Above the tatters of her satin gown.
She overlooked the prying eyes in town,
Drifting in silent dreams of yesterday.

So when she died, crude hands among her things
Seeking a clue to former friend or kin
Found in the remnants of old crinoline
Torn manuscripts and poetry with wings,
Old tales of Bagdad or of dim Cathay,
That yield a fortune to her heirs today.

UNKNOWN.

On a visit years and years ago . . . I asked the question . . . what becomes of love when it dies . . . there were several thousand answers . . . but none better than this . . .

UNDERSTANDING

What becomes of love when it dies? Where does it go?

Dear Heart, love never dies!

But when love is no longer wanted, then it is taken by the Divine Hand that fashioned it from out a human heart and ground into a fine soft scented powder called "Star-Dust".

Hast never heard of Star-Dust, Beloved? Why surely, that's what Star-Dust is. Unwanted love ground to feathery golden bits.

God then puts it in the big blue container which stands always upon the floor beside His throne, and at night when tired old eyes ache for rest, and weeping ones for comfort, when the gossamer film of golden dreams in the eyes of old lovers begins to grow thin and ever anew is lifted the clear questioning gaze of young ones, then God, like a kind old country doctor with one powder for all ills, stoops and gently upends His big bowl so that its contents come sifting out like fairy magic through the myriad star-shaped perforations in its lid.

It's because of the shape of the perforations, Darling, that we mortals call it "Star-Dust".

But God doesn't call it "Star-Dust"—God calls it "Understanding".

IRIS JAMIESON.

Ignorance ... no on second thought ... I mean Innocence ... is bliss ...

QUERY

How,
Then,
Distinguish
(Since they look the same)
The flush
Of Pleasure
From
The blush
Of Shame?

UNKNOWN.

It might be that sentiment of this sort ... twenty-four hours of every day ... would pall ... but for a few hours ... once in awhile mm—m—m—m ...

LOVING YOU

Loving you so that I would steal if you were hungry;
   Loving you so that skies grow gray when you are sad;
Loving you so that I would die to make you happy,
   Die with a smile if dying would but make you glad.

Loving you so that when we walk in crowded places,
   Sudden my eyes grow misted with a veil of tears,
So that I only see a blur where there were faces;
   Loving you so that I am swept with bitter fears.

When you are late or hurried or a bit impatient;
   Loving you so that when my head is on your breast,
Words do not come and sudden thoughts go all unspoken;
   Loving you so that just your reaching hands bring rest—

How can I ever let you know the love I bear you,
   How can I tell you, dear, that true love never dies?
When words are only words and hands are only fingers,
   When lips are only lips, and eyes are only eyes?

UNKNOWN.

LETTER FROM ALICE

Dear Mom:

Today, I found God!
You know how I've looked for him?
For so long . . . In so many places . . .
In churches of every denomination
I've knelt, searching for him;
I've hunted him at the firesides of friends;
I've watched upon the hills at midnight,
I've listened beside the rivers at evening;
Barefooted, I've trudged the sands at dawn;
I've walked bareheaded in the rain
Lifted my face to the snows,
Held out my arms to the wind—
But never did I feel him near me.
I searched with hope at first,
Then fear, and lately, Mom,
With mocking laughter.
Others found him; why could not I?
And now, I have!
This very day!
Upon the street, just at noon,
Amid the clamor and confusion
And hurry and heat.
How strange . . .
He was standing
With Kenny, Mom!
He had on riding boots,
And the sun
Made his hair look almost red,
And his eyes were blue—and glad—
And when Kenny said,
"This is Alice,"
He took my hand
In both his gentle ones
That were as brown
And as hard as Kenny's

392

And said, with a little catch
In his beautiful, beautiful voice,
"Why, Alice, I was beginning
To think you'd never find me!"
Then, I knew!
Oh, Mom, I knew! . . .
Is that what
You've always meant
When you said,
"God is Love"?
Is it, Mom?
Sort of like you always told us
That Santa Claus
Is the Spirit of Christmas?
That way, Mom?
You're wonderful.
And please, may I bring him home
For the holidays?
And Oh, Mom!
You were right!
He's a Methodist!

IRIS JAMIESON.

To "J" . . . to H.A.N. . . . to C.P. . . . to so many . . . from so many . . .

TO "J"

I'm not sentimental, Heaven knows.
And yet . . . today I found, among some books,
A little scrap of paper, with your name,
In dear, familiar, handwriting.   And so
I pressed it to my lips, and held it there
And found myself repeating a small prayer
"God . . . bless him . . . help him . . . keep him as he goes
Through this short life!"
Perhaps you think it looks
Foolish of me, to cherish just a name,
To kiss the paper, and repeat a prayer.

It wasn't just a paper . . . nor a name . . .
You see . . . I know *your* dear hand wrote it there.

E. PEARL DANCEY.

393

INCONSTANT

Inconstant—inconstant, when a single thought of thee
Sends all my shivering blood,
Back on my heart in thrills of ecstasy.
Inconstant—when to sleep and dream
That thou art near me, is to learn,
So much of heaven, and I weep
To think that earth and morning must return.
Inconstant, when to feel that thou has loved,
Will love me to the last,
Is joy enough to steal all joy from life,
The future and the past!
Inconstant? Ah, too true,
Turned from the rightful shelter of thy breast
My tired heart flutters through this changeful world,
A bird without a nest.
Inconstant to the crowd through which I pass,
As to the sky above the fickle summer cloud,
But not to thee, oh, not to thee my love.
I may be false to all on earth beside,
And every tender tie,
Which seems to hold enthrall this weary life
Of mine, may be a lie,
But true as God's own truth
My steadfast heart turns back evermore,
To that sweet time of youth
Whose golden tide beats such a barren shore.
Inconstant! Not my own the hand
That builds this wall between our lives;
On its cold shadow grown to perfect shape,
The flower of love survives.
God knows, I'd give all other joys,
The sweetest and the best,
For one short hour to live
Close, close to thy heart, its comfort and its rest.
But life is not all dark.
The sunlight gladdens many a hidden slope,
The dove shall find its ark
Of peaceful refuge, and of patient hope.
But sacred to this loss

One white, sweet chamber of my heart shall be.
No foot shall ever cross
The silent portal, sealed to love, and thee.
And some time, when my lips
Are to my first-born's, clinging close and long,
Drawing with bee-like sips
At its lily heart, will it be wrong,
If, for an instant, wild with precious pain,
I put aside the truth
And dream it is thy child
I'm fondling with such tender pride?
And when another's head,
Sleeps on thy heart,
Should it ever seem to be my own instead,
Oh, darling, hold it closer for the dream
God will forgive the sin—
If sin it is, our lives are swept so dry,
So cold, so passion-clean. Thank Him,
Death comes at last, and so,—good-bye.

AMY BUFORD COOKE.

Come, come, my dear . . . I swear it isn't true . . . that crush of yours . . . he didn't deserve you . . . be glad he's gone . . . wait until the next one . . . ah me then you will really hear phrases worthy of you . . . resignation rejected . . .

RESIGNATION

I did not know
   That there was star dust in my hair—and wisps of song.
I did not know
   My eyes were amber pools—until you came along.

No one before
   Had ever told me there was music in my name;
I did not know
   My voice was like the summer dusk—until you came.

Now you are gone—
   And no one ever said these things to me, but you;
And now I know
   That no one will again. They are no longer true.

NORA LANE.

RENUNCIATION

Let this good-bye of ours—this last good-bye—
　Be still and splendid like a forest tree;
Or like the hands of Silence holding up
　The blue and burning corners of the sea.

Let there be one grand look within our eyes,
　Built of the wonderment of these past years;
Too vast a thing of beauty to be lost
　In quivering lips and burning floods of tears.

Back to the chaos of the world, we go
　Shining with one sweet secret no one knows;
Crutches of dreams to help us on our path,
　From snow to tender petaling of the rose.

So in places we lift high our heads,
　That none may find within our calm, clear eyes
The secret that two travelers have returned,
　And cast away their key to Paradise.

UNKNOWN.

A BOOK OF REMEMBRANCE

Some, fingering the leaves of memory's book,
Linger at one especial page to look—
Thus visioning again in fancy's way
The vanished gladness of a by-gone day—
Living once more a happy hour, that cheers
The dreary routine of life's emptier years.

To find just one such page, I do not need.
But opening my book haphazard—read
In every chapter, records of dear days
Set with white mile-stones all along their ways—
Because, Dear Heart, the whole thick volume through,
Began, continued, ended—all with You!

MAZIE V. CARUTHERS.

Shine on . . . shine on starvest moon . . .

INTROSPECTION

Ah moon, how slender sliced tonite.
   What lovely grace. I sigh it.
How may I reach thy slimness slightness;
   Without that deadly diet?

RUTH D. McGINNIS.

Make yourself a scrap book of poetry . . . and let this be the theme . . .

BEAUTY

Who scorns
The simple things
Knows not where beauty lies;
A tiny roadside pool may hold
A star.

ALICE BOOTH DAY.

*Here is a creed for living . . . that has lived thirty centuries . . . three
thousand years and in all that time . . . and all the changes of civiliza-
tion . . . no man has improved on it . . .*

LOOK TO THIS DAY

Look to this day!
For it is Life, the very Life of Life.
In its brief course lie all the verities
And realities of your existence:
The bliss of growth,
The glory of action,
The splendor of beauty.

For yesterday is already a dream,
And tomorrow is only a vision;
But today, well-lived, makes every
Yesterday a dream of happiness,
And every tomorrow a vision of hope.

Look well therefore to this day!
Such is the salutation of the dawn.

SANSKRIT.

TO A YOUNG GIRL

Weave lovely dreams, my dear. Use golden strings
  For warp and rainbow stuff and stars for woof,
But make your fairest pictures simple things;
  A little house beneath a low red roof,
A garden running round, a swing where grass
  Is worn away by happy children's feet—
Gay curtains, friendly chairs, and shining glass
  And every joy that makes a home complete.

Dream much of sun and song and being glad,
  Of laughing lips and eyes adoring you,
But weave a share of rain and being sad,
  For never can the dreams of her come true
Who draws too gay a plan for her career,
  Or shuts her eyes to living, O my dear!

ELAINE V. EMANS.

*If when you have finished reading the Album . . . you have found it
replete with pictures . . . then know that these two lines reveal the
secret . . .*

How lovely common things must seem to you
Who have such lovely eyes to see them through.

EUGENIA AND ELFRIEDA GRIESS.

All for you . . .

BENEDICTION

The sun be warm and kind
    To you,
The darkest night, some star
    Shine through,
The dullest morn
    A radiance brew,
And when dusk comes—
    God's hand
To you.

ELEANOR POWERS.

*And so we come to the last page in our American Album of Poetry . . .
before you close the book . . . here are three wishes from the pen of a
poet . . . from the heart of your friend . . .*

THREE WISHES

I wish you Happiness—
Not just the kind that bubbles up
But happiness that is a quiet peace
Within your heart.
Trials will come—
They always do—but somehow
They will go away because that peace
of Happiness is there.

I wish you Faith.
Not the fairweather kind of faith
But faith that faces the blackest sky
and says, "I trust."

I wish you Understanding.
So many dreams are shattered, petal-like
Because we do not try to see the other side.
If we would open our self-blinded eyes
We would see what they see—and seeing
We would understand.

My three wishes for you.
I do not wish you Fame, or Power, or Gold,
But I think what share of these
That comes your way
Will be the brighter and the dearer
And still more sweet—because these
Other three belong to you.

KATHLEEN GARDNER.

G'bye

Ted Malone

399

INDEX

404

409

411

412